INDONESIAN ISLAM
IN A NEW ERA

D1596134

contents

glossary

adat	traditional, customary practices and/or law
adat pepatih	Malay tradition characterised by matrilineal descent in cases of land and property
adat temenggung	Malay tradition characterised by patrilineal kinship
Aisyiyah	Muslim women's organisation; section of Muhammadiyah
aurat	parts of female body that should be covered according to Islamic principles
Badan Amil Zakat (BAZ)	state-based philanthropic organisations
Badan Kontak Majlis Taklim (BKMT)	Associate Board of Majlis Taklim
Badan Koordinasi Organisasi Wanita (BKOW)	Co-ordination Board of Women's Organisations
Baitul Mal wa Tamwil (BMT)	micro-finance institutions
baju kurung	Malay dress
busana Muslimah	Muslim clothing
Dewan Perwakilan Rakyat Daerah (DPRD)	Regional House of Representatives
dakwah	religious proselytising
Dompet Dhuafa Republika	philanthropic foundation
dukun	traditional healer; sorceres; black/white magician; medium
dukun bayi	traditional birth attendant (with or without spiritual abilities)
Fatayat NU	women's wing of the Nahdlatul Ulama organisation
fatwa	religious edict given by Islamic scholars
fiqh	system of Islamic jurisprudence

gotong royong	mutual help in the community or between neighbours/working together
hadis	collection of traditions relating to the sayings and deeds of the Prophet Muhammad
infak	almsgiving
Institut Agama Islam Negeri (IAIN)	State Institute of Islamic Studies
Islam Jawa	Javanese Islam
Islamism	a militant ideology of Islamic fundamentalism
Islamist	a Muslim who uses Islam for political purposes
jilbab	headscarf exposing only the face
jubah	long and loose dress, which hides the whole figure
kampung	urban neighbourhood
kebatinan	mysticism; the study of one's inner world (as spiritual)
kenduren/kenduri	male aspect of *slametan* or *syukuran* rituals
kerudung	a loose headscarf, which exposes the hair and neck
kiai	male religious (Islamic) leader
kitab kuning	Islamic classical literature
kodrat	the natural destiny of women
Kompilasi Hukum Islam (KHI)	Compilation of Islamic Law
Lembaga Amil Zakat (LAZ)	private philanthropic organisations
madrasah	Islamic school
mahar	dowry
mahram	the group of men a woman may not marry because of marital or blood relationships
majelis taklim	local religious organisations/Islamic study forums
menyan	a type of incense

*mitoni (*or *tingkeban)*	life crisis ritual performed during the seventh month of a woman's first pregnancy
Muhammadiyah	second largest Muslim organisation in Indonesia, with a modernist tradition
mukenah	white cloak worn by women for praying
Muktamar	national congress
Muslimat NU	women's wing of the Nahdlatul Ulama organisation
mut'ah	temporary marriage contract
Nahdlatul Ulama (NU)	largest Muslim organisation in Indonesia, with a traditionalist orientation
Nasyiatul Aisyiyah (Nasyiah)	young women's wing of the Muhammadiyah organisation
New Order	Suharto regime, 1967–1998
NGO	non-government organisation
nyai	wife or daughter of *kiai*
Pak Kaum	religious official
Pendidikan Guru Agama (PGA)	Islamic teacher training college
pengajian	religious lesson
Persatuan Perempuan Peduli Melayu Riau (P3MR)	Association of Concerned Malay Women
pesantren	Islamic boarding school
pesantren putri	Islamic boarding school for female students
Portal Infaq	philanthropic foundation
Pos Keadilan Peduli Ummat (PKPU)	philanthropic foundation
Ramadan	Islamic fasting month
Reformasi	the reform period following the end of the New Order in 1998
rewang	literally 'to help': female practice for *slametan* and *syukuran* rituals
Sahabat Pekerja Migran (SPM)	philanthropic program that supports female workers

sajen (sesajen)	ritual offerings (usually made by women)
sakinah	happy, harmonious (eg families)
Salafi	one who believes in returning to the practices of early Islam
santri	male student of Islam (usually those in a *pesantren*)
santriwati	female student of Islam (usually those in a *pesantren*)
sedekah	voluntary giving, almsgiving
selir	secondary wife
setan	Satan
sinetron	Indonesian television dramas, soap-operas
siri	unofficial but Islamic form of marriage
slamet	balance and harmony
slametan	ritual or communal feast performed to mark life crises, particularly death and anniversaries of death
syariah	Islamic law
syukuran	ritual or communal feast performed to mark life crises and celebratory events
tahlilan	male aspect of *slametan* or *syukuran* rituals where men chant the verse *tahlil* from the Qur'an
tudung	loose headscarf that does not tightly cover the hair
ulama	Muslim scholars
Universitas Islam Negeri (UIN)	Islamic State University
wakaf	religious endowment, almsgiving
Wanita Kepala Keluarga (WAKALA)	program that helps widows in Aceh
zakat	almsgiving
zakat fitrah	food or money given at the end of Ramadan
zakat mal	mandatory financial donation for those whose income has reached a particular high level

contributors

Susan Blackburn is an associate professor in the School of Political and Social Inquiry at Monash University, where she teaches Southeast Asian Politics and the Politics of Development. In recent years her research has focused on women in politics and development and her latest book is *Women and the state in modern Indonesia* (Cambridge University Press, 2004).

Amelia Fauzia is a lecturer at the State Islamic University, Syarif Hidayatullah Jakarta, Indonesia. She is currently completing her PhD in the Asia Institute, University of Melbourne. She has an MA in Islamic Studies from the University of Leiden, and was Executive Secretary for the Center for Languages and Cultures of the State Islamic University Jakarta (2000–04), and Project Director of Philanthropy for Social Justice in Muslim Societies (2002–04).

Rachmah Ida completed her doctoral degree in Media Studies at Curtin University of Technology. Her research focuses on Indonesian television drama and the consumption of the urban *kampung* class. She is a lecturer in the Department of Communication Science at Airlangga University in Surabaya.

Nina Nurmila is a lecturer at the State Institute for Islamic Studies, Bandung. She completed her PhD in the Gender Studies Program and the Asia Institute at the University of Melbourne. Her master's degree was in Development Studies from Murdoch University, and her first degree was in Education at the IAIN in Bandung.

Lugina Setyawati is a sociology graduate of the University of Indonesia in Jakarta, where she is currently a lecturer in sociology. She has a Masters in Anthropology and Sociology from the School of Political and Social Inquiry at Monash University, where she is currently enrolled as a PhD candidate. Her thesis concerns regional ethnic identity and decentralisation in the Indonesian province of Riau.

Bianca J Smith is a postdoctoral researcher in Anthropology in the School of Political and Social Inquiry at Monash University. She has a PhD in Anthropology from Monash University. Her research interests include the anthropology of religion and gender, feminist ethnography, Islam, Sufism and spirituality in Indonesia.

Eka Srimulyani is a lecturer at the State Institute for Islamic Studies, Banda Aceh. She completed her first degree in Education at IAIN Banda Aceh and her MA in Islamic Studies at the University of Leiden. Currently she is completing her PhD in the Institute for International Studies, University of Technology, Sydney.

Siti Syamsiyatun is a lecturer at the State Islamic University in Yogyakarta. She completed her Bachelor of Arts with Honours at Yogyakarta's Muhammadiyah University and gained her MA in Islamic Studies at the Institute of Islamic Studies, McGill University. She gained her PhD in the School of Political and Social Inquiry, Monash University.

introduction

Susan Blackburn, Bianca J Smith and Siti Syamsiyatun

Indonesia, the fourth largest country in the world with its population of some 220 million, is also the largest Islamic society, since roughly 90% of its population claim to be Muslims. With the rising interest in Islam around the world, it is timely to publish books about this religion in Indonesia and particularly about that half of the Indonesian population who are women. Unfortunately, the interest of many people in Islam relates not just to its current connection with terrorism, but also to its perceived ill-treatment of women. Given the widespread ignorance about Islam in Indonesia, any publication which can help to correct misconceptions and prejudices about the religion should be welcomed.

This book breaks new ground in several ways. Firstly, although a number of books have been published on Islam and women in Indonesia, they tend to focus on interpretations of Islam rather than on how women themselves experience their religion and actively engage with it in their lives. A view of women as religious agents pervades this book. Secondly, our focus is on women and Islam in Indonesia in the post-Suharto period, since 1998. This is a significantly different period from the New Order, during which most previous books have been written about women and Islam in Indonesia. The situation of both women and Islam has changed, globally and nationally, as the chapters illustrate. While Islam has become even more prominent than before in society and in politics, it has also become far more acceptable, and common, to put forward feminist views in Indonesia—and within Islam. The feminist orientation of most of the Indonesian authors in this book would have been inconceivable just ten years ago. Finally, the book is the product of collaboration between Australian and Indonesian women scholars. It was initiated by two postgraduate students (one Australian and one Indonesian) at Monash University and they drew in a lecturer at that university and other Indonesian postgraduates studying in Australia. The number of Indonesian women pursuing graduate studies in the social sciences has greatly increased in recent years, particularly the number of women from

1

Islamic institutions. While in the past it has been difficult for Indonesian women writing about Islam to contribute to English-language publications, in the future we can expect to see far more of them contributing their views to debates in English on religion and gender. The fact that they are 'insiders' gives their writing extra authority. With their Western training and facility in English, these women help to bridge the gap between Western and Indonesian scholarship on Islam and women, a gap that will be discussed later in this Introduction.

Through its dialogue with Islam's plurality and gendered elements, this book enhances knowledge of Islam and its Indonesian female practitioners. *Indonesian Islam in a new era* demonstrates that by understanding the agentic role women play in Muslim societies and cultures such as Indonesia, we gain further insight into the practice of Islam more broadly, and into the creative lives of women who understand and negotiate their worlds in different ways. More importantly, the fact that, as mentioned, most authors in this book are Indonesian Muslim women means that their perceptions of their own culture and religion significantly contribute to understandings of Islam and women in Indonesia by challenging traditional Western methods that privilege Westerners as researchers who knowingly create knowledge about Third World others.

Some brief introductory discussion is warranted to explain the way this book is situated within a number of overlapping contexts. It can be located within feminist writing, within writing about Islam in Indonesia, and most particularly within discourse about women and Islam in Indonesia. All these areas are controversial and this Introduction will sketch the nature of these controversies. Special attention needs to be paid to the differences between discourses inside and outside Indonesia. Since this book attempts to bridge that division in many ways, readers need to be aware of the debates that have been going on more or less in parallel, in different languages and from different perspectives.

Feminism and the study of Islam in Indonesia

Indonesian Islam in a new era does not deliberately engage with a single critical feminist theory in its representation and examination of Indonesian Muslim women. The book's authors are influenced by feminism rather than explicitly defining themselves as feminist writers. They do not engage in feminist polemics, but they contribute to the diversity of feminist practice and theory by deliberately questioning what it means to be a Muslim woman in Indonesia. By emphasising women's agency they are also reflecting current feminist concerns to show women as actively engaging with their environments rather than portraying women as passive victims of male oppression.

Taken as a whole, this book reflects current feminist preoccupations with diversity by demonstrating the variety of women's Islamic practices and ways of being in contemporary Indonesia. Largely empirical and ethnographic, it details the agency and life negotiations and practices of women as examined by various authors. It particularises how women negotiate their gender, agency and identities as Muslims in diverse spaces including rural and urban environments, through discourses, across ethnicities, in organisations and schools, and in their relationships with men. In doing so it examines the ways in which women express their Islamic identities in different spaces and in particular contexts during periods of change in Indonesia. Women are shown as cultural, social, political, and religious agents who actively interpret discourses on Islam, and Islamic discourse and practice, to shape their roles as women and their sense of self at the intersection of Indonesian society, culture, and Islam in local and national contexts. Beyond this, the book's chapters illustrate the diversity of contemporary Islamic practice in Indonesia and reveal a range of subjectivities, methods for agency, self-expression and negotiations that women in Indonesian Islamic culture create as gendered social actors.

One of the sources of friction between 'Third World' feminists and those in the West has been the past tendency of the latter to assume the superiority of Western women's struggles for liberation as against the 'backwardness' of Third World women, conceived in a homogenised fashion. Inherent power struggles between privileged Western feminists and underprivileged Third World women raise questions about feminist methodologies and research in cross-cultural contexts, as scholars grapple with the politics of global power structures which frame cross-cultural research (see for example Bulbeck 1998; Abu-Lughod 1990; 1993; Stacey 1988). In the past, tension amongst feminist scholars has undoubtedly been exacerbated by the overwhelming numerical dominance of Western scholars. Now, however, the growing number of non-Western women graduating from Western universities is facilitating change, and as this Introduction later reveals, in the case of Indonesia it is Indonesian rather than Western women who are now producing the bulk of scholarship on women and Islam in Indonesia. A few Indonesian male feminists have also played a crucial role in researching women, gender, and Islam.

At present it is particularly valuable to hear these Indonesian voices because of the widespread controversy over the nature of Islam in general and in Indonesia in particular.

The Islamic context

In the current climate of global concern for what is termed 'Islamic terrorism' there is a need to correct misunderstandings about Indonesian Islam. Concurrently, it is important to examine the significant role Indonesian women play in the constitution of Indonesian society and culture as pluralistically Islamic. This sense of urgency in the Asia Pacific region to clarify understandings of the religious environments of Indonesia—the largest Muslim nation in the world—has rapidly developed as a result of terrorist attacks since 11 September 2001, including repeated bombings in Indonesia since 2002.

Dominant Western constructions of Islam are historically situated in the Middle East and through an accumulated tradition of orientalist scholarship have portrayed Muslims and Islam as the Other (see Said 1978). This homogenous construction is also gendered, as Muslim women have been constructed in Western consciousness as oppressed, weak, passive and submissive as a result of sexist practices and patriarchal regimes. (It is worth remarking, too, that in some Islamic circles there is a long-standing tendency to take the contrary view, that is, to represent Western treatment of women as exploitative and immoral as contrasted with Islamic protection of womanhood.) In this context it is important to gain a deeper understanding of Islam in Indonesia and its relationship to women in particular.

The first thing to be noted is that Indonesian Islam is different from Arabian modes of Islam. There is not one way to practise Islam or to be Muslim; Islam is plural. The Indonesian archipelago is ethnically diverse and Muslim practitioners practise Islam in particularised ways unique to their cultural understandings and interpretations of Islam. Within Indonesia this diversity has long been a source of concern in some Islamic circles. Whereas certain regions are well-known for their 'Islamic devoutness' (notably Aceh, West Sumatra, West Java, Lombok and South Sulawesi) others, especially the Javanese heartland, have been labelled as only 'nominally Islamic'. This in itself illustrates a tendency to create dichotomies of 'pure' and 'impure' Islam which are not helpful in understanding how the religion is practised.

The American anthropologist Clifford Geertz (1960) famously characterised Javanese religion as 'syncretistic,' and contrasted modernist (reformist) modes of Islam and 'syncretistic' modes of Islam (Islam mixed with animism and Hindu–Buddhism). Following in his footsteps, Indonesian Islam is still misread as being either 'pure' or 'nominal' in particular contexts (Newland 2000). More recent scholarship on Javanese Islam has not only enhanced and challenged Geertz's observations of Islam, but it has shed light on the complexities of the mystical elements of Islam in Javanese society. Thus, anthropologists now understand how Javanese Islam is diverse in its multiple fields of discursive practice.[1] Despite a plethora of studies on Islam in Java, however, it is still common for scholars to acknowledge Islam's presence in Javanese society but overlook its complex role in local religiosity and ritual, in favour of classifying particular practices as historically Hindu–Buddhist, thus following decades of male scholarship.

The perspective that popular culture rests heavily on Hindu–Buddhism has dominated literature on Javanese religion in general (Howell et al 2001; Newland 2000; Woodward 1989; 1996). Lynda Newland (2000) suggests that scholars' emphasis on describing popular rituals and practices as Hindu–Buddhist has developed from Geertz's (1960) over–emphasis on Hindu–Buddhism, and under–emphasis on Islam, and yet as Julia Day Howell *et al* (2001) and Mark Woodward (1988; 1989) point out, these 'Hindu–Buddhist' practices actually embody aspects of Sufism. As Newland (2000) asserts, although approximately 90% of Indonesians are Muslim, Indonesian Islam's legitimacy is denied when scholars describe particular modes of it as 'not really Islam' or 'syncretic,' and its practitioners as 'nominal Muslims.'[2]

Mark Woodward's (1989) point that Javanese Islam in particular has been misread as 'tradition' or staunchly 'Hindu-Buddhist' is relevant to the reasons nurturing the dearth of Western feminist scholarship on women and Islam in Indonesia. It appears that female students of anthropology have applied the theories of those before them which read 'real religion' as doctrinal, scriptural (for example, Islam) and 'other practices' such as magic, witchcraft or animism as 'not real religion.' In this way, people who do not practise Islam in perceived 'pious' ways are thus not interpreted as Muslims, but as those who practise 'tradition' or 'animism.' Typology, then, plays a strong role in how we understand Islam and its practices. Bianca Smith's chapter in this volume (Chapter Four) takes up this issue in greater detail.

One might almost say that until very recently more effort has been devoted by foreign anthropologists and sociologists to showing that Indonesia is not really Islamic than to discussing how Islam is practised there. Among non-Indonesian feminist writers, for instance, there is a long-standing fascination with the matrilineal practices of the Minangkabau of West Sumatra, which is regarded by most Indonesians as a strongly Islamic area but which departs from strict Islamic legal laws in relation to inheritance. Some writers even like to celebrate West Sumatra as a matriarchy (Sanday 2002) . By largely ignoring Islam, it is easier to make out a case for the undeniable strength of women in Indonesian society.

The example of West Sumatra draws attention also to the longstanding interest amongst many observers in the tension between Islam and *adat* or customary law and culture in Indonesia. In many cases the two conflict. Lugina Setyawati's chapter in this volume (Chapter Three) explores this tension in the case of the Sumatran province of Riau. In terms of understanding the situation of women, this can be a fruitful avenue to follow, particularly in charting the variations between ethnic groups which have different *adat*. The shifting balance between strict interpretations of Islam and *adat* practice helps to explain the erosion or strengthening of women's rights in different regions.

The fact that Indonesian Islam is not as 'strict' as some modes practised in the Middle East may also contribute to the lack of feminist concern for women and Islam in Indonesia. The construction that Islam is lax and predominantly 'nominal' in Indonesia has attributed a set of meanings to Islam which actually reinforce the notion of its illegitimate practice; as somehow less authentic when contrasted to the heartland of Arabian Islam.

Approaching this subject in a different and more positive light, a number of Western political scientists have emphasised the tolerant tradition of Indonesian Islam (for example, Hefner 2000). It is often stressed that Indonesia is not an Islamic state, a decision made at independence. (Neither is it, strictly speaking, a secular state, since the state ideology of Pancasila enshrines belief in God which has justified state support for the five officially recognised religions of Indonesia: Islam, Catholicism, Protestantism, Hinduism and Buddhism.) Religious law prevails only in a restricted way in the realm of family law.

In recent years, however, feminist interest in Indonesian Islam has been triggered precisely because of a perceived rise in Islamic practices in Indonesia, some of them much closer to Arabic customs than in the past. In Java itself, previously seen as only 'nominally Islamic', it is impossible to avoid the evidence of more visibly Islamic ways of being, such as a rise in mosque construction and attendance, the stricter observance of the fast month, and the wearing of so-called 'Islamic' items of dress, in particular by women. Since the fall of Suharto in 1998 the more democratic and open nature of Indonesian society has allowed the emergence of a number of small and dogmatic Islamic organisations which seek to impose their view of Islam on the others, in ways that frequently target women (Noerdin 2002). These organisations have aggressively criticised and even attacked 'un-Islamic' practices like gambling and prostitution and pushed for local regulations to impose curfews on women (perceived as a curb on prostitution) and the wearing of 'correctly modest' clothing which usually includes the requirement that Muslim women cover their heads and most of their body. In 2006 a proposal came before Parliament to introduce a draconian law on pornography that aimed to dramatically control women's dress and behaviour. It provoked such an outcry that these restrictions had to be omitted, yet concern remains that such proposals could surface at all. Moreover, decentralisation reforms and special deals made by Jakarta to pacify troublesome provinces like Aceh have meant that more elements of *syariah* law are being endorsed by local and provincial governments.

Such developments naturally lead to questions about what is happening to Islam in Indonesia, particularly as it relates to women. This book hopes to make some contribution to answering such questions. The chapters by Setyawati, Ida, Nurmila and Syamsiyatun are all concerned with understanding how changing interpretations of Islam in Indonesia are affecting women and, in turn, how women seek to influence those interpretations. Siti Syamsiyatun in particular (Chapter Six) describes the difficult situation of an Islamic women's organisation that tries to steer a middle path between secular feminism and Arabian-influenced Islamism.

Writing about Islam and women in English

In what follows 'writing in English' will often be used interchangeably with 'Western writing', but the dangers of this equation should be born in mind. For one thing, not all 'Westerners' write in English, and a few works on Indonesian women and Islam have been published in other Western languages such as French and Dutch. Moreover, as will be noted, some writing in English is in fact translated from Indonesian, and some writers in English about Indonesian women and Islam are not Western. Two good examples would be Siapno (2202) and Nakamura (1983). However, the purpose of this section is to comment on some major differences (both in volume and character) in writing about Indonesian women and Islam inside and outside Indonesia.

In Western circles, concerns about the connection between Islam and women have revolved around a number of areas in which Islamic practices are felt to oppress women: the inequality of family laws that favour men in divorce, inheritance and polygamy, restrictive views of women's roles that limit them to the 'private' world, the restriction of women's sexuality to marriage, and other practices held to be related to Islam like female circumcision. Particular concern is voiced in the West about the implications of *syariah* law for women, notably its more extreme criminal code such as the punishment of adulterous women by stoning. Are such concerns reflected in Western writing about women and Islam in Indonesia? If not, what does that say about either Western scholarship or Indonesian Islam?

The first thing to be said is that although there is a growing literature on Indonesian Islam, there is a surprising dearth of Western scholarship on women and Islam in Indonesia. When couched in the wider context of Western academia, reasons for this lack of scholarly inquiry could in part be rooted in what has just been discussed: the perceived legitimation of Middle Eastern modes of Islam as 'authentic' and Indonesian Islam as less so, especially given that the Arab world is accepted as the hub or core of the Muslim world in popular and scholarly discourses. The validation and authenticity of Middle Eastern Islam is reflected in scholarly volumes about 'women and Islam,' which rarely include chapters on Indonesia (see for example Kandiyoti 1991; Saliba et al 2002; Moghissi 2005).

Similarly, in volumes on Indonesian women written in English, chapters on Islam are scarce, although this is changing as more Indonesian women write and publish in English, as we examine shortly. The lack of Western feminist inquiry into women and Islam in Indonesia is frequently mirrored in works on women in Indonesia that do not examine the nexus between women and Islam. *Indonesian Islam in a new era* also reflects the lack of Western feminist inquiry, as only one of the seven contributors to this volume is Western. Recent edited volumes on Indonesian women written in English such as *Women and Households in Indonesia* (2000) and *Women in Indonesia: Gender, Equity and Development* (2002) sometimes include chapters on Islam, yet they tend to be written by Indonesian and not Western women. For example, in *Women in Indonesia* Khofifah Indar Parawansa (2002), Edriana Noerdin (2002) and Lies Marcoes (2202) contribute to knowledge about Muslim organisations, the marginalisation of women in *syariah* law, and the changing social role of women's religious organisations in contexts of ongoing political change since 1998. Western authors' chapters in these books do not explicitly address Islam. It may take an editor who is prepared to translate papers from Indonesian or to spend considerable time correcting Indonesian English to ensure the inclusion of chapters on Islam in a book about Indonesian women. Unsurprisingly, then, a recent book on Indonesian women that contains chapters on religion, *Indonesian women, the journey continues* (Oey-Gardiner & Bianpoen 2000) (see the chapters by Rahman and Marcoes) was originally written in Indonesian (Oey-Gardiner, Wagemann et al 1996).

Even among feminist writers in the West, there have been relatively few inquiries into women and Islam in Indonesia (see for example Bennett 2005; Newland 2001; Brenner 1998; 1996; 1995; Siapno 2002; Doorn-Harder 2002; Feillard 1999; Whalley 1993; Woodcroft-Lee 1984; Robinson 2000). Significantly, most are anthropologists whose interest in Islam is incidental to their studies of particular communities. No-one has conducted a systematic study of women and Islam in Indonesia.

There are some obvious reasons for the neglect of this topic in the West. Apart from the entrenched secularist trend in Western scholarship in recent times, it has been notoriously difficult for non-Muslim scholars of Indonesia to undertake study of Islam because it has been assumed that one requires a mastery of Arabic and of what is regarded as an arcane world of Indonesian Islamic theology. Few non-Indonesians gain the necessary expertise to discuss the Islamic texts. Legal experts who are interested in the practical implications of Islamic law, such as Hooker (2003), constitute an exception. Entry into this field is even harder for women than for men, since as a field of scholarship the Islamic religion has been a male preserve.

This is one reason why Western writers tend to discuss Islam and women in Indonesia from the perspective of the social sciences: they are concerned with describing and analysing behaviour rather than discussing theology. Another way of putting it is to say that non-Indonesian writers on Islam and women are almost always non-Muslims. Not only do they have little knowledge of the religion, but for them it is of little importance whether or not Indonesian practice conforms with Islamic teaching. In fact, they may applaud the disjuncture between teaching and practice as an illustration of the flexibility, tolerance and pragmatism of Indonesian Islam. This is not to say that Westerners approach the subject without preconceptions: of course they bring to bear their own historical, religious and personal baggage to the study of Islam in Indonesia. But their preoccupations are different from those of Indonesian Muslims, as we shall see.

Significantly, earlier major volumes in English on women and Indonesia such as *Fantasizing the feminine in Indonesia* (Sears 1996) and *Power and difference: gender in island Southeast Asia* (Atkinson & Errington 1990) do not include any chapters on Islam. The partial exception is Daniel Lev (1996), a chapter that engages in discussion of Islam and women. Lev offers interesting observations about women and Islam in Indonesia. He argues that Indonesian Islam provides women with more freedom than in other Islamic countries, which marks Indonesian Islam as an interesting and isolated case to explore. Indonesian Islam is different from other Islamic nations in its expectations and treatment of women. It is different, writes Lev, because 'the Islamic mainstream in Indonesia has…not produced a campaign to veil women, to keep them at home, or to deny them substantial gains already made…The Islamic wall in Indonesia is relatively low or at least not impossibly smooth' (Lev 1996:194). Lev wrote over a decade ago: he would probably not be so sanguine today when the challenge of dogmatic Islam is much greater in Indonesia, as already pointed out. Nevertheless, it is in this space between Islam's strictness and laxity that this book is situated: exactly how does Indonesian Islam, in its various modes, engage women, and more importantly, how do Muslim women contribute to the shaping of Indonesian Islam?

Much recent writing is triggered by the implications for women of the Islamic revival in Indonesia. For instance, Islamic parties at first prevented Megawati Sukarnoputri from becoming Indonesia's first female president. Ultimately this opposition was overcome and she went on to assume the presidency (2001–04), but the legitimacy of her Islamic identity was challenged in the process, which contributed to ongoing debates about women's roles and positions in Islam (see Doorn-Harder 2002; Platzdasch 2000). Megawati's position was paradoxical because it demonstrated the possibility for women to become leaders, yet those who opposed her because she was a woman only reinforced dominant gendered religious ideologies about women's roles in society and religion.

The issue of Megawati related not only to Islamic views of female leadership but more broadly to the strongly held gender ideology in Indonesia concerning *kodrat* or the natural destiny of women (as opposed to men). *Kodrat* is a case where some Islamic beliefs reinforce existing Indonesian cultural notions that women are dependent on men and that men are natural leaders of the nation, family and religion. A number of writers in English (Feillard 1996; Hubeis 2000; Newland 2000; 2001; Robinson 2000; Siapno 2002; Woodcroft-Lee 1984; Whalley 1993) have examined wide ranging gender issues across the Indonesian archipelago to note women's oppression, agency and cultural identities as Muslims and the position of women in Islam and Islamic law. They have done so in the contexts of literature, politics, nationalism, feminist movements, work and migration, the family and ethnicity. Many Muslim women have faced an uphill struggle contesting ideas about women being restricted to the home, as shown in the chapters in this volume by Srimulyani (Chapter Five) and Syamsiyatun (Chapter Six): the former chronicles the efforts of three women leaders in *pesantren* (Islamic boarding schools) and the latter writes of the work of an Islamic women's organisation to win a place for women in policy-making in Muhammadiyah, one of the largest Indonesian Islamic organisations. Fauzia's chapter (Chapter Seven) also demonstrates how women are winning greater recognition in the running of Islamic charitable institutions, overcoming past prejudices against women in leadership positions. Given the well-known business acumen of Indonesian women, it is surprising that they should have to prove themselves as financial managers.

In the West, polygamy and other forms of inequality in marriage, female circumcision and the wearing of 'the veil,' are perhaps the most controversial issues that generate feminist debate about women and Islam. Feminists have expressed strong opposition to these practices in Africa and the Middle East as Islamic regions, but what is known of these practices in Indonesia, the world's largest Islamic nation?

Relatively little has been written in English about family laws and polygamy in Indonesia.[3] This is surprising given the tremendously controversial nature of these issues in Indonesian society, largely because of their connection with Islam. Perhaps this is because Indonesian marriage laws based on Islam have not been as oppressive of women as in some other Muslim countries like Pakistan. Many observers considered that the passing of the 1974 Marriage Law went a long way (perhaps as far as was possible given Islamic opposition to inroads into Islamic law) to address widespread concerns about inequality in marriage. Moreover, the incidence of polygamy is very low, as discussed by Nurmila in her chapter in this volume (Chapter One). It is in fact not exclusive to Islam: Jennaway (2000; 2002) has written about polygamy in Hindu Bali.

Writing on the topic of female circumcision has been extremely limited both inside and outside Indonesia. Concern over Indonesian women's poor level of reproductive health has drawn attention to the practice in recent years. It has taken research published in English (Feillard & Marcoes 1998) to establish that in Indonesia female circumcision has been widely but varyingly practised and usually located within an Islamic frame of reference. Their research established that it was conducted in a largely symbolic way, without inflicting real harm on girls (although in some cases the practice may be unhygienic and therefore risky). Feillard and Marcoes have questioned the reasons for the lack of research by Indonesians on female circumcision: based on field research and interviews they asserted that there was a general understanding that female circumcision is directly linked to Islam and that the practice is performed across the archipelago, usually in secrecy which makes it difficult to provide accurate statistics.

Both inside and outside Indonesia, the practice of women covering their heads in response to perceived Islamic injunctions has been widely discussed. Western writers have analysed the intersection of Islam, popular culture and modernity in Indonesia that has seen the rise in usually educated middle-class women wearing various forms of head coverings including 'the veil' or headscarves as symbolic of a conscious move from 'the past' into a paradoxical new Islamic modernity (see Brenner 1996; Feillard 1999). The trend in veiling grew stronger with the Islamic resurgence in the 1970s and 1980s which was a direct response to the Iranian revolution.

Women's choice to adopt 'the veil' as a strong marker of their Islamic identity creates social limitations and sets of clearly defined rules that women must follow as good Muslims, particularly in the context of sexuality. Little ethnographic research has been done on Muslim sexualities in Indonesia. Dominant Indonesian and local discourses on sexuality usually describe women as both temptresses who must be controlled, and as wives whose purpose is to reproduce healthy citizens and satisfy their husbands. The sexual expectations of Muslim women are tied into local cultural (*adat*) beliefs and practices and state and Islamic discourses which inform women of their role as mothers, wives and reproductive citizens. (For more on Islam and sexuality see Bennett 2005; Brenner 1995; Santosa 2002). The actions of Islamic pressure groups to control women's bodies and sexuality through legislation (such as the currently debated pornography law) and local regulations reflect the growing influence of puritanical Islam in Indonesia.

Writing in Indonesia about women and Islam

This Introduction has noted that Western writers rarely deal with theological issues when discussing women and Islam in Indonesia. By contrast, the discourse of Indonesian writers on the subject has in the past been heavily theological. A major reason is, of course, that Indonesian writers on this topic are almost exclusively Muslims. It is exceptional for any non-Muslims to comment on Islam in Indonesia. The New Order legacy is strong in this respect: it ruled that religious differences were not to be aired since such debate might threaten national unity. For religious minorities, their own security may be at stake if they are perceived as criticising Islam. Some Muslim writers themselves may find it threatening to undertake the kind of sociological and anthropological inquiry preferred by Western writers precisely because they do not wish to confront the gap between strict Islamic teaching and what happens in practice, to investigate the relationship between religion and culture. In the past their educational training has not prepared them for such critical scrutiny, especially if they have attended Islamic educational institutions where the study of Islam focussed on sacred and legal texts. Writers have preferred to discuss what should be rather than address how and why reality may fall short of Islamic teachings. However, this situation is changing as we explain below.

In any discussion of academic writing in Indonesia we must recognise the constraints there are on research by and about women. If women academics have been late in appearing on the Western scene and feminism even slower to make inroads into Western academic research, the situation has been far worse in Indonesia. Firstly, women have lagged behind men in gaining university qualifications, and secondly the lack of resources in Indonesia coupled with the bias of state funding has meant that few women or men have the luxury of conducting academic research along feminist lines. New Order government interest in research on women was largely confined to their concern about fertility. The world of Indonesian scholarly publishing, too, has until recently been largely closed to women and extremely limited because of the small market for academic works. Indonesia is only just beginning to develop an elite which is accustomed to buying and reading books or scholarly journals. Libraries suffer a severe shortage of funds.

While scholarly writing by women about women and Islam has been restricted, however, it has been a popular topic among male Islamic authors. In any bookshop a multitude of didactic books by men, often translated from Arabic, can be found instructing women how to behave according to Islamic teachings and instructing men how to treat women. Although not in the realm of scholarly literature that we discuss here, these publications serve as a reminder of the popularly available writings against which many academic works have to contend. Just as literature in English is not always written originally in that language, works in Indonesian on women and Islam may well originate from Saudi Arabia. Among male-authored works one can find a clear distinction between those that advise people to follow Arabic-based behaviour and a growing number (although still a minority) of works by male feminists who have joined with women in reinterpreting Islam in ways that empower women. In fact, Indonesian male feminists also play a crucial role in researching women, gender, and Islam in both sociological and theological contexts (on sociology see for example Burhanuddin & Fathurahman 2004; Burhanuddin 2002; Hasyim 2001; on theology see for example Muhammad & Kodir 2001; Mukhotib 2002a; 2002b; 2000c; Umar 1999a; 1999b). Syamsiyatun's chapter in this volume (Chapter Six) acknowledges the common struggle by male and female feminists within Indonesian Islam to eliminate misogynistic practices.

The large gender gap in authorship only began to narrow in recent years. Today it is not as difficult as it was ten years ago to find both popular and scholarly books on various issues written by women, although they remain a minority. Many books produced by these female authors address gender issues. Some scholarly works by women are modified versions of the authors' masters or dissertation theses (such as Ismail 2003; Faiqoh 2003). As these books are written in Indonesian they reach only a limited international readership. Indonesian women producing scholarly works in English are even fewer, and most of them are graduates from overseas universities, such as Yulfita Raharjo, Julia Suryakusuma, Sita Aripurnami, Ro'fah Masduki and Istiadah. This current volume aims to raise the profile of Indonesian women writing in English, as six of the authors of the seven substantive chapters are Indonesian women. Moreover, all writers are addressing women's issues and Islam by using an empirical, sociological approach rather than normative and theological perspectives as used by most Indonesian women authors (for instance, Ismail 2003; Mulia 2005; Munir 1999; Muslikhati). Although there are many factors that give rise to women's authorship in Indonesia, only two intertwined factors will be highlighted here, namely education and the emergence of new feminist activism. While the improvement of girls education was an early demand of the Indonesian women's movement, it has taken decades to reach a stage in which education supports women to speak up and write down their ideas, opinions, concerns and dreams. The contribution of Islamic education in particular to the growth of Islamic feminism is discussed further in Syamsiyatun's chapter in this volume (Chapter Six).

Several groups—feminist, religious and nationalist—have contested women's issues in Indonesia, and the Indonesian government has also been influential in this debate. Although Indonesian feminist activists began to challenge the officially endorsed conservative ideology of *kodrat* in the early 1980s, the New Order government only began to include women in political decision-making and recognise their contribution to national development when it was pressured to do so by international organisations such as the United Nations and foreign donors. Women and their gender interests became part of the movement for democratisation in Indonesia in the latter years of the New Order regime. In 1978 President Suharto had appointed a Junior Minister for the Role of Women; the renaming of the office as the State Minister for Women's Empowerment at the turn of the century illustrates how far gender discourse has officially travelled in Indonesia.

During the 1990s many state and private universities, including some State Institutes for Islamic Studies (IAINs) founded Centres for Women's and Gender Studies. The establishment of these academic centres has strengthened the development of gender discourse initiated by feminist activists in the 1980s, by buttressing it with feminist theories and methodologies. The mutual relationships between feminist activists, women-focused NGOs and organisations, and women's studies centres in universities have fostered the dissemination of gender awareness amongst various segments of Indonesian societies. The involvement of Islamic higher educations such as IAINs in the process of disseminating gender awareness has left a distinct legacy as this Islamic institution has consistently used a religious perspective in approaching gender issues. Another important impact is that Islamic principles and practices on women's issues have also been scrutinised and reinterpreted by various Muslim groups using a gender perspective.

International funding agencies have played a significant role in promoting gender discourse in Indonesia, including in some IAINs. There is evidence that most feminist NGOs founded in the 1980s and beyond have received substantial funds from these foreign funding agencies (Mukhtar 1999:134). They have also made substantial donations to various centres to conduct research on a number of gender issues and to finance the publication of the research findings. The Ford Foundation has assisted in generating discussion on issues relating to women such as reproductive rights. The Asia Foundation is another foreign funding agency that has been active in promoting gender issues in Indonesia. The institution has financed the publication of several books on women's issues from a religious perspective (for example, Munti 1999; Umar 1999b).

The Ford Foundation has also provided financial assistance to several women's centres in Islamic higher education, such as IAINs, and to Muslim organisations to support research and publication on gender and religious issues.[4] The Canadian International Development Agency and DANIDA from Denmark have co-operated closely with the State Islamic University (formerly IAIN) in Yogyakarta on a number of projects on gender and Islam. Several publications by the Centre for Women's Studies at UIN Sunan Kalijaga Yogyakarta were made possible through CIDA's financial assistance.[5] DANIDA has also assisted the Centre in publishing a journal on gender and Islam called *Musawa* (Arabic for Equality). Some of the issues discussed in the journal are polygamy, *mut'ah* (temporary marriage contract), homosexuality, and abortion.

Many IAIN students are now writing their dissertations on feminism, gender and Islam in different faculties. The traditional divisions of Islamic studies applied in IAINs are *Ushuluddin* (Theology), *Syari'ah* (Islamic Law), *Tarbiyah* (Education), *Adab* (Culture, History and Literature) and *Dakwah* (Islamic Mission). Within each of these faculties there are also a number of sub-areas. Some dissertations on women's issues by IAIN graduates from different faculties have been published. The works of Nasaruddin Umar (1999a; 1999b), Yunahar Ilyas (1997) and Ismail (2003) are produced within the tradition of *Ilmu Tafsir* (Qur'anic exegesis), whereas the writing of Khoiruddin Nasution (2002) and Faiqoh (2003) is within the perspective of *fiqh mu'amalah* (Islamic law social relations).

Noting the role of foreign funding agencies in fostering the dissemination of gender awareness from an Islamic perspective through research and publication does not mean that Indonesian Muslims have only been passive recipients or merely taking orders from foreign agents as claimed by many conservative Muslims. On the contrary, long before the involvement of these foreign donors, Muslim women have been engaging in gender issues through collective action in various organisations, such as in *pesantren*, women's organisations or even taking leading roles in practising rituals of local Islamic *Kejawen* as demonstrated in chapters by Smith and Srimulyani in this volume (Chapters Four and Five). It is more appropriate to regard the role of foreign donors as having converged with internal demands for religious reform on gender issues within the Indonesian Muslim community.

The modernisation of Islamic higher education launched by the Indonesian Ministry of Religious Affairs since the mid 1980s has shown results. New approaches to Islamic Studies, including those produced within the fields of sociology, politics and feminism, have been introduced to IAINs and Islamic universities. Both the introduction of gender perspectives and the development of women's studies centres in Islamic higher educations have become important factors in gender mainstreaming within universities management and policies. The gender ratio has become an important consideration for the development of human resources within Islamic universities. Women graduating from these Islamic universities now feel confident to write about women's and religious issues as their qualifications equal those of their male counterparts. Most contemporary Indonesian women writing about these issues are graduates from IAINs.

The chapters

The chapters in this book cover a wide variety of areas where Islam intersects with the lives of Indonesian women: not just the popularly controversial topics of marriage and veiling, but also the media, education, organisational life, religiosity, philanthropy and regional politics. In all of these areas the emphasis is on women's experiences and activism, especially on the way women have negotiated a place for themselves within Islamic discourse. The authors' choice of topics and their approach reflects the post-Suharto era, in which it is possible to question accepted attitudes and break new ground.

Thus the main concern of Chapter One, by Nina Nurmila, is how Indonesian women have experienced polygamy, a subject that has received surprisingly little attention. While the incidence of polygamy is very low in Indonesia, the right of men to take more than one wife at a time has excited enormous opposition from secular women's organisations over the years and great defensiveness on the part of Islamic groups. As Nurmila shows, in recent years there has even been some aggressive promotion of polygamy in newly resurgent Islamist circles in Indonesia. It was timely, then, that she undertook fieldwork on the subject to find out how women not only felt about being in polygamous marriages but about how they actively negotiated the terms of their marriages. As she says, her research shows that wives are by no means just victims in the hands of husbands who are favoured in the current practice of Islam. Some of her informants were well-placed to resist husbands who tried to draw other wives into their marriage.

Nurmila's chapter also shows a strong awareness of the political context of women's encounters with polygamy. It is a feature of many of the contributions to this book that they recognise the importance of wider events for the practice of Islam. Nurmila argues that the end of the New Order regime, which had shown hostility to polygamy, made it possible for pro-polygamy forces to assert themselves. Ironically, it was during the term of Indonesia's first woman president, Megawati Sukarnoputri, that supporters of polygamy were encouraged by the incumbency of the vice-president, Hamzah Haz, who had more than one wife in an open display of polygamy that would never have been tolerated by Suharto.

Rachmah Ida's chapter (Chapter Two) is also a product of its times. It deals with a phenomenon that has long interested observers of Indonesian television— the soap opera or *sinetron*—but it does so with a special twist by drawing our attention to a new type of *sinetron* that is ostensibly aimed at a devout Islamic audience and is shown during the fast month. This study allows Ida to discuss an aspect of Islam that has struck most observers in the last three decades: the spread of the wearing of so-called 'Islamic clothing' by Indonesian women, and in particular the forms of headcovering known as *jilbab* and *kerudung*. In English these are commonly and misleadingly referred to as 'veiling' although in fact the face is never covered: it is merely a matter of how much hair, neck and chest are revealed. Whenever the connection between Islam and women is discussed in Indonesia, this topic is sure to surface immediately and argument will begin as to whether devout Muslim women need to adopt 'Islamic dress'. Thus it is not surprising that 'Islamic *sinetron*' in Indonesia devotes much time to this issue and its actors are used to displaying the attractiveness of highly fashionable versions of concealing costumes, although as Ida notes, the commitment of the 'stars' to concealing themselves is rather dubious. As an example of resurgent Islam, these television *sinetron* appear more determined to exploit the market than to inspire devotion. But what is surprising about that in the context of the mass media? What Ida's chapter does is to tease out the contradictory forces at work here and the interpretations that may be applied: while the phenomenon of 'Ramadan *sinetron*' and the wearing of 'Islamic dress' reflect increasing Islamicisation, the television medium also plays upon rising consumerism and 'celebrity worship' in its approach. Her research also demonstrates how female viewers make their own Islam-based interpretations of what they see on the screen: they are by no means passive consumers of the medium.

Most of these chapters are clearly placed in a post-Suharto context, which is fitting since their subjects and the manner of their research are scarcely imaginable in the earlier period. The New Order placed severe restrictions on research, both by foreigners and by Indonesians. Anything that touched on the controversial was to be avoided in the cause of social harmony and national unity, and preference was given to research that promoted the government's own policies, especially its development policies. The research by Lugina Setyawati (Chapter Three) is new partly because the phenomenon of regional identity has become important in the context of a weak central government and a decentralisation policy that has allowed local loyalties to blossom. In her chapter Lugina Setyawati takes us to Riau, a place where religion has become fused with the ethnic identity of the Malays. In a situation very different from those in other regions, Setyawati shows how the Islamic characteristics of Malay identity have been strengthened by the current resurgence of regionalism. Increasingly, feminist observers like Setyawati are noting the importance of women in this regional resurgence: gender is central to the construction of these local identities, and the part that women play in opposing, supporting and negotiating with this construction is essential for an understanding of the process.

Bianca Smith's ethnological study of women's religiosity in a Javanese village (Chapter Four) belongs to the well-established tradition of studies of Javanese religion of which one of the best-known exponents is Clifford Geertz. But like another Australian feminist anthropologist, Norma Sullivan (1994), Smith is anxious to correct the older tradition by showing the importance of women in Javanese religious life. More than that, Smith wants to correct the Geertzian view of a division between Javanese religion and Islam. Her focus is on the broad notion of religiosity, and she uses her fieldwork to demonstrate that the women in the Javanese village she studied practiced a variant of Islam, not a Javanese form of religion alien to Islam. Thus Smith seeks to confirm the view of Indonesian Islam as a tolerant, inclusive form of Islam, by arguing that Islam (like all religions) necessarily varies with time and place, and its practitioners can validly see themselves as good Muslims. In Indonesia this issue has been divisive, so Smith is contributing to a controversy that encompasses not only gender but also the 'true' nature of Islam.

Smith's chapter is valuable too because of its emphasis on village life. It is a reminder to us that most Islamic women in Indonesia still live in villages. Although influenced by urban and global trends, Islam at that level retains many local variations that can only be understood by the type of careful examination that Smith provides. Her chapter reinforces the point that Setyawati also makes: that the combination of Islam and older traditions in rural areas frequently marks rural practice of religion as different from that in large towns.

In the past almost no attention has been given to women in Indonesian education. What is new about Eka Srimulyani's research (Chapter Five) is her focus on women's leadership roles in the Islamic boarding schools known as *pesantren,* which have been regarded as the heartland of male domination, and one of the places where misogynist Islamic beliefs and practices were nurtured. However, *pesantren* education has been undergoing reform led by a number of feminist Islamic leaders (both male and female) in recent years, and Srimulyani's study shows that women have by no means been absent from leadership of these institutions in the past. She gives us the biographical data on three generations of *nyais,* or female religious leaders in *pesantren.* It demonstrates the conditions under which it has been possible for exceptional women to have influence. In some ways her data resemble those concerning female political leaders in Islamic countries: they rise to the top not only because of their own talents but also because of the legitimacy granted them by influential men to whom they are closely related. Despite their apparent flouting of tradition, these exceptional women have to be careful to abide by gendered Islamic rules in most respects, such as in their dress, in their relations with men and their reputation as household managers. In other words, they have been active in public life, both in educational establishments and in representative political institutions, by negotiating a socially and religiously acceptable niche for themselves.

Little research has been done on Indonesia's large Islamic organisations for women, comprising millions of members. Even less attention has been given to organisations intended specifically for young Muslim women. Siti Syamsiyatun's chapter (Chapter Six) sheds light on the notions of young womanhood in Nasyiatul Aisyiyah (commonly known as Nasyiah), the young women's organisation that was an offshoot of Aisyiyah, the women's wing of the modernist Islamic organisation Muhammadiyah. In recent years Nasyiah's leaders have championed new ideas about women and Islam within the Muhammadiyah family and, as Syamsiyatun shows, they have succeeded in winning a favourable response from male-dominated sections of that family. It is a study of young women negotiating religion. Her chapter is especially important in demonstrating the pressures on a moderate group of Islamic women from both secular feminism and Arabian influenced Islamism: they struggle to keep a middle path between what they regard as two extremes.

Amelia Fauzia ventures into new territory in her discussion (Chapter Seven) of women and Islamic philanthropy in Indonesia. As she says, charity is one of the requirements that Islam makes of its adherents, yet it has been little studied, unlike the well-known philanthropic history of Western Christianity. More than that, however, what Fauzia gives us is a gendered study of Islamic charity in Indonesia, based on a number of empirical surveys and on interviews.

She first examines the pattern of giving by Indonesian Muslims and finds some differences between men and women, which may reflect household decision-making processes. Further, she demonstrates how Islamic charitable institutions are gendered in how they spend their money and how women are employed in them. From her interviews she concludes that in the world of charity, as elsewhere, gender patterns are changing: women are taking a more individual role in giving and playing a more prominent role in charitable institutions.

Although this book makes no claim to cover all the areas of scholarship relating to women and Islam in Indonesia, it does approach well-established topics like marriage and veiling in a new way, reflecting post-Suharto trends in Indonesia, and it shows Islamic women negotiating unaccustomed or unacknowledged roles in public life as well as wrestling with new challenges like regional autonomy. Moreover, these chapters are the contributions to scholarship of a new generation of academics, some of whom we will undoubtedly hear more from in the future. The growing interest in Indonesian Islam and the emergence on the academic scene of increasing numbers of academics with feminist sympathies mean that this book is a sign of things to come.

Notes

1   See for example, Bowen 1993; Hefner 1999; Hodgson 1974; Howell 1998; Roff 1985; Woodward 1988; 1989.

2   See Anderson 1972; Geertz 1975; Jay 1969; Magnis–Suseno 1997; Mulder 1996; Sullivan 1994.

3   Blackburn & Bessel (1997), Butt (1997), Cammack (1999), Feillard 1999, Katz & Katz (1975; 1978), Jones (1994) and Krulfeld (1986) are some exceptions.

4   The following are examples of such works: Soebahar & Utsman (1999); Kadir (2001); Ilyas (2003); Ropi & Jamhari (2003).

5   See Dzuhayatin 2002; Tim PSW IAIN Sunan Kalijaga 2002a; Tim PSW IAIN Sunan Kalijaga 2002b; Tim PSW IAIN Sunan Kalijaga 2002c; Tim PSW IAIN Sunan Kalijaga 2002d; Tim PSW IAIN Sunan Kalijaga 2003a; Tim PSW IAIN Sunan Kalijaga 2003b; Aryani 2004; Sodik 2004.

chapter one

Negotiating polygamy in Indonesia: between Islamic discourse and women's lived experiences[1]

Nina Nurmila

> If ye fear that ye shall not be able to deal justly with the orphans, **marry women of your choice, two, or three, or four**; but if ye fear that ye shall not be able to deal justly [with them]; then only one, or that which your right hands possess. That will be more suitable, to prevent you from doing injustice (Qur'an 4:3) (Ali 1989:184–5; emphasis added).

There is no other verse in the Qur'an that has posed the same religious dilemmas and personal suffering for Muslim women as the above verse and its mainstream interpretations. Among most Indonesian Muslims, polygamy[2] is permitted, while polyandry is prohibited. Many Indonesian Muslims believe that 'polygamy is part of *syariah*'. This statement was commonly made by many of my male research participants as their justification for their polygamy or as the reason for a woman accepting her husband's polygamy. This belief is understandable because the *literal* reading of part of the above verse ('marry women of your choice, two, or three, or four') can result in the understanding that polygamy is permitted and even recommended by the Qur'an, the first source of *syariah*. In addition, many Indonesian Muslims must know that the Prophet Muhammad, the second source of *syariah,* had more than one wife, although only a minority of them would acknowledge that the Prophet was monogamous with his first wife until she died. Moreover, many Indonesian Muslims strongly adhere to *fiqh* (Muslim law) books, none of which prohibit polygamy.

However, a contextual and comprehensive reading of the Qur'an may result in an understanding that polygamy is discouraged and even prohibited. Contextual reading of the Qur'an means that in understanding a Qur'anic verse, Muslims also look at the historical context of the verse revelation. The verse 4:3 was revealed in seventh century Saudi Arabia, after the Muslims were defeated in the *Uhud* war. Many Muslim men were killed in battle, leaving their wives, children and their wealth. At that time, because many women were not accustomed to running a business, other Muslim men were appointed to be guardians to manage the widows' and orphans' wealth (Doi 1989). Some male guardians wanted to have the orphans' wealth for themselves. They tried to take it by mixing their small amount of money with the large amount of the orphans' wealth or by marrying them when they reached puberty. They assumed if they married the orphans, they did not need to pay *mahar* (dowry) and could treat the orphaned wives as they wished because the orphans had no-one to protect them (Tabari 1903). In this context, the following Qur'anic verses 4:2–3 were revealed to guide and prevent male guardians from being unjust towards the orphans:

> To orphans restore their property (when they reach their age), nor substitute (your) worthless things for (their) good ones; and devour not their substance (by mixing it up) with your own. For this is indeed a great sin. If ye fear that ye shall not be able to deal justly with the orphans, marry women of your choice, two, or three, or four; but if ye fear that ye shall not be able to deal justly [with them], then only one, or that which your right hands possess. That will be more suitable, to prevent you from doing injustice (Ali 1989:184–5).

A complete reading of the verses suggests that having only one wife will be more suitable and can prevent a Muslim man from doing injustice. Another verse in the same chapter (4:129) states:

> You are never able to be fair and just as between women, even if it is your ardent desire; but turn not away (from a woman) altogether, so as to leave her (as it were) hanging (in the air). If you come to a friendly understanding, and practise self restraint, God is Oft-forgiving, Most Merciful (Ali 1989:227).

Based on the context of revelation and the wording of verses 4:2–3 and 129, the verses can be interpreted as being not about permission for polygamy, but about the importance of being just toward powerless orphans. If male guardians were afraid of being unfair toward orphans, the Qur'an suggests they marry two, three or four women.[3] However, if they were afraid of being unjust to more than one wife, then they could only have one wife. Being just toward wives, the primary requirement for polygamy, is stated in verse 4:129 to be impossible for men to achieve. Therefore, it can be understood that in effect polygamy is prohibited. Muhammad Abduh (1849–1905), an Egyptian reformist, was the leading proponent of the prohibition of polygamy because he saw many cases of wives and children neglected by husbands who were unable to support even one family. His interpretation of polygamy influenced many Muslim scholars and reformers to legislate against polygamy, especially Tunisian scholars who decided to ban polygamy in 1956 (Jawad 1998:45).

Proponents of the prohibition of polygamy believe that any law can change with changing circumstances. For them, polygamy was offered as a solution to prevent injustice toward orphans. Therefore, if contemporary practice of polygamy causes injustice toward women and children, then, to prevent injustice toward them, polygamy must be prohibited. Opponents of polygamy argue that if the intention of the Qur'anic verse 4:3 is to provide a solution for widows and orphans, then polygamy is contradictory to the intended message of the Qur'an and therefore needs to be abolished (in reality polygamy has been used to fulfil male interest and causes misery for women and children). For them, it is justice to which *syariah* aims, not polygamy itself, because they believe that Islam wants its followers to be happy now and in the hereafter.[4] In addition, they believe that the aim of marriage in Islam is to attain tranquillity, love and mercy.[5] However, looking closely at the women involved in polygamous marriage presented in this chapter, tranquillity in married life is unlikely to be achieved.

Polygamy has been mostly associated with Islam, even though it was practised in the Indonesian archipelago before the coming of Islam in the 13th century. For instance, it was permitted by several customary legal systems, such as the *adat* of Hindu Bali and Chinese Indonesians. Polygamy was practised by Javanese aristocrats, who usually had many *selir* (secondary wives) (Blackburn 2004:113), and by Hindus in Bali (Jennaway 2000).

The incidence of polygamy in the Indonesian archipelago and Islamic world as a whole has been very low. In Indonesia, prior to the enactment of the 1974 Marriage Law, it represented about 5% of all marriages and was assumed to be lower after the 1974 Marriage Law, which made polygamy more difficult (Azra 2003b:89). According to Jones (1994:272), Huzayyin's studies in 1979 found that 1% of men in Damascus, 2% of men in Cairo and 7% of men in Bangladesh were polygamous. Other studies show that around 3–6% of North African and Middle Eastern Muslim men were polygamous, but the percentage was higher (11.7%) among Kuwaiti Muslim men in 1975. It was higher in Sudan in 1956 (15.9%), constituting half of all married men, but, according to Jones (1994:272), this high incidence of polygamy had more to do with African culture than Islamic influence, since 20–30% of Sub-Saharan African men were polygamous.

The above rate of polygamy in Indonesia is far lower than the divorce rate, which in the 1950s in West Java appeared to be one of the highest in the world (Jones 1997:96). Both polygamy and divorce have been considered to be against the spirit of Islam but divorce has been more tolerated. According to Jones (1994:277), there is a correlation between the incidence of divorce and polygamy: divorce could be an escape route for women from the practice of polygamy or from the threat of it. Since the divorce rate in Indonesia and the Malay world was very high, the incidence of polygamy itself, according to Jones (1994:210, 277), could not be a major cause of divorce, but the threat of polygamy—such as when a wife knew her husband's intention to take another wife—could become the cause of divorce. According to Jones (1997:104) and Firth (1966:44), there are many interrelated factors that contributed to the high divorce rate in Southeast Asia prior to the 1950s. For instance, parentally arranged marriages at an early age were vulnerable to divorce. In addition, in Malay society, divorce was socially acceptable, quick and easy. Furthermore, the lack of economic deterrents and post-divorce support, such as childcare arrangements among relatives, as well as easy remarriage, contributed to the high rates of divorce in Southeast Asia.

These interrelated factors have been changing gradually. For instance, according to Jones (1997:105), the rising age at marriage and the increasing number of self-arranged marriages have contributed to the decline of the divorce rate in Southeast Asia. These two major factors, according to Jones, are related to socio-economic development, increasing levels of education of both sexes and women's participation in the labour force. Self-arranged marriages at an older age tend to be longer lasting because of greater maturity and because the marriages are based on love. Also related to the two major factors are other changes, such as strict official regulation of marriage and the preference of parents to support the education and careers of daughters, which gives them economic benefit and prestige (Jones 1997:105). In Indonesia after the enactment of the 1974 Marriage Law, which requires court intervention in cases of divorce and polygamy, the divorce rate decreased dramatically. For instance, according to Azra (2003b:88), in 1955 the divorce rate in West Java was 58% of the registered marriages, but it decreased to 16.53% in 1985 and to 14.05% in 1986. In Jakarta, between 1954 and 1975, the divorce rate was about 26%, but it fell to 11% in 1985 (Azra 2003b:88).

Although polygamy is relatively rarely practised in Indonesia, it has received a great deal of attention from women's organisations, which fear the threat of polygamy (Blackburn 2004). Many would perceive women who are involved in polygamous marriages as the 'victims' of polygamy. However, as shown in the case studies presented here, they cannot merely be seen as passive victims without hope. This chapter shows that there has been continuing protest and resistance to polygamy in Indonesia. It also highlights women's agency in dealing with polygamy. First, this chapter discusses the discourse of polygamy since before independence to show the continuing struggles against polygamy and to provide a context for understanding women's experiences in polygamous marriages, which are presented later. The popular ideas about polygamy and its place in Islam affect the ways in which women respond to a husband's polygamy. Second, the chapter presents and analyses case studies of women's experiences in polygamous marriages to demonstrate their agency in dealing with polygamy.

The case studies presented in this chapter are based on fieldwork that I conducted in Indonesia (Bandung, Jakarta, Bogor and Depok) between December 2003 and April 2004. During the fieldwork, I interviewed 74 participants, male and female, involved in a total of 39 marriages. The sample consisted of three women who had left polygamous marriages because they preferred divorce to polygamous marriage, five women and four men involved in monogamous marriage, 20 polygamous husbands, 18 first wives, nine second wives, two third wives and one fourth wife. As well, I interviewed 11 children from polygamous families and two committee members of the Polygamy Award, one of whom is also a polygamous husband. From the 39 marriages, I could only interview both husband and wife in 16 cases. In the other 23 marriages, I could only interview either the wife or the husband.

Polygamy, women and the law: a history of protest

This section explains the discourse of polygamy in Indonesia since colonial times to show the continuing struggles against polygamy and to provide context to women's experiences in polygamous marriages. The pro-polygamy discourse in Indonesia is highly political. Prior to the enactment of the 1974 Marriage Law, the discourse of polygamy was used by Muslim parties to show their opposition to secular nationalist groups.[6] It will be seen that every time there was a move to abolish polygamy, most Muslim parties and organisations rejected the move. The majority of members of Muslim parties and organisations believe that polygamy is permitted in Islam and therefore prohibiting polygamy is regarded as against Islam or as an attack on Islam.

Polygamy was rarely practised in the Dutch East Indies (now Indonesia). Its incidence varied from region to region. For instance, the 1920 Population Census showed that 1.5% of Javanese husbands were polygamous. Consistently, the 1930 Census showed that 1.9% of Javanese husbands had more than one wife, while the rate of polygamy in the Outer Islands was about double that in Java (4.4%). The highest incidence of polygamy in 1930 was in Nusa Tenggara (Sumba 13% and Flores 12%), where traditional beliefs were more prevalent than the Islamic influence. In more Islamised regions, the highest incidence of polygamy was in West Sumatra (9%), followed by Lampung (5.9%) (Jones 1997:269–70).

Polygamy was more commonly practised by elite families. For instance, Sutherland (cited in Jones 1994:270) reported that almost all Javanese regents in the 19th century had more than one wife. This practice of polygamy among aristocratic families features in Kartini's letters. In her letters to her Dutch friends, Kartini (1879–1904), one of the pioneers of women's emancipation in the Dutch East Indies, expressed her opposition to the local Javanese aristocratic traditions of women's seclusion, parentally arranged marriage and polygamy. In her opinion, polygamous marriage served only to fulfil male interests, and offered nothing to women. Herself raised in a polygamous family, Kartini could see directly the misery of women living with a co-wife under the same roof. They had to compete with each other to gain the attention of their husband. Despite her rebellion, she was finally married to a man who already had three wives and six children. She felt powerless to resist polygamy because she perceived that it had been protected by Islamic law (Kartini 1964:69).

Prior to 1974, there was no codified marriage law for Muslims. Muslims mainly referred to Islamic law, which was written in *fiqh* books for matters related to marriage (Azra 2003b:80). *Fiqh* books were mostly written by male Middle Eastern *ulama* (Muslim scholars) as the products of their interpretation of the Qur'an. In these books, which many Muslim feminists argue are male biased, divorce and polygamy are often regarded as men's right. Also, because none of the *fiqh* books prohibit polygamy, most Muslims regard the prohibition of polygamy to be against Islamic teaching; for them, Islamic teaching is what is written in the *fiqh* books. They assume that *fiqh*, which literally means 'understanding', is the same as the Qur'an itself and therefore both are regarded as infallible.[7] The Qur'an, according to them, can only be understood/interpreted by certain people who have certain qualifications, which most Muslims cannot achieve.

A similar objection to that made by Kartini against the Muslim law in relation to marriage was also expressed by members of Indonesian women's organisations in the colonial period. The un-codified Muslim marriage law resulted in uncertainty for Muslim women regarding their rights and how to protect them. The Muslim marriage law, which was written in *fiqh* books, allowed men to marry and to repudiate women, as well as to practise polygamy against women's will. As a result, there were many cases of divorce, under-age and forced marriage (or parentally arranged marriage), and polygamy without adhering to Islamic regulation, which requires a husband, in practising polygamy, to treat his wife justly and, in the case of divorce, to give maintenance to his former wife during her waiting period (Katz & Katz 1975:656). The crucial problem of polygamy in the 1930s was represented in a number of periodicals published at that time. Polygamy had become an issue of burning interest for women's organisations because of its negative consequences for women and children. For instance, Selegoeri, an outspoken writer, expressed her criticism of polygamy in *Soeara Kaoem Iboe Soematra*. She claimed that in Minangkabau polygamy had caused neglected children not to know their father and women who were co-wives to be unhappy (Hatley & Blackburn 2000:53).

Women's organisations held their first congress on 22–25 December 1928 in Yogyakarta. Thirty organisations participated in the congress (Soewondo-Soerasno 1955:128). During the congresses of 1928, 1935, 1938 and 1941, women continued to put pressure on the government to reform the marriage law (Katz & Katz 1975:657). Polygamy was a sensitive and divisive topic among members of women's organisations: secular nationalist women argued against polygamy and proposed the abolition of polygamy in the marriage law, while members of Muslim women's organisations such as Aisyiyah, Muslimat (women's section of Masyumi), Muslimat NU (women's section of Nahdlatul Ulama) and GPII (Indonesian Islamic Youth Organisation) preferred the restriction of polygamy, not the prohibition of it (Nurdin 2003:42–43).

It was not only women who expressed their resistance to polygamy, but also some secular Muslim nationalist men, such as Bahder Djohan. In his speech at the first Kongres Pemuda Indonesia (Youth Indonesian Congress) in 1926, Djohan expressed his opposition to polygamy. In his view, polygamy was an obstacle to achieving equal partnership between a man and a woman in building a happy household. He suggested that polygamy was only a temporary solution to solve the problems of powerless widows and orphans whose husbands/fathers had died in the war at the time of the verse revelation. According to Djohan, the provision for polygamy could be changed with the passing of time. He supported the views of the Egyptian reformist Muhammad Abduh and Said Amir Ali, an Indian legal expert, who opposed polygamy: they regarded it as a violation of the true spirit of Islam, which gives equal rights to men and women (Djohan 1977:26–7).

In 1946, after the establishment of the Ministry of Religion in the first independent government of Indonesia, the administration of Religious Courts was moved from the Ministry of Justice to the Ministry of Religion. In an attempt to unify the administration of Muslim marriage and divorce throughout the country, the Minister of Religion enacted Law No. 22 of 1946, which required all Muslims to register their marriages, divorces and *rujuk* (reconciliations) with the local religious officer appointed by the Minister of Religion. To implement the law, the Ministry of Religion issued regulations that gave advisory power to registrars in cases of forced marriages, divorces and polygamy.

In 1952 the Indonesian government issued a regulation that gave pensions to multiple widows of polygamous civil servants. This regulation, which indicated the state's support for polygamy, was protested by several women's organisations, which were outraged at the regulation (Blackburn 2004:129). In 1954 the Ministry of Religion founded a marriage guidance council, which gave advice to married couples to help them resolve their internal marriage conflicts as a way to avoid divorce and polygamy. The foundation of this marriage guidance council, according to Blackburn (2004:129), indicated the state's concern over the high divorce rate, which might have been connected with polygamy. In 1958 Sumari, a member of the Nationalist Party, submitted her own private bill. This bill stipulated that marriage should be monogamous, and polygamous marriage should not be permitted. As with previous attempts to prohibit polygamy, this bill, which was discussed by the parliament in early 1959, was rejected by members of Muslim parties who believed that it violated Islamic law (Blackburn 2004:129).

Under the New Order regime, the proposal by women's organisations to reform the marriage law was supported by nationalists, who wanted to unify the law throughout Indonesia and to eliminate the influence of the Dutch colonial law. They thought that the colonial law was divisive and discriminatory (Azra 2003b:81–2). As a result of this support, in July 1973, 45 years after the first women's congress, the Suharto government agreed to reform the marriage law (Katz & Katz 1975:657, 660).

However, the process of reforming the marriage law took a long time. There were several factors that prolonged the process. First, it was not easy to reconcile the conflicting interests of Muslims, secularists, Christians and Chinese. Muslims were afraid of the 'veiled Christianisation' in the Marriage Bill draft proposed by the government. Christians and Chinese, who comprised only a small proportion of the population, were afraid of the increased influence of Islam in Indonesia if the marriage law derived from Muslim law (Azra 2003b:82). Second, some Indonesians were in favour of legal diversity, whereby different religious groups were governed by different marriage laws. On the other hand, others preferred the unification of law so that different religious groups were subject to the same marriage law. Third, the issue of polygamy was also hotly debated. Many women's organisations and secular nationalists opposed polygamy, while members of Muslim parties and organisations wanted to retain it. As stated earlier, members of Muslim parties and organisations could not accept the abolition of polygamy because they perceived polygamy as part of Islamic teaching. They seem to have also used the issue of polygamy as a weapon against secular nationalist groups, which rejected the inclusion of the implementation of *syariah* in the Indonesian Constitution.[8]

Finally, the new marriage law was passed by the parliament and signed by President Suharto on 2 January 1974. To implement this new marriage law, the government issued its Implementing Regulation, Government Regulation No. 9/1975, in April 1975 (Azra 2003b:84). The 1974 Marriage Law aimed to reduce the occurrence of divorces and polygamous and child marriages. It also aimed to unify Indonesian marriage law (Cammack 1989:53).

The 1974 Marriage Law stipulates that marriage is legal if it has been performed according to the religious requirements of the parties involved. It sets the minimum age of marriage at 16 for females and 19 for males. It also requires court intervention for divorce and polygamy. Even though polygamy is legal, the law discourages and restricts its practice. On polygamy, the law states (Department of Information 1979:10–11):

Article 3:

1   In principle in a marriage a man shall be allowed to have one wife only. A woman shall be allowed to have one husband only.

2   A Court of Law[9] shall be capable of granting permission to a husband to have more than one wife, if all parties concerned so wish.

Article 4:

1   If a husband desires to have more than one wife, as referred to in Article 3 paragraph (2) of this Law, he shall be required to submit a request to the Court of Law in the region in which he resides.

2   The Court of Law referred to in paragraph (1) of this article shall grant permission to the husband wishing to have more than one wife if:

a   his wife is unable to perform her duties as wife;

b   his wife suffers from physical defects or an incurable disease;

c   his wife is incapable of having descendants.

Article 5:

1   In order for a request to be submitted to the Court of Law as referred to in Article 4 paragraph (1) of this Law, the following requirements shall be obtained:

a   the approval of the wife or wives;

b   the assurance that the husband will guarantee the necessities of life for his wives and their children;

c   the guarantee that the husband shall act justly in regard to his wives and their children.

2   The approval referred to in paragraph (1) under the letter a of this article shall not be required of a husband if it is impossible to obtain the approval

of his wife or wives and if she or they are incapable of becoming partner or partners to the contract, or if no information is available with respect to his wife or wives for the duration of at least 2 (two) years, or on account of other reasons requiring the judgment of a Judge on the Court of Law.

Members of Muslim parties and organisations were generally happy with the new marriage law. The government achieved its aim of unifying the marriage law. However, the law as enacted failed to eradicate discrimination against women in marriage, leaving women subject to the religious codes that, for instance, obliged them to accept polygamy and made divorce easier to initiate for husbands than wives (Blackburn 1999:190).

To further restrict polygamy, in the early 1980s government regulations were enacted requiring members of the armed forces, police and civil service to ask permission from their superior before divorcing or taking or agreeing to become an additional wife (Jones 1997:247). The enactment of these regulations shows the state's disapproval of polygamy and decreased social tolerance of the practice of polygamy (Blackburn 2004:133). However, the tight restrictions and the difficult procedures for legal polygamy might have increased the incidence of high officials taking mistresses or practising secret polygamy. Secret polygamy occurs when a man takes an additional wife without the consent or knowledge of his established wife. He cannot register an additional marriage because he has not followed the legal procedure for polygamy. This secret polygamy, even though it may be considered religiously valid, is not legal and therefore it disadvantages women and children involved in the marriage. These women and children cannot claim maintenance and inheritance if a problem arises from this marriage because they have no legal document to prove that the marriage is valid. The unregistered second marriage of Moerdiono, a prominent official in the Suharto era, and Machicha Mochtar, a famous *dangdut* singer, is an example of secret polygamy, which disadvantaged Machicha and her son. They were abandoned without any clear status because she had no proof of her marriage (*Cek & Ricek* 1999a, 1999b; *Aura* 1999).

In 1991, in a further attempt to create political stability through the unification of law, the Indonesian government enacted *Kompilasi Hukum Islam* (KHI, the Compilation of Islamic Law) through Presidential Instruction No. 1/1991. This Compilation, which is derived from diverse materials of *fiqh*, was recommended as a practical guide for judges in Religious Courts in resolving cases related to marriage, inheritance and *wakaf* (endowment/foundation). The Compilation has similar stipulations on polygamy as that of the 1974 Marriage Law, except that the Compilation gives authority to Religious Courts to grant permission for a husband to take an additional wife if his established wife is reluctant to give the permission, after examining the circumstances of the wife (Article 59) (Salim & Azra 2003:8, 289–90).

The end of Suharto's authoritarian regime (1967–98) opened up a different milieu for Indonesians in which they enjoy freedom of expression. In this new situation, some Muslims raised the issue of an Islamic state and expressed their desire to include the implementation of *syariah* in the Indonesian Constitution. Many of them also objected to the restriction on practising polygamy because they believed that polygamy is part of *syariah*. The new freedom of expression was also used by Puspo Wardoyo, a successful restaurateur (who in 1999 had four wives), to promote polygamy in Indonesia. Wardoyo began promoting polygamy in early 2000 by sponsoring talk shows on radio and television and by organising seminars in which he and his wives were speakers. He even sponsored the Polygamy Award night on 25 July 2003 at Arya Duta, a five-star hotel in Jakarta. On this occasion, Wardoyo gave 37 awards to polygamous husbands. The aims of the award night were to promote transparent polygamy[10] and to improve Indonesian Muslims' perception of polygamy, which until then had been generally negative (interview with Darso Arief, head of the committee of Polygamy Award night, 30 March 2004).

The Polygamy Award night provoked public demonstrations and controversy. Up until the general election in April 2004, polygamy was a hot topic in newspapers, magazines, radio, television and internet mailing list discussions. During this time, the supporters of polygamy became more open in expressing their support for polygamy, especially during the era of President Megawati (2001–04), whose Vice-President, Hamzah Haz, reportedly had three wives. My fieldwork took place within this context of freedom of expression and the increasing confidence of the proponents of polygamy in expressing their views against the government restriction of polygamy. It would have been difficult for me to find research participants who were involved in polygamous marriage if I had done my research during the New Order period. Even when I conducted my research in 2003–04, some people refused to be interviewed. They seemed to be aware of the negative attitude of Indonesian society in general to polygamy.

Women's experiences in polygamous marriages

As stated earlier, it may be easier to see women who are involved in polygamous marriages as merely victims of a husband's betrayal. However, as MacLeod has pointed out, writing about veiling in Cairo, women can be both active subjects and objects of domination at the same time (1992:534). This can be seen from the following case studies of women who are involved in polygamous marriages. Even though their marriages are dominated by their husbands, they can also be considered as active subjects who are struggling to make their marriages work or to improve their emotional well-being by seeking divorce rather than accepting polygamous marriage. This section analyses five case studies of polygamy in which I highlight women's agency in dealing with polygamous marriages. It is shown, for instance, that the case of Tuti[11] fits well with the argument by MacLeod (1992:534) that:

> women, even as subordinate players, always play an active part that goes beyond the dichotomy of victimisation/acceptance, a dichotomy that flattens out a complex and ambiguous agency in which women accept, accommodate, ignore, resist, or protest—sometimes all at the same time.

Arsa, Jajang and Lia: 'I want to smell the fragrance of heaven'

Arsa (32) was a slim and modest person who had a Diploma in Business from a private university in Jakarta. She was friendly and talkative. She wore loose clothing and a headscarf that covered more than half of her upper body whenever she went out and when she met guests at home. Arsa met her husband, Jajang (34), in 1996 through a friend, just after Jajang broke up with his girlfriend. A month after their meeting, Arsa and Jajang, who was a senior high school graduate, decided to get married. They did not celebrate their marriage because of conflict between Jajang and Arsa's parents about the wedding arrangements.[12] Jajang wanted male and female guests to be separated, while Arsa's parents wanted the standard arrangements in which male and female guests could mingle.

Arsa had been married for four years when Jajang told her of his intention to take another wife. Arsa was shocked by the news. She felt that she had not yet had a chance to enjoy her marriage because Jajang had been sick for one and a half years after the marriage and economically unsettled, and, therefore, they were often dependent on Arsa's parents. Arsa's parents had even built a house for her. Arsa expected Jajang to postpone his intention to take another wife until their children had grown up. However, Jajang could not wait that long and he said that he was afraid his children would disagree with his intention when they grew up (interview with Arsa, 11 February 2004).

Jajang said that he took another wife because of his high level of sexual desire, especially during Arsa's menstruation and after she gave birth. At these times, according to Islamic teaching, men should refrain from sexual intercourse. He had already met his chosen second wife, Lia, several times when he told Arsa about his intention to take another wife. He believed that he did not need his wife's approval to take an additional wife. However, Lia requested that he formally follow the 1974 Marriage Law requirements before taking a second wife. Jajang, Lia and Arsa went to court hearings to obtain approval. Having done so, Jajang and Lia were married in 2000, several months after Arsa gave birth to her second daughter (interview with Jajang, February 2004). Lia's request to have her acceptance of polygamy registered is rare because many women, especially uneducated ones, still seem to be unaware of the importance of marriage registration. Lia, whose sister was also a second wife, seems to have been advised by her parents or her sister to have her marriage registered for her own benefit.

Arsa was unhappy with Jajang's polygamy. She said, however, 'Rice has become porridge [*Nasi telah menjadi bubur*].[13] All I can do now is how to make the porridge tasty to eat and not to make it worse.' This means that Arsa considered she had no alternative but to accept her husband's polygamy and to try to make the polygamous marriage work. Therefore, she tried to make friends with Jajang's second wife, Lia, and invited her to discuss any problems arising from the marriage.

> When there was a problem in our polygamous marriage, I usually called Lia to resolve the problem. However, when the problem was too complicated to discuss on the phone, I invited Lia to spend Saturday night in my house. After several such invitations, however, Lia seemed to enjoy spending the night in my house, which was a five-minute walk from her rented house. Lia often came to my house on Saturday night even without my invitation. I feel that my privacy and my time to be together with my husband had been reduced and disturbed by Lia's presence. I usually sleep with my husband on Saturday night. When Lia was present, however, I had to sleep with Lia in one room, while Jajang slept in another room with our children [Arsa's house has two bedrooms]. For my privacy, I plan to move to another rented house, which is far from Lia's house (interview with Arsa, 11 February 2004).

Arsa seemed to be becoming weary of her husband's polygamous marriage but she also wanted to be a devout woman by not asking for divorce.

> My husband told me a saying of the Prophet that a woman who asks for divorce for no reason cannot smell the fragrance of heaven. I accepted my husband's polygamy, hoping for a long-term gain in the hereafter. My husband told me that for women, polygamy is like a test of their belief in their religion. I feel that this test is hard for me but I believe that I can endure it because I do not want to be judged as an unbeliever for not being able to accept polygamy which is part of *syariah* (interview with Arsa, 11 February 2004).

Arsa seemed not to realise that her husband's polygamy can be a strong ground for divorce. She forced herself to be strong in dealing with her husband's polygamy because she believed in what her husband told her about polygamy.

Tuti, Rosyid and Nuri: 'I feel like I am the manager of my husband'

Tuti (37) had a Diploma in Dance from a higher education institution in Bandung. She had been married to Rosyid since 1991 and had three children. She was a dancer but her husband asked her to stop dancing and requested her to wear a headscarf. One day in 2002, Rosyid told her that his relationship with his girlfriend, Nuri (27), had become too close and asked Tuti's permission to marry Nuri. Tuti was reluctant to give her husband permission. However, Tuti was afraid of the consequences if her husband continued his illicit relationship with Nuri behind her back. Therefore, she finally agreed to give her husband permission to marry Nuri on condition that if his additional marriage negatively affected the first marriage, Rosyid must choose to divorce either Nuri or Tuti. Rosyid agreed to the condition. Tuti's conditions for Rosyid's additional marriage shows that she could not simply accept his polygamy.

To accommodate Rosyid's desire to marry Nuri, Tuti was willing to attend the hearings for court approval and helped him get ready for his second wedding.

> During the court hearings, it seemed to me that the judge of the Religious Court was surprised to see my willingness to permit my husband to take a second wife. On the day of my husband's marriage, I prepared and ironed his clothes. I helped him get dressed. It was also I who provided money to pay for Nuri's *mahar* (dowry)[14] because my income was higher than that of my husband. My husband kissed my feet to ask for my forgiveness before he went out for his second marriage. I could not stand to attend the wedding. I stayed at home with my children who asked where their father was when he did not come home that night. I said to them that their father was attending a meeting. I could not sleep that night. I felt that my heart was very hot. To cool down my feelings, I spent that night praying and reading the Qur'an. My husband told me that he felt that his body was very hot that night and he could not stop thinking about his children and me (interview with Tuti, 23 February 2004).

Tuti not only took control of making the second marriage happen, but also was able to end the second marriage by asking Rosyid to divorce Nuri four months after the marriage.

> Several months after his second marriage, I noticed how tired my husband was, physically and mentally. I saw that my husband was struggling to keep both marriages working. When he was with me, Nuri often called him and asked him to accompany her to go to a wedding or to go shopping. Sometimes, when he was with Nuri, I did the same thing. My husband had less time to work or to put his energy into the development of his art career. As a result, he had financial difficulties looking after his two households. Actually, my husband earned only a small amount of money, not even enough to look after one household. Several months after his second marriage, he had large debts and his children's tuition was unpaid. With that large debt, I thought that I had to stop my husband's second marriage before his economic condition deteriorated. I then reminded my husband of the condition of his second marriage and asked him to choose either to divorce

Nuri or me. My husband rejected the idea of divorcing either Nuri or me but I insisted that he kept his promise (interview with Tuti, 23 February 2004).

With Tuti's help, Rosyid agreed to divorce Nuri. Tuti accompanied Rosyid to his divorce hearings in the court. She also paid his divorce fees, including Rp5 million (about AU$650) of the divorce settlement for Nuri. At the time of the interview, Tuti told me that Rosyid still had a debt of Rp7 million (about five months of his salary). However, Tuti said that she was happy with her current marriage because there was no other woman in it. She also told me about her pride and satisfaction on her ability to end her husband's second marriage: 'I feel like I am the manager of my husband [*Saya merasa seperti menjadi menejer suami saya*]' (interview with Tuti, 23 February 2004).

Ema, Hanny and Risa: 'I prefer divorce to being married polygamously'

This section presents three case studies of women (Ema, Hanny and Risa) who preferred divorce to being married polygamously.

Ema (43) was a plump woman who appeared to be depressed. She was wearing loose, dark clothing when I and Hanny, one of my research participants (whose case will be discussed), visited her. She had a tertiary education and was working as a primary-school teacher. She had an arranged marriage with Husen. Husen had been the husband of her older sister, who had died in a car accident and left three small children. For the sake of the three children, Ema's parents arranged for Husen to marry Ema, even though Ema had a boyfriend at that time. From her marriage with Husen, she had three children, the youngest being 18 years old at the time of our interview. Ema told me about her conversation with her former husband before he took another wife.

> In 2002, Husen had had an affair with Elsa, a married woman with four children. Husen asked my consent to marry Elsa, who asked for divorce from her husband on the grounds of her affair with Husen. However, I preferred divorce rather than to share my husband with another woman. Husen assumed that I refused to be married polygamously because I have my own income. Husen said to me: 'The reason why you do not want to be married polygamously must be because you have your own income.' I answered, 'What woman wants to be betrayed? [*Perempuan mana yang mau dihianati?*]' (interview with Ema, 14 February 2004).

Hanny (42) was a beautiful, tall and energetic woman. She cared about her appearance, dressed well and put on a head-covering whenever she went out. She had just divorced after 23 years of an unhappy marriage. Her ex-husband, Asep (46), had claimed that he was a single man when he married her in 1980, but he was actually a married man with two children. Hanny found out about

Asep's previous marriage when she visited Asep's parents about six years after her marriage.

Hanny met Asep, a handsome and attractive person, when Asep was an undergraduate student undertaking *Kuliah Kerja Nyata* (social work placement) in the village of Hanny's parents. They were interested in each other. Hanny's parents also liked Asep's talent in religious preaching, so they supported Hanny's relationship with Asep and arranged for them to get married. The marriage was celebrated by Hanny's rich parents, but neither of Asep's parents nor any of his relatives came to the celebration. Later, Hanny could assume that Asep probably kept his marriage with Hanny secret from his parents until he divorced his first wife. Hanny told me about her unhappy marriage with Asep.

> Throughout my marriage with Asep, he often had affairs with other women such as his colleague, Yanny (39), and his student, Dina (23). Knowing my marriage was in jeopardy, I prepared myself by continuing my study in tertiary education. In 2001, one early morning, I found my husband asleep in Dina's room. I did not know whether Asep had married Dina or not. In 2002, I found out that Asep had married Lely (46), a widow, during his pilgrimage in Mecca. Since I found out about Asep's additional marriages, I refused to sleep with him, feeling disgusted and fearing I might get AIDS. I often asked for divorce but Asep always refused to divorce me. He said, 'Why do you want divorce while what you can do after divorce is selling vegetable salad?' I was furious by his undermining [of] my ability to survive after the divorce. I said, 'No, but you will see me playing golf in Karawang [small city located near Jakarta]'[15] (interview with Hanny, 30 December 2003).

After her divorce, Hanny stayed in her big, luxurious house with her oldest daughter and her grand-daughter. Her other three children were studying and living away from Bandung. Asep continued to support his children, while Hanny began to run a small business to support herself. She realised that divorcees are socially stigmatised and therefore she avoided going out with a man, especially at night.

Risa (35) was a beautiful, slim and attractive woman who looked five years younger than her age. She had a Masters degree in law from Sydney. At the time of interview, she was preparing for her departure to undertake doctoral studies in Sydney. She had been active in an NGO before working as a university lecturer. Risa had been married to Ramli (37) for 12 years (1989–2001) but she preferred divorce to being married polygamously. Risa met Ramli through a friend when she was an undergraduate student. Three weeks after the meeting, they decided to get married without courtship or a chance to really know each other. The marriage was not celebrated and it was only attended by Ramli's parents and relatives. Risa's parents did not know about the marriage. As a newly converted Muslim, Risa thought that her parents, who are non-Muslim, could not be the guardians for her marriage.[16] Her marital happiness lasted only a short time because she soon found out that she could not get along with Ramli. Risa told me about Ramli.

> Ramli is a quiet person so I did not have someone to share my feelings or discuss the problems we faced. Many of our marriage problems were left unsolved because of the absence of communication. I had a higher income than that of Ramli and I mainly supported our nuclear family needs. My unhappiness culminated in 2001 when I found out that Ramli had secretly married another woman, Mamah. I could not share my husband with another woman, so I preferred divorce (interview with Risa, 21 February 2004).

About a year after her divorce from Ramli, Risa married Cecep, who was doing his doctoral studies in Sydney. The marriage with Cecep was celebrated and attended by Risa's and Cecep's parents. Risa said that she was happy with her marriage with Cecep.

Analysis of the case studies

The case of Arsa, Jajang and Lia highlights several important themes. First, Jajang's assumption that he did not need to ask the permission of his wife before taking another wife indicates his resistance to the government-enacted law, the 1974 Marriage Law, and the generalised belief that polygamy is his right. It shows us also how Lia was able to use the law as a form of protection as a second wife. This also points to the attitude, shared by a number of my research participants, of making the best of a difficult situation. For instance, being a second wife might be better for Lia than being a single woman in very poor economic circumstances. Arsa also may not have been as confident as the other three women who preferred divorce to polygamous marriage. She might not be ready to face the challenge of the cultural assumption that it is a woman's fault if a marriage fails, and she might be worried about the stigma attached to the alternative option of divorce. Arsa's belief, stressed by her husband, that by not asking for divorce and by enduring the situation she would be rewarded spiritually, is supported by many male religious preachers, who sometimes encourage women to accept polygamous marriage by saying they will be rewarded in the hereafter by entering paradise (Jones 1994:279).

There are similarities between the cases of Arsa and Risa. Each decided to get married before knowing her intended husband very well. Each married without *pacaran* (courtship) because she disagreed with the idea of courtship before marriage; each believed that Islam does not favour courtship because it may lead to *zina* (illicit sexual relationship). The price each had to pay for not spending enough time getting to know her intended husband before marriage was that she did not know much about his character. Therefore, it is likely that each found it difficult to build a strong emotional bond. This especially applied to Risa: the absence of a strong emotional bond between her and her husband appeared to open the door to the possibility of the presence of a third party in the marriage.

Further, Arsa and Risa did not celebrate their marriages. This created uneasiness, especially for Arsa: some of her neighbours were suspicious that she might have already been pregnant before her marriage, which was a reason for not holding a wedding celebration. The neighbours did not know that it was the conflict between Jajang and his father-in-law about the wedding arrangements that prevented the celebration. However, it is also possible that Jajang might have had his own unstated reason for not celebrating his marriage with Arsa. It is possible that Jajang requested an 'unusual' guest arrangement to prevent the celebration occurring because he was embarrassed to hold a wedding without contributing any money to it.

> When I married Arsa, I only had Rp2,250,000 [about AU$300]. I spent this money to pay for marriage administration and to buy Arsa's *mahar*. Therefore, on the day of my marriage, I did not have any money at all. During the first three years of my marriage, I was mostly economically supported by my father-in-law (interview with Jajang, February 2004).

Another similarity between the cases of Arsa and Risa concerns their levels of education and income. Arsa's and Risa's level of education was higher than that of their husbands. Arsa had a three-year diploma in business, while Jajang had only spent several months in tertiary education because of economic hardship. Risa gained a higher level of education than Ramli after her marriage: she had a masters degree, while Ramli had a bachelor's degree. In terms of income, Jajang had a very low income, so most of Arsa's household needs were supported by her parents. Similarly, in Risa's case, her income was higher than Ramli's, and it was she who mostly provided for the economic needs of her household. It is possible that Jajang and Ramli felt inferior to their wives because of their lower levels of education and income. In Indonesia a husband usually has a higher level of education and income than his wife because he is expected to be the head of the household and therefore superior to all members of his family, including his wife. It is also possible that Jajang and Ramli felt inferior to their wives because of their inability to properly fulfil their expected responsibilities of supporting their households. Their failure to provide enough money for their household members and their lower levels of education may have violated their sense of masculinity. These feelings of inferiority vis-à-vis their wives, together with the social factors conducive to polygamy in the post-Suharto era, may have encouraged Jajang and Ramli to take additional wives to show their superiority as men over women. Similarly, Rosyid, whose income was lower than Tuti's, may also have felt inferior to her. Here, the three men have done something (taking another wife) that is not possible for Muslim women in order to show their superiority in the Indonesian Muslim context. Three of them have taken additional wives with similar characteristics: they are educationally and economically lower than their husbands. By having 'inferior' wives, their male superiority may have been confirmed and their sense of masculine pride sustained.

Ema, Hanny and Risa were well aware of the negative image attached to being *janda* (divorcees) in Indonesia. However, each was ready to face the challenge of being stigmatised rather than sharing her husband with another woman. Since their divorces, both Ema and Hanny have had marriage proposals. However, they said that they want to enjoy the freedom of not having to 'serve' men[17] until they are really ready to get married again.

> I am afraid that I might not be able to get along with my new husband. I am afraid that my new husband would not like my cooking and would complain about it. Therefore, I prefer to be alone for a while and enjoy the freedom of not needing to serve a husband (interview with Hanny, 14 February 2004).

From the case studies of the three women above, it is obvious that education and economic independence play important roles in saving women from unwanted marriage. Three of them are tertiary graduates and even though Hanny had never worked for money during her marriage with Asep, her education and her savings allowed her to run a small business to support herself economically after the divorce.

Tuti, Arsa, Ema, Hanny and Risa can be seen as victims of their husbands' polygamy. However, they are not merely victims. They actively resisted polygamy even though the degree of their resistance varied. Arsa displayed the weakest resistance by trying to make her marriage work well in order to reconcile her religious belief on polygamy and the bitter reality of sharing her husband with another woman. Tuti exercised moderate resistance: she initially accommodated her husband's polygamy but finally brought the second marriage to an end. The strongest resistance was shown by Hanny, Ema and Risa, who preferred divorce to involvement in polygamous marriage.

All the women mentioned in these case studies believe that Islam permits polygamy on condition that a husband must be just to all his wives. Both Arsa and Tuti believe that, as good Muslim women, they have to be able to accept polygamy; otherwise they would feel that they have failed in religious devotion. This feeling seems to be stronger for Arsa than Tuti because Arsa lives among people who strongly suggest that women should accept polygamy as part of *syariah*. Jajang, as we saw, had frequently advised Arsa to accept polygamy as a test of her belief in Islam. Therefore, even though Arsa is unhappy and emotionally weary of her husband's polygamous marriage, she stays in her marriage out of religious devotion and for the sake of her children. Tuti also told me about her regret at not being able to accept her husband's polygamy and her fear of being labelled non-devout for not accepting polygamy. Tuti's initial accommodation of her husband's polygamous marriage and her later attempts to resist it show the religious dilemma she experienced. On the one hand, she might have felt that she was a devout woman when she supported Rosyid's polygamy. On the other hand, her support for polygamy caused her personal suffering and economic hardship.

However, unlike Arsa who lived among militant Muslims, Tuti lived among moderate Muslims who seemed to have negative attitudes about polygamy. Therefore, Tuti experienced less social pressure than Arsa to accept polygamy as a sign of religious piety. Only Ema, Hanny and Risa appeared unafraid of being labelled un-Islamic in not accepting polygamy. Even though the three of them believed that Islam permits polygamy, they interpreted the Qur'anic verse 4:3 contextually. This means that they believe that polygamy is permitted in Islam only in certain situations described in the context of the revelation of the Qur'anic verse 4:3. Thus, the way the women responded to polygamy was very much affected by their beliefs about polygamy in Islam and the attitudes of people who live around them.

Epilogue

In September 2004, Susilo Bambang Yudhoyono, who has a military background, was elected president of Indonesia. Puspo Wardoyo, who seems to be politically savvy and aware of the changing political climate, has been silent during the era of Mr Yudhoyono, who appears to share Suharto's opposition to polygamy. The discussion on polygamy re-emerged after 4 October 2004 when Kelompok Kerja Pengarus utamaan Jender (The Gender Mainstreaming Work Team), Department of Religious Affairs, chaired by Siti Musdah Mulia, submitted a Counter Legal Draft of KHI, which proposed that polygamy be abolished. This draft was submitted as an alternative to the new draft of KHI (namely *Rancangan Undang-Undang Hukum Terapan Peradilan Agama Bidang Perkawinan* or the Applied Legal Draft of Religious Court on Marriage), which was proposed to be elevated from a practical guide for judges of Religious Courts into a codified law (*Swara* 11 October 2004). The submission of the Counter Legal Draft caused public controversy. Islamist[18] groups such as Majelis Mujahidin Indonesia[19] and Islamist magazines such as *Majalah Suara Hidayatullah*[20] accused the team that wrote the Counter Legal Draft of attacking *syariah* (Thalib 2005) and regarded the draft as an *halusinasi* (hallucination) of the opponents of *syariah* (Awwas 2004). Disagreements about the Counter Legal Draft were also publicised by senior female Muslim scholars such as Huzaemah T Yanggo, Nabilah Lubis and Zakiyah Darajat, all three of whom had doctoral degrees from Egypt. According to Huzaemah, the draft caused uneasiness among Indonesian society, which is understandable, according to her, because the draft contradicts the Qur'an, Sunnah and other reliable sources of Islamic law (*Republika* 18.2.2005).[21] As a result, the Minister of Religious Affairs rejected the Counter Legal Draft on 14 February 2005 on the grounds that it contradicted the Indonesian mainstream interpretation of the Qur'an (Rokhmad 2005; Surur 2005).[22]

Even though the Counter Legal Draft proposing the abolition of polygamy was rejected, the Applied Legal Draft of the Religious Court on Marriage put further restrictions on polygamy by stipulating a punishment of three months' imprisonment or a Rp3 million (about AU$400) fine for any man who takes an additional wife without the permission of his established wife (*Gatra* 7 December 2003). In addition, even though the Counter Legal Draft was rejected, its existence shows that there is an alternative interpretation of polygamy to the existing mainstream one. The working team of the Counter Legal Draft seemed to approach Qur'an *contextually*, not *literally*.

The Minister of Religious Affairs is right—the interpretation that Islam prohibits polygamy is held by a minority of people. These people approach the Qur'an comprehensively and contextually. They include young Muslim scholars, both men and women. Some of them work in NGOs such as Rifka Annisa, Yasanti and Lembaga Bantuan Hukum Asosiasi Perempuan Indonesia untuk Keadilan, while others have been actively engaged in teaching and research in IAINs and the UIN throughout Indonesia, mainly in Jakarta and Yogyakarta. Their active engagement in teaching and research opens up the possibility that the minority interpretation, some day in the future, may become more acceptable among Indonesian Muslims.

Notes

1   I would like to thank Associate Professor Susan Blackburn and my supervisors Associate Professor Maila Stivens, Dr Kate McGregor and Professor Abdullah Saeed for providing insightful feedback on this chapter.

2   *Polygamy* refers to a marriage in which a spouse of either sex has more than one mate at the same time. The term *polygamy* encompasses *polyandry* and *polygyny*. *Polyandry* refers to marriage between one woman and two or more men, while *polygyny* refers to marriage between a man and two or more women (Jones 1994:268). For the purpose of this chapter, the term *polygamy* will be used to refer to a man who has more than one wife at the same time.

3   Having an unlimited number of wives was common in pre-Islamic tradition.

4   Qur'anic verse Al-Baqarah:202 states: 'Our Lord! Give us good in this world and good in the Hereafter, and defend us from the torment of the Fire!' (Ali 1989:82).

5   On the aim of marriage, Qur'anic verse Ar-Ruum:21 states: 'And among His Signs is this, that He created for you mates from among yourselves, that ye may dwell in tranquillity with them, and He has put love and mercy between your (hearts): verily in that are Signs for those who reflect' (Ali 1989:1050).

6   Indonesian nationalists were against Dutch colonisation and aimed at building an independent Indonesian state based on nationalism. Endang Saefuddin Anshari categorised Indonesian nationalists into secular and Islamic nationalists. Secular nationalists could be Muslims, Christians or others who argued for separation between religion and the state, while Islamic nationalists argued that state and society must be governed by Islam (Anshari 1986;8–9).

7   For further information regarding Muslims' confusion between Qur'an and its interpretation, see Barlas (2002).

8   On the debates between secular and Islamic nationalists on the inclusion of the implementation of *syariah* in the Indonesian Constitution, see Anshari (1986).

9   A Court of Law here means a Religious Court.

10 Transparent polygamy refers to the practice of polygamy in which a husband asks his wife's consent before taking another wife or lets his established wife/wives know that he has married (an)other woman/women. He may also let his wife/wives know of his arrangement for visiting each of his wives.

11 All participants' names are pseudonyms.

12 Islam recommends that marriage is to be celebrated (*dirayakan/walimah*). Indonesian Muslims generally celebrate their marriage right after they sign the marriage contract by having a marriage ceremony. They usually invite neighbours, friends, relatives and colleagues to the wedding ceremony. The invited guests come to congratulate the newly married couple, who sit side by side in a decorated room, and to give them presents, and then they have a meal provided by the host. It is unusual that a Muslim marriage is not celebrated. Therefore, when this happens it often becomes the topic of gossip. Neighbours of the bride or the groom may wonder

why the marriage took place secretly. They may suspect that the bride was already pregnant before the marriage, which is considered shameful.

13 It is an Indonesian proverb that means that we cannot undo something that has happened.

14 *Mahar* is a compulsory gift from the groom to his bride, usually in a form of money or jewellry.

15 Hanny contrasted Asep's assumption of her selling vegetable salad, a low-income occupation that was usually undertaken by poor and uneducated women, with playing golf, an elite sport usually undertaken by rich and high-class people.

16 In a Muslim wedding, the bride's consent is given on her behalf by her guardian (usually her father).

17 In the Indonesian context, a wife's expected role is to serve her husband, such as to serve his meals and clothes and to serve him sexually.

18 Tibi (2002:xiv) differentiates between Islam and Islamism. For him, Islam is a great, tolerant faith, while Islamism is a militant ideology of religious fundamentalism. According to him (2002:xxv), 'religious fundamentalism—as a political phenomenon not restricted to the World of Islam—is an aggressive politicisation of religion undertaken in the pursuit of nonreligious ends'. Thus, Islamists are Muslims who use Islam for political purposes.

19 Majelis Mujahidin Indonesia, short for Majelis Mujahidin untuk Penegakan Syari'ah Islam (The Council of Mujahedeen for Islamic Law Enforcement), established in 2000 in Yogyakarta, is a small organisation and regarded as extremist by the Muslim mainstream.

20 *Majalah Suara Hidayatullah*, or *Majalah Hidayatullah*, is the magazine of an Islamic organisation called Hidayatullah. Between 50,000–55,000 copies are distributed throughout Indonesia and neighbouring countries. First published in 1988, the magazine belongs to Hidayatullah Islamic Boarding School in Balikpapan. In 1989 its office moved to Surabaya (Majalah Suara Hidayatullah website, 2006).

21 This comment shows her tendency not to differentiate the Qur'an from its interpretation, the problem addressed by Barlas (2002). Huzaemah is one of the senior female scholars who strongly adhere to *fiqh* books. This may be because of her academic background as an Al-Azhar University graduate.

22 The reason given by the Minister of Religious Affairs for the rejection of the Counter Legal Draft shows his understanding of the difference between 'Qur'an' and 'its interpretation'. Unlike many Islamists who cannot differentiate between Qur'an and its interpretation and who often claim that their interpretation is the only true Islam, the Minister did not say that the Counter Legal Draft was rejected because it was contradictory to the 'Qur'an': he said that the Counter Legal Draft contradicted 'the mainstream interpretation'. Again, the rejection of the Counter Legal Draft shows that the discourse of polygamy is highly political. To avoid social chaos, the Minister preferred to reject the abolition of polygamy.

chapter two

Muslim women and contemporary veiling in Indonesian *sinetron*[1]

Rachmah Ida

The practice of veiling, which in Indonesia usually means wearing the *jilbab*, has grown rapidly among urban middle-class women in contemporary Indonesia since the 1990s. This reflects new patterns of consumption among the urban middle classes, along with the popularisation of Islamic religious iconography in the mass media. The practice of wearing the *jilbab* reflects shifting meanings, from religious devoutness to a mode of cultural consumption, as evidenced in advertisement images and media coverage. However, it is still debatable as to whether the practice of veiling is just another fashion trend that could disappear, or whether it does indeed represent a collective religious awareness, one that challenges globalisation, Westernisation or de-Islamisation movements among urban middle-class women.

Veiling has also become significant in the process of *otonomi daerah* (regional autonomy) in several provinces such as Aceh, Padang and Banten, and in Riau, as discussed by Lugina Setyawati in this volume. These regional governments have issued regulations requiring women to wear the veil in public spaces. Questions arise as to whether or not this political arrangement creates more challenges for women. It is clear that nowadays the adoption of *jilbab* has a new meaning, which reaches far beyond the religious need to cover the female *aurat* (any part of the body which should not be visible according to Islamic interpretation). Rather, the practice of wearing the *jilbab* (and the politics associated with it) taps into significant issues of female bodies, sexuality and subject identities.

This chapter examines the practices of contemporary veiling among urban middle-class Muslim women as they are represented in the Ramadan television dramas, locally known as *sinetron*. It aims to understand how religious iconography is utilised to construct Muslim female identities and questions whether the practice of veiling reflects the rise of a collective religious/Islamic faith awareness or if it is simply a new trend and consumption pattern among urban middle-class women. I argue that the practice of veiling as shown on the televisual texts (the *sinetron*) signifies the problematic relationship between the need to promote a moderate Islamic look and the challenge to conserve meanings of veiling as adherence to the Islamic principle of covering the female body to conceal it from the male gaze. In fact, the wearing of *jilbab* articulated throughout the serials suggests that the practice of veiling is simply utilised to differentiate 'devout' Muslims from 'ordinary' Muslims.

In this chapter, I use three highly rated 'Ramadan *sinetron*' texts—which are categorised as 'religious' (Islamic) drama productions—that were broadcast on the national private channels between 2003 and 2004. The three *sinetron* productions, *Doa membawa berkah* (*Prayer brings blessing*, 2003), *Doa dan anugerah* (*Prayer and bestowal*, 2004) and *Maha pengasih* (*All-loving God*, 2002–03), have had notable success and have been very popular with *sinetron* viewers in recent years. All these *sinetron* serials have been re-run soon after the Ramadan fasting season has ended. Sequels have also been produced. The analysis of these three televised fiction productions, together with my field research on the audience's reception, is also an attempt to unpack whether and how these Islam-themed television serials, which are exclusively produced to run during the holy month of Ramadan, have participated in (re-)constructing images of contemporary urban Muslim women, particularly their Muslim fashion culture in the era of post-authoritarian Indonesia.

Islam on television

Religious programs on Indonesian television have been broadcast for a long time. Every day, Islamic sermon and proselytising (*dakwah*) programs are broadcast as early as 5 am. Previously, the state-owned station, TVRI, which had about 2.4% of audience share (meaning the station was watched by three million people (*Media Scene* 2004:34)), had broadcast a weekly religious program called *Mimbar agama* (*Religious rostrum*) dedicated to the five major religious practices that were formally acknowledged by the New Order government as 'religions' of Indonesians. For instance, Sunday night was designated for the Catholic and Christian faiths, Wednesday was for the Hindus or Buddhists, and Thursday night was for Muslims. The programs were mainly designed as a one-way *ceramah agama* (lecture model). Exclusively for Islam, as the major religion in Indonesia, every private television station has morning sermon programs such as *Kuliah subuh* (*Morning lecture*), *Hikmah fajar* (*Dawn wisdom*) and *Siraman rohani* (*Religious shower*), which are broadcast between 5 am and 6 am daily.

Further, there has been a trend every Ramadan for all private nationwide television stations to broadcast particular programs covering specific issues on

Islam. The programs range from talk show programs and sermons to quizzes, music and *sinetron*. All channels reschedule their daily programming patterns and prioritise such religious programs during the Ramadan month, including Ramadan cooking shows, Ramadan celebrity shows, Ramadan current affairs and even some off-air *dakwah* programs (Pudjiastuti 2002). Islam is strongly prominent during the Muslim fasting month, as all the female performers—including the newsreaders, program hosts and the actresses—wear Muslim clothing (known as *busana Muslimah*—literally Muslim women's dress) and *jilbab* (a full headscarf that exposes only the face) or *kerudung* (a loose headscarf). The Indonesian television channels seem to become such 'religious channels' just for the holy month.

A survey by ACNielsen shows that several Ramadan programs gained high ratings, particularly early morning quizzes broadcast between 2 am and 4 am (during *sahour* or morning breakfast) and the locally made *sinetron* broadcast in the evenings between 5 pm and 7 pm (before *iftar* or evening break of fast) (Muzakki 2003:4). Said Ramadan (2003:4) also suggests that this trend is a 'temporary market culture phenomenon'. The audience share of private stations has grown. For instance, during 2002/2003 they were watched by more than 50 million people (*Media Scene* 2004). Consequently Ramadan programs are projected to gain more revenues from advertising.

The broadcast time allocated to Ramadan programs on all national private television stations amounts to approximately 44 hours per day. This large time allocation has also resulted in massive profits for the stations. Although exact figures have not been publicised by the private television stations, *Kompas* (*Program* 2002) reported that the advertising revenue of private channels in 2002 was calculated at around Rp1.2 billion (AU$240,000) per day; this figure rose to about Rp3.6 billion (AU$720,000) during the month of Ramadan. Audience numbers watching the Ramadan shows reach a peak between five and ten minutes before the evening breaking of fast, so advertisements placed between these times are expensive. For a 30-second advertising time slot, the advertisers paid between Rp15 million and Rp18 million (AU$3,000–5,000). Thus, Ramadan has been used by the capitalist media not for religious considerations but, rather, for commercial motives: 'Television itself is as a type of surrogate popular religion closely linked to the values of consumer capitalism' (Ruthven 2002).

Normally pictures of Islamic cultures and identities on television are marginalised, compared to foreign productions and the abundance of Western adaptation programs. As Wardhana (2002) suggests, Indonesian television appears to air issues of Islam and religiosity only when the Ramadan holy month is close. According to him, during the Ramadan month and for other

Islamic events such as *Ied Mubarak* (known as *Idul Fitri,* end of Ramadan) or *Maulid* (birthday) of Prophet Mohammad, the television programs are filled with images of Muslim women in Muslim clothing and *jilbab*, and Arabian music programs (known as *irama padang pasir* or *gambus* music) are shown frequently (Wardhana 2002:148). Although Islam is the religion of the majority of Indonesians, the national television channels appear to work in a secular idiom in a social context where religious practices and identity are important to many of the multicultural viewers. Subsequently, when these Islamic events are concluded, the television channels return to 'normal' business. Like other capitalist media, the Indonesian private television stations do not want to lose their consumers, so they have to conform with issues relating to moral and religious values found in the wider culture of Indonesian society.

The subject-position of Muslim women in contemporary Indonesia: an overview

Issues of identity politics in Indonesia have long been unchallenged. Under the New Order regime, individual subject-positions were under the authority of and defined by the state. The creation of different identities was subtly denied. Discussing the condition of Muslim women in Indonesia, one should consider the relationship between Islam and the state. Hefner (1993) observes that in the New Order era, Islam was considered as the opposition by the regime and it was marginalised within the state political system. Influential Muslim leaders were even restricted from exercising their civil rights.

However, since the late 1990s, the Islamic movement, pioneered by some prominent Muslim leaders and academic scholars such as Abdurrahman Wahid, Nurcholish Madjid, Quraishy Shihab and others, has forged a new relationship between Islam and the state. This development offered significant opportunities for Muslims to play a role in the socio-political system of the New Order and it has gone further in the current era of the so-called *Indonesia baru* (new Indonesia).

Responding to this phenomenon, Istiadah (1995) argues that Muslim women in Indonesia have also attempted to challenge patriarchal domination. Her argument derives from her optimism that, first, through writings, biographies and autobiographies, devoted Muslim women, individually or collectively, have presented a challenge to advance women's status beyond the state ideology and conservative Islam in Indonesia. Second, changes in socio-political and economic circumstances have encouraged Indonesian women to gain more access to participation in the work force and education. Lastly, the rise of liberal Muslim intellectuals in the country has provided more opportunities for the transformation of Muslim women in the Indonesian context (Istiadah 1995:1).

However, many Indonesian Muslim women still interpret and define the subject-position of women in different ways. Some Muslim women continue to believe that Islam requires a woman, especially as a mother and a wife, to carry household responsibilities and to look after the children. For instance, one Muslim mother argues: 'The role of the husband is as leader in the house and in society. In Islam a woman has no obligation to work for money, that is her husband's role' (Williams 1998:273). This notion implies that a woman in Islam needs the support of her husband in order to have a job outside the home, because a woman is not required to look for a job to earn money. The responsibility to earn an income for the family rests on a man's shoulders. Another Muslim woman says:

> We are not superwomen...so if I want to work then I must compensate for my absence by providing a maid to do my [house] work. Islam doesn't say that a wife has to do all the work herself...The husband isn't actually doing any of the domestic work himself (Williams 1998:272).

In contrast to these two women's views, some Muslim leaders and scholars have argued that Islam does not restrict the relationships between husband and wife in terms of responsibility for bringing in the family income or in terms of role distribution in the household. Also, Islam has never prohibited women from working outside the home or going out in the public arena. Islam may even encourage women to have a job outside the home. Abdurrahman Wahid, also known as Gus Dur, one of Indonesia's prominent Muslim leaders and previously the Indonesian President, claims:

> You have to look at the issue with [a] wider sense of the meaning of Islam in Indonesia...We are conscious of the threat of being uprooted by modernisation and rapid social change...Personally, I believe that the Prophet demands interpretation from us, not just blind following, and I think this illustrates the differences in the perceptions of women in the religion. But, also, I do have to say this frankly, many Muslim leaders still look at women with degrading attitudes, they still believe that the rights of women are not equal to the rights of men (Williams 1998:278–9).

The *Reformasi* (Reform) era in Indonesia since 1998 has offered opportunities for some Muslim women activists to expand the position of women in the state and society. On the issue of Islam and women's development in Indonesia, for instance, the State Minister for Women's Empowerment during Abdurrahman Wahid's presidency, Khofifah Parawansa (an NU female activist), attempted to set a new direction in state policy for women's advancement. Yet she became aware of particular Islamic communities and institutions that are not yet supporting the effort to improve the status of women in society:

> religious teachings have strongly influenced society's mind-set and the way of life in Indonesia. Unfortunately, many *Ulama* (Muslim religious scholars), preachers, and religious leaders do not have enlightened views on gender. Even though the new president of Indonesia is a woman, gender mainstreaming will still be required to effect a change in attitude (Parawansa 2002:73).

The New Order determination of the ideal image of women has been challenged by various independent women's organisations and feminist activists. In post-Suharto Indonesia, official policies challenging the existing stereotype of women's position in society have been issued. Attempts to empower women within the national development and socio-political discourses have also been endorsed during this transitional period. However, this raises the question of whether Indonesian society, as well as the media, has responded and negotiated the issue of Islam and the position of women in the post-*Reformasi* era of Indonesia as part of the discourse of democracy in the country.

Muslim women's position and the practice of veiling

In the early 1980s, the practice of veiling among Muslim women in Indonesia was limited and seen as a form of Muslim fundamentalism, but some Muslim women, particularly university students, started to wear long dresses and the *jilbab* over their necks and bosoms in public arenas. During this time the practice gave rise to extreme points of view concerning 'oppression' and 'lack of freedom'. Muslim women wearing *jilbab* were considered conservative by the Indonesian society.

However, the social conditions of the 1990s seem to have been in direct contrast with the conditions of the 1980s. Until the mid-1990s, the number of Muslim women wearing Islamic clothing remained a small minority of the population, most visible around Islamic schools and university campuses. The trend towards wearing Islamic clothing has increased in recent years in Indonesia. More and more women, particularly the young and the urban middle classes, have chosen to conceal their bodies and heads as a sign of adherence to the Islamic faith and belief.

Formerly, in the mid-1990s, the wearing of a 'modish' headscarf became popular when the youngest daughter of New Order President Suharto, Siti Hardiyanti Rukmana (popularly called Tutut), began wearing *kerudung* (a loose headscarf, which still exposes the hair and neck) for her official dress. The way she dressed with *kerudung* became the fashion model for (mature) Muslim women during that time. Lies Marcoes Natsir (2004) argues, 'Indonesian fashion designers as well as the garment industry geared up both to follow and steer her example and a veritable Indonesian Islamic fashion started to develop' (Natsir 2004:3). This 'politics of dressing' was seen as one of the political attempts of the Suharto New Order family to gain a positive image for their practice of Islam in the eyes of the public. Natsir claims that this political attempt marked an active involvement of the New Order regime in religious (Islamic) rituals and its support of particular Islamic groups, which resulted in the trend to acknowledge 'Islam' as part of national identity. In accordance with this attempt, in 1990, for the first time in the Suharto era, the Department of National Education and Culture allowed the wearing of *jilbab* in state schools.

Since the end of the New Order, the socio-political situation has become more favourable towards the wearing of *jilbab*. According to Lyn Parker (2005:21), the wearing of *jilbab* in some schools in Indonesia has even become a compulsory part of the school uniform. 'The dramatic turnaround in *jilbab*-wearing reflects the Islamisation of Indonesian society, and is part of the so-called Islamic resurgence worldwide' (Parker 2005:21). Several regional areas in Indonesia have initiated regulations requiring the wearing of the *jilbab*. For instance, in Tasikmalaya, a sub-region of West Java, formal requirements to wear the *jilbab* have affected women's positions. The Tasikmalaya government issued Policy No. 451/SE/04/SOS/2001, which requires all female Muslim students of primary schools, junior and high schools, colleges and universities to wear the uniform that covers their *aurat* ('*Otonomi*' 2004). This policy has been translated as obliging all Muslim female students in the Tasikmalaya region to wear the *jilbab*.

In several *kabupaten* (provinces and regions) where the practices of Islamic norms and principles are intense, the wearing of *jilbab* has been included in the legal policy of the regional governments through the so-called *Peraturan Daerah (Perda) Syariah* (Regional Syariah/Islamic Law). In the province of Aceh, for instance, the application of *syariah* law requires all Acehnese women to wear *jilbab*, even visitors who enter this province. However, Harsono (2004) found that there have been different interpretations concerning the wearing of *jilbab* in Aceh. Harsono showed that there are Acehnese women who wear a *jilbab* as their everyday dress code, and who disagree with the government regulation that requires all Acehnese women to wear *jilbab* when appearing in public. For these women, since the wearing of *jilbab* relates to the 'faith', and they believe faith is an individual matter, so it is up to the individual woman whether she wears *jilbab* or not. One woman among Harsono's informants said, 'Islam is flexible. Islam does not force people. *Jilbab* or not, it's your own business with God' (Harsono 2004:1). Lugina Setyawati's chapter in this volume shows a similar trend requiring the wearing of the *jilbab* at official functions in Riau.

Indeed, there is still a dichotomy in perceptions relating to the wearing of the veil in Indonesia. There are people who consider that a Muslim woman is required to wear a veil and others who believe that wearing a veil is not mandatory and depends on the belief of a Muslim woman. Many women think that a woman wearing a *jilbab* will be considered 'fundamentalist' or 'traditional' or 'revivalist'. One Indonesian Muslim woman, cited by Williams, responded to the issue by saying, 'It is a requirement to wear *jilbab* but not all women do. Maybe they think that it makes them look old, or maybe they like European or American clothes' (Williams 1998:277). This comment is typical of the attitude of those women who are strongly committed to Islam, but realise the persistence of modernisation and global social change, which have affected women's views about Muslim women's dress and veil in Indonesia. It is also representative of the Muslim woman who remains essentially conservative, but who is tolerant of moderate views regarding the code of conduct for Islamic women. Abdurrahman Wahid, who has been perceived by Indonesian society as a 'democratic' Muslim leader, comments on the issue of veiling as follows.

> We are conscious of the threat of being uprooted by modernisation and rapid social change and one way to go back to our roots is by wearing clothes that are as close as possible to what is prescribed by the prophet. But that doesn't mean women want to accept domination by men. Even some men have adopted Muslim garb like a tunic because they want to be identified as Muslim (Williams 1998:278–9).

Wahid seems to recognise that Indonesian Islamic women are divided about the requirement for women to conceal their bodies completely, including the head and shoulders, by wearing Muslim dress and veil. On the one hand, he acknowledges that, as part of the modernisation process, there are women who do not want to practise veiling. On the other hand, judging from the coverage of media and advertisements in Indonesia, Wahid also remarks that there has been a 'shifting' phenomenon in which more urban middle-class women are starting to wear the *jilbab* to consolidate their identities as devout Muslims. Commenting on the rise of this social phenomenon among middle-class women, Wahid states:

> At one level the interpretation of a woman's image seems to have polarised: on the one hand skimpily clad girls are gracing all kinds of consumer goods in advertisements splashed across billboards, but on the other hand more and more women are choosing to wear the *jilbab* (Williams 1998:278).

This issue has also been picked up by the Indonesian media and by capitalist manufacturers. Challenged by the increased practice of veiling among middle-class women, Indonesian magazines and other printed publications show in their fashion pages contemporary styles of Muslim women's fashions and other 'new' looks of Islamic clothing for women, men and children. The designs represent a combination of 'traditional' Muslim women's dress and Western-style ideas of fashion.

Various kinds of *busana Muslimah* and *jilbab* are created and promoted for urban middle-class women, the target market of those magazines and tabloids. *Busana Muslimah* and *jilbab* have become the new mass-marketing fashion trend for urban Indonesian women. The model of Muslim female dress has been modified to create a contemporary look. Some of the designs are expensive and only affordable for the elite. Elsewhere, however, outlets and do-it-yourself patterns make the designs of veiling generally available for middle- to lower-class women. Therefore, the *jilbab* has developed into an indispensable part of Muslim female fashion. The wearing of *jilbab* has not only acted as a strong expression of one's identity and individual choice, but also has become part of the occasional costumes of Muslim women for events such as *pengajian* (congregation) and funerals and during the month of Ramadan.

Accordingly, in many new designs of *busana Muslimah*, parts of a woman's body, like the neck and hair, are still uncovered. For devout women, this model of fashion is extremely controversial. According to common interpretation of the Qur'an (particularly, chapter An-Nur 30–32), the female *aurat* (which is concealed during prayer) is shameful and must be covered (Harsono 2004). A female's *aurat* is considered to go from her hair to her knees. However, the stricter interpretation says that a female's *aurat* even includes her feet and her face, so prompting some women to wear socks and *jalabiya* (dark robe) and *cadar* (face cover). This different interpretation is thus quite different from *busana Muslimah*. On the one hand, some devout women choose to wear the design of *jubah* (long and loose dress) and conventional, long *jilbab*, often in dark-coloured material. (This *jubah* is mainly a 'do-it-yourself' model and is less often found in retail shops.) On the other hand, the popular designs of *busana Muslimah* and *jilbab* available in the market places are mainly a combination of pants and long jackets or blouses in fine, multi-coloured fabrics and sometimes even silk.

The wearing of *jilbab* has received massive media coverage, and it has become a central interest of the fashion industry in Indonesia. However, few studies explore how women in *jilbab* are portrayed in relation to women's femininity, sexuality and identity. This chapter thus fills a gap by studying women and the media in Indonesia in terms of *jilbab* and the construction of women's identity. How, then, do television dramas represent the issue of veiling throughout their stories and visual creations? The following part of the chapter examines the televisual construction of veiling among affluent urban middle-class women.

Images of women and veiling in *sinetron*

For the most part in Indonesia, images of women wearing *jilbab* can only be seen in particular Islamic-themed programs or in melodrama *sinetron* television programs, which are run only during the Ramadan fasting month. These Muslim females wearing either the *jilbab* or *kerudung* in the television programs, particularly in teledramas, represent the contemporary look of the urban veiling fashion. Their styles of Muslim dress and the veil do not represent the articulation of the established meaning of veiling as a sign of adherence to the Islamic principle of covering the body to conceal it from the male gaze. Rather, the wearing of a loose scarf with hair still shown conveys the impression that the wearing of the *jilbab* is only a matter of 'body accessories'.

As such, the wearing of *jilbab* in melodramas suggests a weak relationship with the devoutness of the person. The *jilbab* as presented on the screen reinforces the picture of moderate Muslims in a secular-based and capitalist media landscape. Although, sometimes, women are represented wearing *mukenah* (a white cloak covering a woman's head and body, which is worn only at the five prayer times), the *sinetron* producers seem to suggest that the wearing of *jilbab* is not mandatory for Muslim women. Although it is prescribed in the Qur'an chapter An-Nur 30–32 that Muslim women are required to conceal their bodies, the interpretations of the chapter itself are diverse and contradictory, and the *sinetron* producers appear to reflect this varied discourse.

The practice of wearing *jilbab* depicted in *sinetron* also appears to denote the difference between pious or devout Muslim women and 'ordinary' Muslim women. The figure with the *jilbab* is presented as a 'holy' person who surrenders and submits her destiny and fate only to Allah Almighty. Aisyah, the prominent character in *Doa dan anugerah*, is depicted as a devout woman who has never removed her veil on any occasion; she is conservative, submissive and is leaving her fate and destiny to her Almighty. Aisyah (played by a talented singer and popular celebrity, Krisdayanti) is a confident figure and strongly believes that her body is created by, and therefore belongs to, God. Her fate as a Muslim, and as an orphan stricken with cancer, and her veiling of her body are all given, and not part of her choice, as a creature of God. Thus, wearing the *jilbab* for Aisyah is presented as a consequence of her fate as a Muslim, as *hamba Allah* (God's slave).

The way Aisyah wears her own style of *busana Muslimah* and *jilbab* signifies the popularisation of contemporary Muslim fashion by middle-class women in Indonesia. Muslim women's fashions and veils worn by Aisyah in the *sinetron* have reproduced the more popular fashions in which women's *aurat* are still seen through tight-fitting designs and the use of sheer fabrics that sometimes expose underwear. During the series, the veiling fashions seem to be utilised as a fashion marketing space. Moreover, by creating these contemporary styles of Muslim women's fashion, the *sinetron* creators seem to wish to promote the notion that wearing this style of *jilbab* does not mean that the image of 'modern' women is erased.

In recent years, the capitalist media and the fashion industry in Indonesia have re-designed the style of Muslim women's fashions to create 'new' and flattering images for a wide range of Muslim women. This not only challenges the more conservative Muslim fashions, but also encourages middle-class Muslim women to be more accepting of the practice. However, for some Muslim fundamentalists, these styles of *jilbab* wearing (as shown in the images reproduced here) are extremely controversial and unacceptable; for them, the practice of veiling, as defined by the Qur'an, is essential and necessitates covering the female body to conceal it from the male gaze. They insist on women wearing the veil as an obligation, as a true way to practise Islamic principles in everyday life, instead of just following a fashion trend.

To continue promoting the images of moderate and non-conservative Islam, the producer of *Doa membawa berkah* created the figure of Tarisa (played by Indonesia's top-earning actress, Tamara Blezynski, who converted to Islam). Tarisa is a liberated and rebellious woman from an upper-class family who converted from Christianity to Islam. Tarisa is portrayed as a Western-oriented person who is just starting to learn how to be a Muslim woman. She married a man from a conservative Muslim family background. During her 'journey' to learn about Islam, Tarisa is shown learning about the basic principles of Islam, such as prayer five times a day and fasting in Ramadan, and about how to be a good wife, a good daughter-in-law and a good sister-in-law as prescribed in Islam. She has to adapt her previous lifestyle, as an upper-class woman who graduated from an American university, to her husband's family style of life, practising conservative Islamic principles and norms. Tarisa is required to act and behave properly, including the way she dresses in public. She personifies Hegel's 'eternal irony of femininity', projecting an image of an obedient and faithful Muslim wife, yet leading a double life. At first, she misses the frenzy of aspects of upper-class life, such as the discotheque, until she becomes the epitome of a dominated daughter-in-law as her wish to live separately from her mother-in-law diminishes.

In this melodrama, Tarisa is rarely represented as wearing the veil. She is shown covering her head with the *kerudung* when she goes to the mosque and when she prays and talks to God about her problems, fate and destiny, and particularly when her husband has a lover. The wearing of the headscarf in this drama seems to occur only when the Muslim woman is in trouble. With the headscarf, her identity as a devout Muslim seems perfect and complete. The headscarf thus symbolises the crowning touch in the formation of a perfect devout Muslim identity.

Sinta (played by the popular film actor Paramitha Rusadi), the prominent female character in a *sinetron* melodrama titled *Maha pengasih*, is personified as a devout Muslim, a successful and determined career woman. Although she comes from an educated and well-off family, her marriage to a man from the same social background was arranged by her parents. Sinta differs from her mother-in-law and her sister-in-law, who do not work outside the home. Sinta personifies the typical upper-class woman who has just started to practice as a 'true' Muslim and to consider Islam as the ideology in her life: happy or sad, religion is the best way to resolve her problems.

The way Sinta wears her *jilbab* exemplifies the moderate use of veiling. She wears a *jilbab* when she goes to public spaces. Her *jilbab* does not tightly cover all her head: once again, it represents an Islamic accessory. To show her devoutness to Islam, in terms of her fashion style, Sinta always wears long-sleeved clothes and skirts, without covering her head with a veil. This style is also used by the *sinetron* creator to differentiate Sinta, a successful career woman, from her mother-in-law and sister-in-law, who are housewives. As a career woman, Sinta wears various fashionable and colourful *busana Muslimah* and veils; the two other women appear in a traditional style of veiling, which is plain and ordinary. The fashion for veiling in this context is utilised to emphasise the difference between a career woman and a housewife.

In the same way as the idea of going to Mecca and fulfilling the fifth principle of Islam has become more and more widely desired and seen as a social status symbol among urban upper-class communities, the *jilbab* is being worn by most members of that class more and more often. This phenomenon has received massive media coverage. Images of women wearing modern *jilbab* behind the wheels of BMW or Mercedes Benz sedans can be seen more often in the fashion pages of Indonesian women's magazines and tabloids. The *sinetron* creators use this trend in their productions by frequently showing images of Sinta with her 'modern' style of *jilbab* and driving a Mercedes Benz.

Religious iconography, Islamic faith, and pop culture

Women's magazines and other women's commercial publications are loaded with various styles, models and designs of contemporary Islamic clothing. The flourishing images of women in *busana Muslimah* and veils are an indicator of the rise of a new consumer trend towards *jilbab*-wearing in the country. Fashion shows and new designs of Muslim clothing in the media mainly target young urban middle-class Muslim women. However, there seems no close relationship between veiling and Islamic faith; the veiling fashions function merely as women's costumes and accessories.

Particularly, the wearing of *jilbab* in the *sinetron* appears to have become an 'exotic' fashion show that lures Muslim women viewers. The *sinetron* creators are less interested in relating the practice of veiling to religious affiliation. Fashion for veiling is not shown to convince the audiences that the person with the *jilbab* has committed herself to practice Islamic principles. Rather, the *jilbab* tends to be utilised as a way of differentiating one female subject-position and identity from another. In fact, as Brenner observed about the practice in the Javanese community, the case of veiling women is not simple and is completely different from the media construction:

> Although veiling is a marginal practice that continues to be regarded with suspicion in Javanese society…the resistance that veiled women encounter often seems to strengthen rather than weaken their resolve and their sense of identity as Muslim women…They refashion themselves to fit their image of modern Islamic womanhood (Brenner 1996:691).

The wearing of Islamic clothing and veils in Ramadan *sinetron* also distinguishes these serials from ordinary melodramatic serials. As 'religious' serials, Ramadan *sinetron* are supposed to address the issues of Islam more frequently and obviously than *sinetron* broadcast daily on private channels. However, as criticised by journalists and scholars in Indonesia, Ramadan *sinetron* are considered 'religious' televised fictions only because of the presence of Islamic clothing and prayer. The story lines and themes resemble the mainstay of everyday melodramatic *sinetron*.

In addition, the *jilbab* in *sinetron* such as *Doa dan anugerah* represents modernisation among young urban middle-class Muslim women in Indonesia. Aisyah's veils and clothes and other models and designs worn by female characters in *Maha pengasih* have become promotional sites for the capitalist fashion industry to attract the target market. Such models and designs are exclusive and expensive. Nevertheless, the Muslim women in the *sinetron* have been idealised as devout supporters of religion (Islam) and have become agents for the popularisation of Islamic ideology in an attempt to penetrate both the public and private spheres.

The representations of women and their veiling styles in these Islamic-themed melodrama productions suggest that social class and the status of women are significant in defining the degree of individual attachment to Islam as a religion. The wearing of the veil in the *sinetron* productions, once again, goes far beyond addressing Islamic ideology as a political movement of Islamic revivalism or Islamic fundamentalism in the country. Rather, the practice is utilised to meet the desire of women to consume. In other words, this creation suggests that there is a complex relationship between the identity politics of those Islamic communities and the forces of market economics and consumer culture in regard to the religion, faith and beliefs. The pictures of *jilbab*-wearing women in the *sinetron* suggest that the capitalist media supports the view that the basic landscape of Islam in Indonesia is moderate and not monolithic.

Moreover, in some scenes, the *jilbab* or *kerudung* is worn on particular occasions, such as religious services for weddings and funerals, and in prayer congregations. The headscarf tends to function as an accessory for Muslim women in attending religious services. The wearing of a loose veil or a headscarf on such occasions has become a national image everywhere in Indonesia. The headscarf seems to have become a 'formal accessory' of ordinary Muslim women for certain occasions.

The audience's responses: *kampung* Muslim women talk about veiling in the *sinetron*

The following analysis of audience reception is based on fieldwork I conducted in one *kampung* (urban neighbourhood), a crowded middle- to lower-class housing complex in the eastern area of the city of Surabaya, from January to May 2003. The *kampung* is a migrant neighbourhood, with about 40 households living in a narrow lane. The average size of houses is about 21 square metres. The inhabitants are mainly young couples whose children are still small. Here, I examine the 'reading practices' of women viewers of the *sinetron* entitled *Doa dan anugerah* and *Doa membawa berkah*, which were re-run on the private television channels *Indosiar* and *RCTI*.

The *kampung* residents are typical urban middle- to lower-class Muslim families of the kind known in Indonesia as 'Islam secular' or '*Islam KTP*' (KTP is an acronym of *Kartu Tanda Penduduk* or citizen identity card). They profess to be Muslims, but are rather casual about observing basic Islamic requirements such as prayer five times a day. Even though there is a *Mushalla* (Muslim praying place) nearby, which always sounds *adzan* (the call for praying) loudly, some *kampung* Muslim people are not willing to go there to pray together with neighbours or to pray in their own homes. Only in a few houses, the family members pray together in their small living rooms every evening when *adzan Maghrib* (evening prayer) sounds.

Although many *kampung* people only occasionally practise the requirements of Islam in their everyday lives, they fast during Ramadan. Muslims of the *kampung*, as well as elsewhere in Indonesia, practise Islam according to traditional Javanese beliefs—what is called *Islam Jawa* (Javanese Islam). (See Bianca J Smith's chapter on Javanese Islam in this volume.) Although *kampung* residents are Muslims who profess their faith in a single God, some of them also still believe in the supernatural spirits in their environment.

In addition, there are several *kampung* women, particularly middle-aged women, who are active members of a women's prayer congregation with other women from a different *kampung*. Only the *kampung* males sometimes attend neighbourhood congregations, particularly when there is a *slametan* (a communal ritual meal for a deceased relative). Usually the family that holds the *slametan* invites neighbours, relatives, *kiai* (Islamic teacher) and *amir Mushalla* (the *Mushalla*'s committee) to eat and chant Islamic prayers and Qur'an for the soul of the deceased (known also as *tahlilan*). Both in congregation and *slametan*, Muslim women usually wear a headscarf and long dress. A headscarf is also worn when they go to *takziah* (visiting relatives or others to present condolences).

What has been obvious for the viewers of the Ramadan *sinetron* is the *jilbab*-wearing practised by several female protagonists. However, the viewers recognised that the wearing of *jilbab* by the actors was part of the costume requirement. A 26-year-old woman with two small children said, 'The wearing of *jilbab* is just…a mask. They [*sinetron* players] look as if they are devout Muslims, whereas in fact they dress up in Western-style fashions on any occasions outside the shows.'

Similarly, two other women told me that the female characters who wear *jilbab* in shows like *Doa dan anugerah* were portrayed in a manner contradictory to how veiling women should be treated; 'Women wearing *jilbab* in *sinetron* are not represented as pious women: instead, they appear to be hated and harassed by other women who do not wear *jilbab*', a 24-year-old housewife stated. She emphasised that Muslim women who decide to wear *jilbab* must be strongly committed to Islamic principles, though she realised that veiled women are not always pious. She continued by noting that Aisyah's character in *Doa dan anugerah*, for instance, was mistreated by her mother-in-law because she wore a *jilbab*. In an evening talk with several *kampung* women, another woman added, 'Her clothes show that Aisyah is a devout Muslim. Those who hate Aisyah do not have any Islamic principles.' For this woman, the *jilbab* worn by Aisyah in the drama represented the identity of a good Muslim woman. For her, when Muslim women wear *jilbab*, they should be humble and show strong commitment to Islamic principles. Although she recognised that the presentation of Aisyah's clothes and veils in the drama reflected the fashion trend in veiling, which has been remarkable in Indonesia, she considered that the treatment of the individual who was wearing a *jilbab* was wrong.

A 27-year-old woman in the *kampung* believed that wearing the *jilbab* is an obligation for Muslim women and it aims to cover the *aurat*. However, for her, who had been wearing the *jilbab* since she was in high school, if a woman has decided to wear a veil, she must practise the principles of Islamic *syariah*: 'It is better not to wear it [*jilbab*], if we think we are not ready to commit to the religion [Islam], especially those actresses.'

This woman admitted that when her father, a *pesantren* graduate and an activist of NU, strongly encouraged her to wear *jilbab*, she was reluctant to obey the order in the beginning. Later, when she entered high school, she converted to the practice of veiling. She believed that the decision to wear the veil should come from the individual herself, not because of the force or influence of other people, including parents. She understood veiling as a matter of individual commitment to religion. Therefore, she was disappointed with the practice of veiling as shown in the television dramas that she watched, because the portrayals of veiled women were not encouraging.

A 35-year-old married woman declared that *jilbab*-wearing in the Ramadan *sinetron* should not be designed to present merely an aspect of conservative Islam. Though this woman does not wear *jilbab*, she is concerned that *jilbab*-wearing should be promoted as an obligatory *syariah* for Muslim women. She declared that she did not wear *jilbab*, as she believed that veiling was still considered conservative by the society. She gave the example of one of her friends, who encouraged her daughter to convert to veiling; the daughter refused and told her mother she was conservative. She argued, 'I think that is why many of my neighbours are still reluctant to convert to the practice of veiling, because many people still have [a] view like that [as conservative]…Only old women like to wear it.' She said that surely *jilbab* for Muslim women was good, as it covered the head neatly, especially for a mature woman like her. However, this mother of four small boys admitted that she had not yet taken the decision to wear it, as she felt embarrassed to wear it within the *kampung*. She would not know how to respond if someone asked the reason why she wore it. However, sometimes this woman wore a headscarf when she went outside, as she wanted to fulfil a request of her late husband, before he died, that she conceal her head with a scarf.

Another viewer, a 25-year-old woman, considered that veiling symbolised Muslim womanhood, that those who wore *jilbab* should understand *syariah*, and that women who wore a veil, as represented through the Aisyah character, must be well mannered in public. This young mother told me she used to work in a supermarket, where she once caught a veiled woman stealing goods and hiding them under her long coat. She also added that she read in the newspapers that veiled women commit crime in public places. Based on those experiences, this woman concluded that women who wore the *jilbab* were not always devout, pious and well-mannered women.

This *kampung* woman also acknowledged that today many Muslim women wear the *jilbab* in a 'modish' and fashionable style. Unlike previously, when a woman wearing a *jilbab* was considered out-of-date, this woman noted that veiling is not considered conservative anymore by society: 'Nowadays, there are various modes of veiling. Veiling is now getting modish and stylish. [Veiled] women do not need to hide and be embarrassed about their decision to wear the *jilbab*.'

Another woman in the *kampung* who wore a *jilbab* was a university student of 23 years of age. She declared that although she was still an imperfect Muslim woman, she tried to be an ideal Muslim woman as represented in the drama: 'Frankly, I feel that I am too far away from being a perfect Muslim, but I am still learning to be…one.' She agreed that the *jilbab* was compulsory for Muslim women, and that veiling would cover a woman's *aurat* from public eyes. She preferred that women who were not mentally ready to adopt the *jilbab* should dress in 'proper' clothing. This young woman, who boarded in the *kampung*, also observed that she found it remarkable that nowadays there is endorsement for Muslim women to dress in more fashionable Islamic clothing, including the *jilbab*. For her, the *jilbab* was supposed to cover the woman's whole upper body, but now women considered that *jilbab* was worn only to cover the head, leaving their necks and bosoms uncovered. According to her, the clothes worn by veiled women, like her friends and other university students that she saw frequently, looked tight and tended to show the woman's shape. She considered that Muslim women should wear looser dresses to conceal the shape of the body.

This woman wanted Indonesian female celebrities in *sinetron* to become good trendsetters in veiling for Indonesian women more broadly. She remarked that society, particularly urban women, actually liked to copy what celebrities wore:

> For instance, when Inneke [a popular female celebrity previously known as a pornographic actress] converted to wearing the *jilbab*, many women seemed to follow her. Just like Krisdayanti [cast as Aisyah in *Doa dan anugerah*] as well. The *mukenah* that she wore in the *sinetron* soon became a model of *mukenah* in the fashion market everywhere.

This university student maintained that the way the public treated veiled women and non-veiled women was not the same. In her everyday life, she found that people greeted her with '*assalamualaikum*' (Arabic, meaning 'peace be upon you') when she passed them. Yet she had never heard non-veiled women being greeted like that. However, she was not sure whether this sort of Muslim greeting was intended to respect her as a Muslim or whether it was just a form of teasing her, since she wore the *jilbab*. She considered that by wearing the *jilbab*, a Muslim woman could be protected from predatory men, especially when walking alone at night. This woman also emphasised that a veiled woman needs to be consistent about her decision to wear the *jilbab*: 'The *jilbab* cannot be put on and off. Wearing the *jilbab* means we ought to implement Islamic law.' She was concerned and disappointed about unpleasant behaviour by young veiled women: 'Often I see a veiled young woman having bad manners in public such as holding her boyfriend's hands or even kissing her boyfriend publicly, or sometimes a woman is laughing loudly.'

Like this university student, another *sinetron* viewer in the *kampung* observed that there were women in her *kampung* who wore the *jilbab* only during Ramadan fasting month, and she disapproved of this: 'They are just following what celebrities do. Sometimes they wear the *jilbab* and other times they just leave it off. The worst case that she found in her *kampung* was of several neighbours who do not perform prayers but who wear *jilbab*.

From all these Muslim women's viewpoints, the practice of veiling clearly is not expected to be part of a costume contest or a social trend. The practice of veiling carries a consequence for the individuals who adopt the practice. Though the media have bombarded viewers with pictures of devout women and stylish modes of contemporary veiling, these women viewers were deeply concerned about the pictures represented. They realised that the images shown in the media were a representation of reality, but these women viewers expected both the media portrayals and the veiled women themselves to recognise and be aware of their behaviour in public places.

In addition, regarding the compatibility of contemporary Islam shown in the Ramadan *sinetron* with the essential Islamic values, the *kampung* women noted that Islamic values should mean upholding *syariah*, and in general the *sinetron* should also carry such meaning. Though some Islamic values are presented in the show, such as caring for and helping others, *syariah* principles should also be performed. One *kampung* woman, who wore a *jilbab* as everyday practice, disagrees with the way Islam is represented in Ramadan *sinetron*:

> I see the *syariah* is not completely presented in the *sinetron*…the good side is the producer showed religious behaviour to challenge bad habits such as snatching and drinking alcohol…this [bad manners] is supposed to be the spice to enrich the story, but I found this feature [bad manners] is more prominent than the practice of *syariah*.

Moreover, this woman considered that Ramadan *sinetron* portrayed only the life of the 'haves' or urban elite classes, whereas, in fact, the viewers are mostly from middle to lower classes. Another important fact that was underlined by this woman viewer was that the rich people are represented as not following the *syariah* principles and tend to be hypocritical. In her opinion, focusing on the elite classes in *sinetron* was inappropriate, as it did not reflect the audience's lives. For her, Islamic *sinetron* should be telling stories about faithfulness, as Islam does.

The *kampung* women viewers also observed that religious Islamic *sinetron* represent idealised Islam as currently practised among the upper classes, rather than the 'real' Islamic society of Indonesia. Islam, according to them, is not the religion of those well-off communities, but the religion of the poor, of *kampung* people like themselves. They viewed Islamic-themed *sinetron* as representative of contemporary Islam as practised exclusively by the elite. Meanwhile, the poor or the middle- to lower-class communities, like those in the *kampung*, seemed to be still practising 'traditional' Islam. As one *kampung* woman viewer commented, 'They [the upper class people] seem reluctant to stay close to the poor, they look like exclusive Muslims, and they appear to have to maintain their prestige as exclusive Muslims'. The viewers also remarked that essential Islamic values received less emphasis throughout the show. Although the viewers recognised that the image of contemporary Islamic society as shown on *sinetron* looked moderate, fashionable, not too rigid and not too conservative, the practices of contemporary Islam represented in the televised productions appeared to be exclusive and unique.

Conclusion

Although not all female characters in the Ramadan *sinetron* are depicted covering their heads with the veil, they dress in Islamic clothing styles that are modified to fit the trend of Islamic fashion in Indonesia. The female characters in these popular dramas are portrayed as adopting contemporary Islam dress to promote the image of non-conservative Muslim women. Yet the wearing of the veil and women's Islamic clothing continues to be a marginal practice in these religious-themed dramas. The *sinetron* producers, the makers and the actors seem to be intent on maintaining a 'moderate' image and not adopting extreme styles of veiling.

In recent years both the capitalist media and the fashion industry in Indonesia have re-designed the style of Islamic women's clothing to create a 'new' look for contemporary urban Muslim women. In order to challenge the notion that wearing *jilbab* makes Muslim women look conservative or fundamentalist,

Muslim dress has been presented as fashionable. The practice of veiling has been a remarkable trend in Indonesia. Ranging from veiling for official costumes and for leisure activities, contemporary veiling styles have become common and can be found everywhere. The media have provided alternative images of the contemporary look in veiling styles to adapt to the dynamic of global-modernised fashion culture in the country, particularly since the late 1990s.

The representations of contemporary Islam and the practices in the *sinetron* are indulgent, even excessive within the context of contemporary structures of Islam in Indonesia. However, the construction of Islam and Muslim society as shown in the television productions does not derive from actual social conditions; instead, the media producers appear to utilise features of Islam and its adherents (predominantly urban middle-class Muslims) to support the economic interests behind the productions.

Notes

1   This chapter was part of my research project on 'the construction of contemporary Muslim women in Indonesian television' as a Young Muslim Research Fellow of the Asian Muslim Action Network of the Asia Research Foundation in Bangkok, Thailand, in 2004.

chapter three

Adat, Islam and womanhood in the reconstruction of Riau Malay identity

Lugina Setyawati

You are entering a Malay dress code area.
Character of Malay dress:
1. Long-sleeved tunic (symbol of being covered according to *adat* and *syariah*)
2. Cover parts of body that should not be visible
3. Loose/not tight
4. Not transparent
(Council of Indonesian Ulama of Pekanbaru)[1]

The statement above can be seen on a billboard on the road from the airport into Pekanbaru, the capital city of Riau province. It reminds people who are visiting the city that Pekanbaru is characterised by Malay (and Islamic) cultures. The dress code is quoted from a *fatwa*[2] of the Majelis Ulama Indonesia (Council of Indonesian Ulama) in Pekanbaru. Majelis Ulama Indonesia is an institution that was established by the state in 1975 to deal with religious issues that develop at national or regional levels, such as issues of interfaith marriages and relationships. It has a regional office in with the responsibility of dealing with religious issues at provincial level.

Adat[3] and Islam are two important components in Malay culture. This is expressed in a Malay proverb, '*Adat bersendi Syarak, Syarak bersendikan Kitabullah, Syarak mengatakan, Adat Memakai*' (customs are based on *syariah*, *syariah* is based on the holy Qur'an, *syariah* provides the rules, custom implements the rules) (MS, Suwardi 2003:52). *Adat* and Islam influence economic, social and cultural aspects of people's lives.

Although Malay *adat* is dominant in Riau, the Malay ethnic group does not constitute the majority in this province. According to the Central Statistic Bureau of Riau Province (*Biro Pusat Statistik Propinsi Riau*) (2000:40), Malays make up approximately 38% of Riau's population of 4,755,176, which makes them the largest single ethnic group.[4] Of this percentage, most of the Malay

69

population is concentrated in the districts of Kampar, Bengkalis, Rokan Hilir, Pelalawan, Indragiri Hulu and Kuantan Singingi. In other districts, however, Malays are dominated by other ethnic groups: Javanese constitute the largest group in the districts of Rokan Hulu and Siak; Minang (from West Sumatra) dominate the population of the capital city of Pekanbaru; and Banjarese make up the largest ethnic group in the district of Indragiri Hilir. Accordingly, though Malay *adat* is respected as the native tradition in Riau, it is not the only *adat* practised in the areas. As an illustration, in Pekanbaru the Minang language has been the major language used in public areas, such as in the market. Although in terms of ethnicity Riau's population is diverse, the vast majority (almost 90%) is Muslim.

Although *adat* and Islam are supposed to support and complement each other, according to Karim (1992) there are some conflicts and contradictions between *adat* and Islam.[5] Negotiation may occur when such conflicting ideas appear. In this regard, consensus or *mufakat* (a traditional way of problem-solving) is often selected by people as a strategy for compromise between *adat* and Islam. In *mufakat*, *adat* and Islam are negotiated in order to find the most harmonious and convenient ways of practising both *adat* and Islam. This negotiation process occurs in different times and contexts. These two components of Malay culture contribute to the construction of gender relations in a dynamic process. At one time and/or in one place, it may be *adat* that is strongly dominant, while at other times and/or other places, Islam defines gender relations.

This chapter aims to examine notions of womanhood in the current reconstruction of Riau Malay identity. Indeed, Islam and *adat* have played a significant role in this process. However, various other factors also contribute to the process, such as the global Islamic resurgence that has influenced the way Islam is practised in Riau. This is obvious in regard to the practice of veiling among Muslim woman in Riau. In addition, the Indonesian state's ideology on womanhood has shaped the process. My focus in this study is, first, on the way the reconstruction of Riau Malay women's identity occurs through various channels, such as through the implementation of the dress code. Second, since women have been the subjects of the reconstruction of identity, I am interested in the ways women respond to and interpret the ideas of womanhood that are being promoted by the elite. I contend that women's responses, both individually and collectively, are varied according to time and place. At present, this reconstruction of identity is occurring in the context of democratisation in Indonesia since the end of the New Order era. As will be seen, democracy has permitted the process of reconstruction but my concern is that, to the extent that not everyone is able to participate equally in the process, democratisation is also restricted by it.

The chapter is divided into three sections. The first section focuses on the dynamic relationship between Islam and *adat* in Riau Malay identity. This section aims to contextualise the interconnection between Islam and Malay culture in Riau. It also shows the heterogeneous nature of *adat* in Riau, which has two variants—*adat pepatih* and *adat temenggung*. Notions of womanhood in Riau are signified differently by these two forms of *adat*.

The second section concerns women's identity. A portrait of the ideal Riau Malay woman has been developed on the basis of Islamic and *adat* principles. Since Riau is a part of the Indonesian nation-state, the dynamics of these notions are influenced to some degree by the interplay between *adat*, Islam and the Indonesian state's ideology of womanhood. However, the Islamic resurgence at the global and national levels that took place in the 1980s has also affected Islamic practices in Riau. Since the 1990s the *jilbab* has become a popular fashion among Riau Malay women. Currently, in the reconstruction of Riau identity, the *jilbab* has been used as a means of delineating an 'ideal' portrait of womanhood. The *jilbab* has modified Malay dress. It is even seen as perfecting *adat*.

The final section examines the roles of women as agents in the reconstruction of Riau Malay women's identity. Women contribute to the process of reconstruction by campaigning and promoting the ideal picture of womanhood as currently reconstructed in Riau. In addition, at a practical level, women apply various strategies to negotiate the reconstructed identity on their own terms.

This study is based on fieldwork conducted for my doctorate degree, entitled 'Regional ethnic identity and the unity of Indonesia, a case of decentralisation in Indonesian Riau province 2000–2005'. I carried out fieldwork for a period of eight months from November 2003 to July 2004, and subsequently visited Riau to update my data in June 2005 and December 2005. During my research, I mostly stayed in mainland Riau areas (in the districts of Pekanbaru, Kampar, Pelalawan, Kuantan Singingi and Tembilahan), though I visited Riau islands (Penyengat, Tanjung Pinang and Batam) three times. Since my research focuses on the reconstruction of Riau identity, I selected my informants on the basis of their relationship to this issue. Thus, I dealt mainly with elites including academics, NGO activists, *adat* and community leaders, and government officials. However, I also interviewed members of the community when it was relevant to the topic. I recruited my informants based on a snowball method, using my networking with NGO activists and academics in Pekanbaru, who then introduced me to other informants. They included both men and women in order to provide a comprehensive understanding of the way the reconstruction of identity is taking place in Riau. Moreover, in this process, it is men who are most active.

Islam and *adat* in Malay culture in Riau: between *pepatih* and *temenggung*

Islamic symbols and values are currently being adopted in the expression of ethnic identity in various Indonesian regions, especially those where the majority of the population is Muslim, such as Tasik Malaya (in West Java), Cianjur, Banten, Aceh, Gorontalo and West Sumatra. This is also happening in Riau. Veiled women and Arabic lettering/script in public places are some indications of the way Islamic symbols are increasingly employed in the community.

In many areas of Sumatra, including Aceh, Palembang, Bengkulu, Jambi, West Sumatra, Riau and Lampung, the phenomenon of drawing on Islamic symbolism is a common trait, because *adat* and Islam have merged and been practiced side by side for a long time.[6]

Figure 1: Riau is located in central Sumatra. In the north it borders the province of Sumatera Utara (North Sumatra); south of Riau is the province of Jambi; in the west it borders the province of Sumatera Barat (West Sumatra).

Map©Monash Asia Institute

The strong association between Islam and *adat* is shown in *Tunjuk ajar Melayu* (a guide to behaviour), which comprises norms and principles for Malay peoples. It provides guidance for many aspects of people's social, cultural, economic and political lives. *Tunjuk ajar Melayu* is traditionally transferred from the older to younger generations through local legends, epics, poetry, poems and proverbs. This quotation from *Tunjuk ajar Melayu* indicates the interconnection (Effendy 2004:9):[7]

> What is the content of our guide to behaviour?
> *Syariah* and *Sunnah*, the knowledge of truth.
> What is the content of our guide to behaviour?
> All guidance towards the right track.
> What is our guide to behaviour?
> *Syariah* as the head, knowledge as the body.

Previously, during the period of the Sultanate, in Malay communities a person who converted to Islam would be described as *masuk Melayu* (becoming Malay) (Effendy 2004:31; Yegar 1979:17). Thus Malays identify themselves as Muslim. For instance, it is common knowledge among Riau people that Chinese who convert to Islam are labelled as *masuk Melayu* (Hamidy 2000:3).[8] Two of my informants, Siti (from Bagansiapi-api, in northern mainland Riau) and Aisyah (who lives in Batam, Riau islands), support this common knowledge by referring to such cases in their villages. In contrast, it is said of Malays who convert to a non-Islamic religion that *gugur Melayunya* (his/her Malayness is disappearing).[9] The most obvious Islamic legacy in Malay culture is the Arabic script, which was previously used for writing Malay literature.

Compared with Sumatra, the interconnection between *adat* and Islam is not so strongly integrated into Javanese culture (Brenner 1996). For example, it is possible to be a Christian Javanese without being considered 'un-Javanese'. This is not possible for Riau Malay. There are various other elements that construct the Javanese culture. Woodward (1989) discusses the complexities of Javanese history that affect the development of Islam in Java. The significant influences of Hinduism and *kejawen* (Javanese religious practice) on Javanese culture should be taken into consideration in describing the characteristics of the relationship between Islam and *adat* in Java. Like Sumatra, Java is not a homogeneous island; it contains various subcultures. Each subculture has its own historical background that has shaped the relationships between *adat* and Islam. For instance, the practices of Islam and *adat* in West Java are different from those in East or Central Java. A common belief present among those who live in Java is that Sundanese are generally more religious than Javanese, as they follow Islamic principles more strictly (Kipp 1987).

This description of relations between *adat* and Islam in Sumatra may explain the current phenomenon of employing Islamic symbolism. Hence, what is going on in Sumatra (such as in Aceh, which applies *syariah* law, West Sumatra and in Riau) may be regarded as an *adat* revival, which has strong Islamic characteristics. In this respect, Islamisation had taken place in the past.

In the case of Banten, Cianjur and Tasik Malaya, on the other hand, it is Islam that is resurgent. Thus, in these areas of Java the adoption of Islamic symbols and icons demonstrates a process of the Islamisation of *adat*.[10]

Despite the differences between Sumatra and Java, in general the dynamic interaction between Islam and *adat* may be seen as a celebration of Islamic revival in Indonesia, since in the past the state prevented Muslims from expressing and practising their Islamic principles freely. The state's increased respect for Islam is indicated in various ways.[11]

Basically, *adat* exists in all Malay areas in Sumatra, Malay Peninsula, Malacca and the surrounding areas. However, Malay *adat* is heterogeneous. There are two forms of Malay *adat*: *pepatih* and *temenggung*. Despite similarities, there are differences between them. *Adat pepatih* is characterised by matrilineal descent, particularly in regard to land and property rights. Meanwhile, *adat temenggung* is more associated with practices of the patrilineal kinship system (Stivens 1996; Peletz 1998). Peletz (1998:15) refers to *adat temenggung* as a 'social structure that is usually characterised as bilateral (cognatic)'. In the case of Riau, I prefer to describe *adat temenggung* as patrilineal Malay in accordance with my informants' terminology in referring to their own form of *adat*.

The difference between the kinship systems of *temenggung* and *pepatih* contributes to the way scholars treat both forms of *adat*. Most of them tend to contrast or highlight the differences between the two in regard to their systems of descent. This kind of comparison, according to Peletz (1998:15), is 'misguided', as there are also similarities with respect to other aspects of *adat*, such as in terms of women's status and gender roles. In this discussion, however, I compare the way the followers regard their *adat* at the practical level. They make comparisons between both forms of *adat* for the purpose of claiming Malayness. My purpose is to show how these *adat* are used for identifying Malayness, and to show how these *adat* regard women.

Allegiance to *adat pepatih* or *temenggung* is connected with the geographical setting of Riau. Those who live on the mainland and/or near the border with West Sumatra, in areas such as Kampar and Kuantan Singingi, mainly adopt *adat pepatih*. *Adat temenggung* is found among communities that live in the islands and coastal areas (and in the majority of Riau areas) (see Figure 2). Jamil et al (2001) associate *temenggung* with *adat* that is practised among Malays in Sarawak, Brunei, Singapore and Malaysia Peninsular, while the Minang have influenced *adat pepatih*, which is mainly followed by Malays in Negeri Sembilan.

Figure 2: Map of Riau province

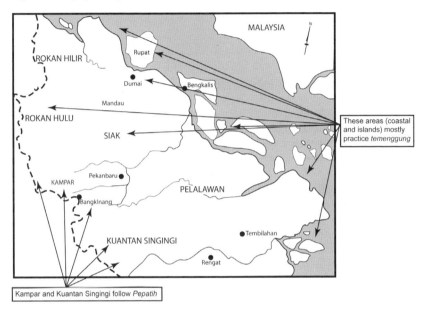

Map©Monash Asia Institute

The areas in Kampar and Kuantan Singingi districts mostly follow *adat pepatih*, while the majority of communities in the districts of Rokan Hilir, Rokan Hulu, Siak, Pelalawan, Bengkalis, Dumai, Tembilahan and Indragiri practice *adat temenggung*. In several areas located in the borders, such as in Langgam, a part of its community, which is close to Kampar, practises *pepatih*, while another part is characterised by *adat temenggung*.

The basic similarities of *adat pepatih* and *temenggung* are that they share a common language (Malay), associate with Islam, and respect *adat* as their cultural reference for their social activities (Peletz 1998; Effendy 2004). Nevertheless, the followers of *temenggung* claim *pepatih* does not represent Malay *adat*, because its matrilineal descent is not in accordance with Islamic patrilineality. Hence, the difference between *adat pepatih* and *temenggung* is used in making claims about Malay identity. Some of my informants from both *pepatih* and *temenggung* groups described how this claim is made. Achmad,[12] an activist from Kuantan Singingi, explained his feelings of being marginal, since he was treated as less Malay. Achmad, who was born in Taluk Kuantan (in the district of Kuantan Singingi) and studied for his tertiary degree in Pekanbaru, stated:

> Sometimes I was made to feel different [being from Taluk Kuantan]. Moreover when I studied in the city [Pekanbaru], I made friends from other areas [those who come from coastal areas and islands]. They sometimes insinuated that I was not Malay (Achmad, interviewed 9 January 2004).

A strong feeling of being different exists among the two groups, and is continuously transferred to, and internalised by, the younger generation. During my fieldwork, this feeling was even stronger when I visited the Riau islands. Most of my informants in the islands claimed that they were more Malay than those who lived on the mainland.

Most people I dealt with during the fieldwork, both from *pepatih* and *temenggung* backgrounds, described how they are taught to be 'aware' of being different from one another. Among *pepatih*, parents advise their daughters to avoid finding a husband from Minangkabau or West Sumatra. Similarly, among the Malay families in coastal and island areas, parents repeatedly advise their daughters not to marry a man from Kampar. In this case, in both *adat pepatih* and *temenggung*, daughters become the main targets of socialising such ideas. This is because women have two burdens of responsibility: for collective continuity and for maintaining collective unity. Women should maintain the existence of the group. These women's burdens are applied in both *pepatih* and *temenggung* groups.

Yuval-Davis (1997) argues such obligations are caused by women's position as a symbol of collective unity. Women's duty is to maintain and secure the collective boundaries, as well as to maintain the collective identity. These roles are performed in their capacity as mothers of their children. Therefore, women's sexuality is controlled and managed by the group, and parents raise their children in the family within the traditions.

Claims about who are more Malay than others have particularly been experienced in the current decentralisation period, during which the discourse of Malay identity has resounded strongly. The majority of Riau Malays follow *temenggung*; consequently, in the present reconstruction of Malay identity, *adat temenggung* is used as the main reference. Moreover, the elites, activists and academics mostly originate from areas where *adat temenggung* is practised. The ritual, the dress code and other activities related to *adat* are designed by the elites and those involved in the Riau revival movement in Pekanbaru. Basri, a lecturer at the UIN in Pekanbaru who came from Kampar, expressed his feelings about Malay dress, which differs from Kampar's style of clothing:

> Nowadays everything related to *adat* in Riau is defined by the centre [elites] at Pekanbaru. The kind of *adat* that is used as reference is patrilineal Malay. In Kampar, however, our system of *adat* is different. For example, in the case of Malay dress code, what is meant by Malay dress at official events [in Riau currently] differs from what we in Kampar mean by Malay dress. The top of Kampar Malay dress, for instance, should have no pocket, as a symbol that we are supposed not to accept money. This is not the case in the concept of Malay dress to which the local government [of Riau] refers (interview with Basri, 15 September 2005).

In the current period of decentralisation, there is friction among Kampar peoples. Although they follow a matrilineal form of *adat*, members of the younger generation are more likely to identify themselves as Malay rather than Minang. They refuse to be called Minang. Meanwhile, members of the older generation mostly identify themselves as part of West Sumatra. This is because Kampar is positioned geopolitically as part of Riau, while geo-culturally it is closer to West Sumatra.

Gender relations in Riau Malay communities are illustrated in the Malay proverb usually referred to by parents when they teach children how to behave as husbands and wives:[13]

> Husband's debt to wife:
> indebted to fulfil physical and mental needs,
> indebted to provide love and affection,
> indebted to provide guidance and lessons,
> indebted to provide advice and trusteeship,
> indebted to provide a place for living,
> and a field as a place to rest and take it easy.

> Wife's debt to husband:
> indebted to provide support and care,
> indebted to be loyal and obedient,
> indebted to watch out for each other
> indebted to protect from disgrace,
> indebted to be thrifty and careful.
> Because the wife is at her husband's command,
> Because fortune is shared,
> Share in protecting children,
> Share in happiness and sadness.

Based on *Tunjuk ajar Melayu*, men's and women's roles are designed to complement each other: there are distinct roles for men and women. For example, in the proverb above, women's roles are to serve, care for and support their husbands. Women are also responsible for providing meals for the family, while the husband should fulfil the financial needs. These roles obviously assume that women are homemakers and that men are breadwinners.

In the past, women in Riau also had access to power in political, economic and socio-cultural affairs. In the 19th century, for example, Engku Puteri Raja Hamidah (1824–1913), a consort of Sultan Mamud, who ruled the Kingdom of Riau-Lingga, had authority to hold the *Regalia Kerajaan* (insignia) of the kingdom, by means of which she had authority to make decisions (Junus 2002; Hamidy 2001). A similar status was also assigned to Putri Reno Intan, who lived in Kuantan Singingi in the early 18th century. She occupied the position of *Orang Gedang* (a person who holds supreme power in *adat* and is awarded the title of *Datuk*—head of the clan). Women held that position until 1905, when the Dutch government determined that only men could occupy such a role (Hamidy 2002:64).

Although women have specific gender roles according to *adat pepatih*, their status is relatively higher than that of women in *temenggung* communities because the structure of society is based on matriliny, particularly in regard to clan property such as land, houses and paddy fields, which are inherited by the female line. Therefore, women's position is significant. Reenen (1996:3) argues that in at least two ways women are the foundation of the family, since 'the line of descent is traced through women' and 'they are the custodians of ancestral property'.

Adat pepatih, as practised in Kampar, divides property into two kinds—clan property (ancestral inheritance of the clan) and earned property (individual family property). The latter is passed on to the children of the family (rice fields, houses and yards are inherited by daughters; plantations and forests are passed on to sons). Meanwhile, the clan property or collective property is inherited by women. This land can be accessed by members of the clan, and each clan's land has a chief who manages and co-ordinates the usage of the land. The chiefs are men from the female line: the position is passed on to the male from his sister's or mother's line, a person referred to as *mamak* (brother from mother's line) (interview with Basri, 15 September 2005). This is similar to Reenen's (1996:3–4) description of the matrilineal system of Minangkabau people in West Sumatra, 'where the senior women are honoured members of the community, yet the chiefs—or, to use a more appropriate term: the representatives—the matrilineages and clans are male'. Thus, according to *adat pepatih*, to some degree men remain powerful, as it is they who hold the central power.

Basri illustrates the practices of matrilineal tradition in daily life in Kampar. According to him, men and women have an equal role as income-earners. There is no restriction on women working in the public sphere. Women in many cases are even more active economically than men. Particularly in the villages, every morning the men and women go to the paddy field together. But women should prepare breakfast before they leave the house. Also, when they return from the field in the afternoon, women have to cook, clean up the house and do other domestic tasks, while men are free and may take a rest. Women's activities continue into the evening, when they have to teach recitation of the Qur'an to their children. Moreover, regardless of women's contribution to the family income, men retain control and dominate the decision-making process in the family.

In this regard, women both in *adat pepatih* and *temenggung* occupy a relatively lower status than men. Matrilineality does not necessarily provide women with control and power in the family decision-making process; instead, power remains in male hands. This is similar to the case of matrilineality in the Minangkabau tradition, as highlighted by Reenen (1996:3) when she describes the position of *Bundo kanduang* (woman, mother or senior woman) in matrilineal *adat* as powerless:

> *Bundo kanduang*, the legendary queen, is depicted as the source of knowledge and the mother of the Minangkabau World, but she does not possess the power to take decisions on her own or to act independently. She is an honoured advisor, but she does not function as an executor.

The unequal position between men and women in both *adat pepatih* and *temenggung* is continuously reshaped by various factors. The change of family structure to a nuclear form has made the role of husband more dominant than the clan (Reenen 1996). Consequently, women's roles in *adat* have diminished. Likewise, state interventions in family affairs through regulation and laws have positioned Indonesian women as subordinate to men. For example, the Family Law of 1974 (*Undang-Undang* No: 1 *tahun* 1974) clearly declares that the husband is the head of the family. The subsequent section elaborates the aspects that affect the current reconstruction of Riau Malay women's identity.

'Perfecting *adat*': veiling and modification of Malay dress

In this section I discuss the current reconstruction of Riau Malay identity with a special focus on women. Women have been the main objects in this process, particularly through applying a dress code. Since the topic is about reconstruction of identity of Riau Malay women, *adat pepatih* and *temenggung* are not specifically discussed: the notions apply to followers of both *adat*, in a process mainly led by the elites in Pekanbaru, the capital city of Riau. Instead, I point out various elements that contribute to the process. Hence, various factors, such as Islam, state ideology and *adat* feature in the reconstruction of notions of womanhood.

Some scholars of women's roles and status in Malay communities (particularly those which practise matrilineal descent) to some extent agree that although women have a degree of authority and power, particularly in economic activities, women remain subordinate to men (Stivens 1996; Whalley 1993; Karim 1992; Azra 2003b; Blackwood 2000). However, there are disagreements between scholars as to whether it is *adat* or Islam that most influences the subordination of women. Karim claims Islam has negative impacts on women in matrilineal society. She describes the roles of *adat* and Islam in constructing gender relations as follows (Karim 1992:14):

> Malay value preferences describe a system where hierarchical distinctions are not easily created on the basis of biology or sex...Malay metaphorical statements, however, emphasize the contribution of women to social formation process... Islam cannot, ideally speaking, be construed as a liberator of female oppression. Indeed theoretically, it introduces so many more ways of dichotomizing male and female relationships in domestic and public terms that it may have an adverse effect on women's position...

My case study in Riau, however, shows that to posit Islam as the only contributor to women's marginality in the Malay community in Riau is to over-simplify the issue. I argue that it is the interplay between *adat*, Islam and the state ideology of womanhood that has affected women's position in Riau. Here, I agree with the argument of Stivens (1996;14) regarding matriliny in Negeri Sembilan. She gives a comprehensive explanation of the reconstitution of matriliny that has taken place throughout Negeri Sembilan's history from the colonial through to the post-colonial period. She points out the role of modernity and capitalism in shaping such a process of reconstitution.

In the same way, in the case of Riau, the interplay between *adat*, Islam and the Indonesian state's ideology of womanhood has continuously reconstructed gender relations among Riau Malay communities (those who practise both *adat pepatih* and *temenggung*).

Under the New Order, Indonesia's official ideology of womanhood included 'five major duties of women: to be a loyal supporter to her husband; to be caretaker of the household; to produce future generations; to raise children properly; and to be a good citizen' (Blackwood 1995:135). This notion was propagated by the government with the aim of supporting its national program of development. It was applied and disseminated down to the village level through three main programs of the state—Dharma Wanita (the association of civil servants' wives),[14] Pendidikan Kesejahteraan Keluarga (Family Welfare Program) and Integrated Posyandu—Pos Pelayanan Terpadu (Community Service). During the period of the New Order, elites, bureaucrats, and community and religious leaders at the local level were the channels and mediators of the programs. The wives of local leaders were also involved in the implementation (Blackwood 1995): for them, to be a member of these organisations was compulsory.

The institutionalisation of the Dharma Wanita, Pendidikan Kesejahteraan Keluarga and Posyandu programs effectively positioned women as subordinate to men. In many cases such programs added to the poverty of women who lost access to economic activities because of the burden of their duties. Additionally, various studies show the domestication of women caused by such programs. The state systematically promoted such a hegemonic ideology, and it was internalised among citizens, both male and female. The current movement of reconstruction of Riau identity in many ways also adopts that ideology of womanhood, although the current movement aims to challenge the nation-state of Indonesia. For example, women have been the main targets of the reconstruction of Riau identity. Also, the provincial government makes use of women, particularly the women of elite groups, to mediate its programs. This is obvious in the case of the programs of the Persatuan Perempuan Peduli Melayu Riau (P3MR, the Association of Concerned Riau Malay Women), which are directed to support the Riau government program. Hence, women's duties remain unchanged—women are expected to support development programs (this issue is elaborated in the last section of this chapter).

Notions of Islam and its growth in Indonesia have shaped concepts of womanhood in Riau. The effects of global Islamic resurgence are also experienced in Indonesia. One of the impacts of this movement is the *jilbab* as a style of dress for women. The *jilbab* has been accepted as part of Islamic practice among women. Subsequently, the *jilbab* has signified current ideas of womanhood among Muslims in Indonesia. It has become a new symbol of Muslim women's identity. (See Chapter Two by Rachmah Ida in this volume.)

The interplay between Islam and the state contributes to the way Islam is practised in Indonesia. To give an illustration, the ban on Muslim women students wearing *jilbab* at public schools in 1982 showed discrimination by the state against Islam (Effendy 2003:161). At that time, those who wore the veil felt marginalised, as described by one of my informants:

> When I was in the secondary school, there were only a few students who wore the *jilbab*. We could not wear the *jilbab* at school. I had to uncover my head while I was at school. It contrasts with the current situation, in which school or tertiary students wearing *jilbab* are common and accepted. Previously, we were not confident to wear it in public, because we felt different (interview with Rahma, 2 September 2005).

Rifka shared a similar experience As one of my informants (and also as a friend), Rifka was a significant resource person for my fieldwork, as her life experiences provided a good case study of how the discourse of women's identity is working in Riau. A 40-year-old woman, Rifka was a lecturer in a state university in Pekanbaru. She was Malay and came from Bagan Siapi-api (in the district of Rokan Hilir, the northern part of Riau province). She was married with three children. Her husband was a Javanese and worked for a government institution. I selected Rifka because her case was noteworthy for various reasons. She was Malay and lived in a village before moving to the city of Pekanbaru. Her experiences of living in these two locations were diverse and, in turn, influenced her response to, and understanding of, the discourse of reconstructing Riau Malay identity. She had experienced and was able to share the dynamics of notions of womanhood in Riau Malay identity. Moreover, as she was an open, talkative, friendly person, she was willing to share her views and experiences on the issue of Malay dress. Her experiences are referred to several times in this chapter.

Regarding the issue of the *jilbab* in the public schools, Rifka describes how at one point when she attended secondary school, she was expected to uncover her head to follow the state regulation. She did not wear a *jilbab* (a scarf that is wrapped around the head and neck), but wore a *tudung* (a loose shawl, which does not tightly cover the hair), a Riau Malay traditional head-covering. Although the *tudung* did not cover the whole of her head, the government regulation disallowed the *tudung*. Therefore, most of her friends who strictly practiced such a style of clothing preferred to enter an Islamic school, such as *madrasah* (interview with Rifka, 5 September 2005).

The restriction on wearing *jilbab* by the government regulation caused young women to define the *jilbab* as a symbol of struggle against the state. This cause was particularly popular among women in the urban middle class, such as tertiary students (Brenner 1996; Natsir 2004). The situation changed in the 1990s when the Indonesian government became more accommodative to Islam. As Azra (2004:138) argues:

> The retreat of political Islam during much of the New Order period...provided a momentum for the rejuvenation of cultural Islam. This began with Soeharto's more accommodating and reconciliatory attitude towards Islam and Muslims in the period after Muslims' acceptance of *Pancasila*.[15]

Since that time, the *jilbab* has been worn not only as a symbol of resistance, but also as a fashion trend. It is not only practised among urban middle-class women, but also among women in the villages. Television and mass media are effective and strategic in spreading the idea of the *jilbab* to the whole of Indonesia. Religious programs, which provide *dakwah* (religious proselytising), have become part of television programs in all private and state television channels. Subsequently, the *jilbab* has also become part of the lifestyle of celebrities, actresses, business women, models and the elite. Designers and boutiques offer various models of modern *jilbab* (Natsir 2004). The acceptance of the *jilbab* as a symbol of new Muslim women in Indonesia was officially legitimised when it was worn by Tutut, a prominent daughter of President Suharto.

In Riau the *jilbab* phenomenon emerged in the 1980s, although only in limited circles, such as among students of *madrasah* and IAINs. Elsewhere, the *jilbab* was not yet popular, particularly in the villages. Malay women's style of covering the head was more associated with the *tudung* or *selendang* (a long shawl that is draped over the head and crossed loosely at the front of the neck). The *tudung* or *selendang* were more familiar among Riau Malay women, as they made up part of Malay dress (the rest being a long-sleeved loose tunic worn over a sarong or long skirt). Jamil et al (2001:13–14) classify *baju kurung* (Malay dress) into five types: daily clothes, formal costume, wedding dress, ritual dress and *adat* ceremonial costume. These costumes are applied differently for each age category (child, teenager and adult). For female teenagers and adults, *baju kurung* for all occasions usually includes a *selendang*, *tengkuluk* or *kain tudung lingkup*—different kinds of cloth used as head coverings. Thus covering the head is common among Malays, particularly for grown-up women.[16] Imam, a prominent NGO activist who was born and grew up in Lirik (in the district of Indragiri Hulu), and Basri, who spent his childhood in Kampar, supported my observation concerning this *jilbab* phenomenon. They said when they were young they were more familiar with the *tudung* form of the headscarf, since their mothers wore it. They rarely found women in their villages wearing the *jilbab*. *Tudung* were usually worn when women went out of the house, such as to market, the paddy field or other public areas.

Among younger girls the regulation was not so strict: they might use only a sarong to protect their heads from the sun, as Rifka did when she played with her friends at school. But when she got older, her father asked her to wear the *tudung* and a long skirt or *sarung*. Her father applied such a rule when she reached puberty, when she was expected to protect and cover her *aurat*. The *tudung* was respected as a form of self-protection and socially it designated a 'good woman'.

Rifka stated that she and her teenage friends sometimes complained to their parents about this tradition because they could not show off various hairstyles. If someone had a new hairdo, she was only able to show and share it with girlfriends. For instance, a classmate who had her hair waved (at that time, curly hair was trendy) asked Rifka to visit her house to see her new hairdo.

When Rifka was ready for senior school, her parents sent her to study in the city of Pekanbaru. In the first month she still wore the *tudung*, as her father reminded her not to forget to put it on. However, since only a few of her house and schoolmates wore the *tudung*, she did not feel confident to keep wearing it. She saw it was not popular among girls in the city and a friend often criticised her when she wore it. Since that time she took off her *tudung*. She only wore it when she went back to visit her family in the village, in order to avoid her father's criticism and also to respect his rules (interview with Rifka, 5 September 2005).

Unlike the *tudung*, the *jilbab* phenomenon originated in the city. It was popularised by young Islamic middle-class women in Pekanbaru. Rifka said the *jilbab* was introduced to her village by IAIN students in the 1980s, when they stayed there during their fieldwork.

Since 2000 the *jilbab* has been a common fashion among Riau Malay women, both in the cities and villages. Various models of *jilbab* have been introduced. Now the *jilbab* has become incorporated as part of the 'new' Riau Malay identity. Malay dress has been redefined as *baju kurung* plus *jilbab*. The head of P3MR asserts that Malay dress currently has been modified to be similar to *baju muslim* (Muslim dress).[17]

This new version of Malay dress is confirmed on formal occasions. Rifka reported that invitations to official events, particularly those conducted by the government, usually mentioned the dress code. Although the code did not specify that the *jilbab* was compulsory, this form of head-covering has gradually become a convention among Riau people, since the elites recommended and practised it. Rifka, who on many occasions had been appointed the master of ceremonies by the municipal government office of Pekanbaru, also had to wear the *jilbab*, although in daily activities she did not wear it. She followed the rule to maintain her relationship with the office so that she secured her access to casual work there.

Most of my women informants agreed that the *jilbab* was not originally part of their local tradition. My male informants, Imam and Basri, also claimed that wearing the *jilbab* is something new, influenced by Arabian or Middle Eastern culture. However, they supported the incorporation of the *jilbab* into Malay culture because in their view it represents a better understanding of Islam. According to them, it reflects a proper form of Islamic dress. Since Malay *adat* is based on Islam, in their view the *jilbab* will strengthen the Islamic characteristic of Malay *adat*. Thus, they regard the *jilbab* as 'perfecting *adat*'.

The meaning of the *jilbab* phenomenon in Riau is different from what happened in the case of veiling among young Javanese women as discussed by Brenner (1996). She argues that veiling among young urban Javanese women reflects the reconstruction of self and society. According to Brenner (1996:673), veiling among Javanese women reflects a 'new historical consciousness', as it is not 'deeply rooted in the local tradition'. In the case of Riau, however, veiling has strengthened the Islamic element in Malay *adat*, since the style of Malay clothing is constructed on the basis of Islamic principles. The head of the tourism division in the office of the Riau islands province supports this by pointing out that the top of male clothing has five buttons as a symbol of the five pillars of Islam (interview with Nurminsyah, 9 February 2004). Jamil et al (2001:21), in their book about Malay dress, also refer to Islamic principles when explaining the meaning of each element of clothing. A Malaysian government website asserts the history of Islam's influence on Malay dress:

> Prior to the 20th century, Malay women [wore a] bodice wrap (kemban) [wrapped around the upper part of a woman's body] with their sarong. In the late 1900s the Sultan of Johore deemed this costume inappropriate according to Islamic law, as a result the baju kurung was adopted (Muzium Negara Malaysia 2005).

The discussion in this section shows how the interplay between the Islamic movement at global, national and local levels and the state ideology of womanhood has reshaped and reconstructed Malay *adat* and the way it is practised among women. The issue of the *jilbab* is raised again in the next section, where I discuss the Riau government regulation on Malay dress.

Negotiation and agency in the reconstruction of Riau Malay women's identity

In the previous section I discussed the phenomenon of the *jilbab* and its effect on the modification of Riau Malay women's dress. This issue is currently at the centre of discourse concerning the reconstruction of Riau Malay women's identity.

The decentralisation policy, which began to be implemented in 2000, provides more space for expressing local identity. In Riau this is manifested in the resurgence of *adat* with additional Islamic nuances. As in Aceh and West Sumatra,[18] this revival of *adat* is formalised in local government regulations. The province of Nangroe Aceh Darussalam, as an example, has implemented *syariah* law as its local legal system, which includes flogging as a punishment.[19] In Riau the provincial government underlines the importance of the religious character of the region in its 'Riau Vision of 2020', the guidelines for development programs. This document states, 'The Riau Vision of 2020 is to develop Riau province as a centre of Malay culture and economy in an ethos that is religious, prosperous and healthy in body and mind in Southeast Asia in 2020' (Pemerintah Provinsi Riau 2002 ch 2:1). Although this statement does not explicitly mention Islam, the way the policy is applied and transferred through the discourse of the elites and community and *adat* leaders, and subsequent local government regulations (at municipal/district level), clearly indicates that Islam is considered to be basic to Riau identity. They refer to Malay language, Malay *adat* and traditions, and Islam as essential to Malay character.

In countries that are applying *syariah* law, such as Bangladesh and Pakistan in South Asia or Iran in the Middle East, dress code, particularly as applied to women, has been a major concern of governments (Shaheed 1998; Gardner 1998; Moghadam 2002). According to Moghadam (1994), veiling is associated with a portrait of 'ideal society'. Women's duty is to represent the concept of 'ideal society'.

Reconstruction of identity is a political and cultural project (Moghadam 1994:14). In the context of Riau, it has a political meaning and consequence, as it redefines the relationship between Riau and the Indonesian nation-state. The process of reconstruction of Riau identity is an attempt to revive 'authentic' local culture. This involves contesting the authority of the Indonesian nation-state because, previously, local identity was suppressed by so-called national culture. Women have been the objects of the process, and women's identity and images are created through ruling their appearance. Weedon (2004:7) argues that 'identity is made visible and intelligible to others through cultural signs, symbols, and practices'. Thus dress code in Riau is a symbol of Malay *adat* identity in that region.

As a member of a cultural or ethnic group, a woman's duties are as a biological and cultural producer (Yuval-Davis 1998). Women's duties as biological producers are associated with women's capacity to give birth, which involves the women's task of producing new members of the community to secure its continuity. As cultural producers, women are also responsible for preserving the collective norms and traditions from one generation to another (Yuval-Davis 1993; 1994; 1998; 2001). Thus women are crucially associated with collective continuity. Dress code among Malay women on the one hand is aimed at providing the role model for the community, and on the other hand at disseminating Malay cultural identity.

In regard to implementing the 'Riau Vision of 2020', rules of clothing among Malay women are applied particularly in government institutions, both at the provincial and district levels. At the provincial level, *peraturan berbusana Melayu* (Malay dress code) is imposed in government institutions and schools. Every Saturday students in all areas of Riau province, from elementary to senior high school students (both public and religious schools), have to wear Malay dress. As well, staff members at government offices wear Malay dress. At district level the execution of this policy is carried out on different days. In Pekanbaru, for example, Malay dress should be worn every Friday according to the municipal government's Regulation No. 12 of 2001 concerning wearing Malay dress in educational institutions, the civil service and government institutions. The regulation specifies that the dress is compulsory in those institutions:

> From 2002 on, it is compulsory to implement the wearing of Malay dress in educational institutions, among civil servants, and in private institutions or companies owned by the local government in the city of Pekanbaru, and offenders will incur sanctions (Pemerintah Kota Pekanbaru 2001:4).

This regulation also stipulates the criteria of Malay dress:

> a. For males, *baju kurung cekak musang* [a type of Malay male dress with a high collar] and a headdress called *kopiah*, and wear *kain samping* [a short sarong worn around the waist with the hemline just above the knee]; b. For females, *baju kurung labuh* [a type of *baju kurung* for women], and head covering; c. Malay dress is principally loose and not tight, not transparent, and covers the *aurat* (Pemerintah Kota Pekanbaru 2001:4).

Thus the regulation explicitly determines head-covering as part of Malay dress.

Generally, Malay dress code is also required on formal, official and ceremonial occasions, such as seminars, Riau anniversary day, during the fasting month, and at other social, cultural and political events. As stated above, head-covering is an inseparable part of Malay dress. Even though the regulation does not specify that the *jilbab* should be worn, it is highly recommended, particularly for those who are Muslim.[20] The fact that it is not compulsory is intended to show that Malays also tolerate other religions.

Most of my Malay informants from government institutions agreed that the implementation of this regulation is aimed at preserving Malay *adat*, which should be respected by whoever lives in Riau, including members of non-Muslim and non-Malay communities. They refer to a Malay proverb, which states, '*dimana bumi dipijak, di sana langit dijunjung*' ('wherever you live, you should respect and follow the traditions of that place').

As a matter of fact, cases of *adat* resurgence vary among districts in Riau. Some districts apply a strong Islamic inflection in their regulations, while others do not. In the district of Kampar, Islamic principles are forcefully spelled out in the regulations. My informant who used to work as a staff member at the government office in Kampar referred to the daily practice of *sholat Subuh* (early morning praying) for male staff. This was a verbal order from the *bupati* (head of district) of Kampar district and was conducted during his period of office in 2003–04. However, this regulation was not compulsory for female staff because, according to his version of Kampar tradition, women should stay home in the early morning to prepare breakfast for the whole family (interview with Basri, 15 September 2005). The *bupati* urged female staff to wear the *jilbab* while in the office.

Women from different socio-economic backgrounds respond in different ways to the dress code. Also, the practices of women in towns differ from those who live in rural areas. In urban areas, such as Pekanbaru, the resonance of dress code is stronger. In the villages, particularly among women who live in remote areas, far from the district offices, the regulation is not well executed. Dress code applies mainly to women who work for government institutions such as schools, public health centres and village offices. Not all women in the villages understand and know about the dress code, which is promoted by the government in Pekanbaru. The enforcement of dress code, however, is not strict· there is no formal punishment, only social sanction.

Negotiation and agency are important elements of identity. To show how negotiation and agency work in the reconstruction of Riau identity, I refer to the case of Rifka. She was proud of being Malay, and supported the revival of Malayness that was taking place in Riau, although her husband was Javanese. Rifka came from a religious family. Her father worked for the regional office of the Ministry of Religion and applied strict Islamic rules in the family, although she did not wear the *jilbab*. According to her, since her marriage, her father had no authority to control her style of dress. This authority had shifted to her husband. Soon after her wedding day, she asked her husband for permission not to wear the *jilbab* and her husband allowed her to choose her own form of dress. Rifka explained that in Malay *adat*, restrictions were greater for young unmarried women; for married women the rules were looser. This was because young unmarried women should protect their virginity. The *jilbab* was utilised to protect young women from men. According to those who wore the *jilbab*, men showed them more respect.

Although she is not accustomed to wear the *jilbab*, as a Malay Rifka respected the government promotion of the new style of Malay dress, which included the *jilbab*:

> I am happy that the government has initiated a dress code among people who live in Riau, not only among Malays. Also I support the government initiative to recommend the *jilbab* as part of Malay dress. That makes Malays more visible. The *baju kurung* as Malay dress has its philosophy. It is not only meant as a body covering. *Kurung* means being covered. It symbolises that we should protect

ourselves by not inviting men to see our *aurat*. Thus the *jilbab* perfects Malay dress (interview with Rifka, 5 September 2005).

Since Rifka did not wear the *jilbab*, she tried to negotiate with such a regulation. In daily practice she strategically exercised the dress code in the way she found most convenient. For routine activities on the campus, she did not necessarily wear Malay dress, or she wore Malay dress without veiling. Occasionally, in formal and official events both on campus or in family affairs, she donned the *jilbab*. In this regard she was showing her capability as an active agent able to decide for herself how to deal with the dress code (Badran 1994; Weedon 2004). Mahmood (2005:8) defines agency as 'the capacity to realise one's own interests against the weight of custom, tradition, transcendental will, or other obstacles (whether individual or collective)'. Rifka's case, however, illustrates the complexity of agency, as each individual may respond in varied and different ways. Here, I refer to Rifka as a specific case, not as a general portrait of women in Riau: she should not be seen as a representative of all Riau women.

Rifka exercised a strategy of veiling or unveiling when wearing Malay dress while working as master of ceremonies for the *Kantor Walikota Pekanbaru* (municipal government office of Pekanbaru). She earned a second income from this profession, besides teaching. In this position, according to her, performance and physical appearance, including clothing, were important. The municipal office quite often hired her, and for that reason she needed to maintain the relationship by voluntarily following the rule of the office regarding the dress code. By adopting this strategy she showed, first, her respect as a Malay for her own cultural identity, and, second, she secured access to government employment.

Despite her ability to strategically practise the dress code, she frequently found it inconvenient that she did not consistently wear the *jilbab*, particularly in places where most women were veiled. Her students criticised her for being unveiled. In the written evaluation for her course subject, many male and female students wrote, 'It would be better if you were veiled'. These complaints are mainly associated with her identity as a Malay and a teacher. Being Malay, she should respect her own culture; being a teacher, she should be a role model for her students.

Rifka is known as an expressive person. She voices her complaint about the strict *jilbab* regulation by criticising the policy. Every time she is criticised by her colleagues for her style of Malay dress, she replies by saying that the *jilbab* is not a representation of 'proper womanhood'. She even criticises the policy as merely concerned about covering the head but not about the religiosity of *jilbab* users.

Agency is exercised not only at the individual level, but also at the collective level. This is true in the case of the women's organisation P3MR, which is based in Pekanbaru. P3MR has branches in districts, municipalities and villages. It was established in March 2003 and the majority of its members come from academia and government institutions. Although the organisation aims to empower Malay women, its members come from different ethnic backgrounds. There is no ethnic requirement in recruiting its membership, although P3MR is affiliated with Lembaga Adat Melayu Riau (Riau Malay *Adat* Institution), an institution consisting of Malay *adat* leaders. According to the head of the organisation (interview with Maemanah Umar, 18 January 2004), membership is open because the organisation is concerned about preserving Malay culture, not about Malays as an ethnic group. As a women's organisation, P3MR presently plays significant roles in reproducing notions of womanhood in Riau.

P3MR underlines the roles of women in the community. According to the head of P3MR, women as part of the society have to support government programs such as 'Riau Vision of 2020'. As a supporter of the government, the organisation's program is directed to preserve Malay traditions and:

> to support government's program in preserving Malay culture. This should be expressed in daily activities that reflect Malayness. [This] may be seen in *adat* activities from birth to death, and in Malay dress code, although presently the dress has been modified, to be more Islamic in nature (interview with Maemanah Umar, 18 January 2004).

Financial support for this organisation is still limited, and comes mainly from local government. P3MR actively promotes Malay cultural practices among women and organises various programs for women.

Another women's organisation that also actively supports the government policy on dress code is the Badan Koordinasi Organisasi Wanita (BKOW, Co-ordination Board of Women's Organisations) in Riau, which has been the umbrella organisation for local women's organisations. Members include religious and non-religious women's organisations in Riau, such as Pendidikan Kesejahteraan Keluarga, Dharma Wanita and the Badan Kontak Majlis Taklim (BKMT, Associate Board of Majlis Taklim). BKOW mainly involves wives of political elites and government officials.

BKOW is based in Jakarta and had been a significant mass organisation in support of the state's program of development during the New Order. In Riau the position of the head of BKOW is occupied by the wife of the governor, a tradition established by the New Order. To support the new dress code, BKOW organised various programs. For example, at the beginning of 2005, BKOW, in collaboration with BKMT, conducted an event called '*Gerakan 1000 Jilbab*'

('The 1000 *Jilbab* Movement'), described below. In this program, while its involvement was significant for the success of the program, BKOW mainly acted as the sponsor, while members of BKMT actually implemented it.

BKMT is also based in Jakarta. It was established in January 1981 as an initiative of Tutty Alawiyah, who was later Minister of Women's Affairs in the Habibie government. BKMT was started as a forum for *majelis taklim* (local religious organisations) in order to develop their roles in the community, not only as clubs for the recitation of the Qur'an, but also in social activities. At its inception it was supported by 732 *majelis taklim* (*Republika* 2005a). Nowadays BKMT has branches up to district level. In Riau, at the province level, BKMT is led by Roslaini Ismail Suko, the wife of a former member of the Regional House of Representatives (DPRD), the mother-in-law of the present governor and the mother of the head of BKOW. Its official connections are thus as strong as they were in the New Order period.

BKMT initiated *Gerakan 1000 Jilbab* in 2005 to collect donations for tsunami victims in Aceh, and to celebrate the Islamic New Year and the anniversary of Riau province. At the provincial level, it was mainly aimed at collecting *jilbab* to be sent to Aceh. However, this program continued to be implemented at the level of the Pekanbaru municipality through the distribution of *jilbab* to women in that city. In this context, *Gerakan 1000 Jilbab* Pekanbaru was aimed at raising awareness of wearing the *jilbab* among women in Riau. In this city, *Gerakan 1000 Jilbab* was conducted for three days, during which members of BKOW rallied across the city, stopped unveiled women on the main road and distributed *jilbab* freely to them (excluding non-Muslim women). The reason behind this program was to remind Riau women to practise their religion properly. Wearing the *jilbab* was seen as one way of practising Islam. According to the members of BKMT, the tsunami in Aceh was a warning from God to Muslims to obey His command. In distributing *jilbab*, they found that most women openly accepted the way they were urged to wear the head-covering. Because they realised some women felt offended, they did it without intimidation. Moreover, as the *jilbab* was free, most women were happy to accept it. A woman informant who was not used to wearing a *jilbab* but who had received one from the campaign, said that she took for granted the distribution of *jilbab* in Pekanbaru because Islam had coloured the daily activities of the city and the majority of its female population wore veils. However, there were women who avoided the roads where the rally passed. They apparently did not want to accept the *jilbab*. One informant related to me that when she was stopped and given a *jilbab* by the members of BKOW, she accepted it but complained to them about the program. She suggested that the members should concentrate their activities more on those involved in the sex industry, such as prostitutes and their clients. According to her, that was the way to uphold Islamic principles.

The case of *Gerakan 1000 Jilbab* reflects, on one hand, the role of a women's organisation as the mediator and channel of the government in supporting a program promoted by the male elite. On the other hand, the responses of women to the event indicate different interpretations about such a program. One woman accepted that it was a normal activity and did not really care about the agenda of the program, while another woman seriously criticised the approach and target of the activity. These different views illustrate women's ability to deal with the issue: as agents, they interpret and respond to the issue in accordance with their perceived interests.

Gerakan 1000 Jilbab indicates that the Riau government has used a strategy similar to that applied by the New Order, which is to make use of women as their supporters. Consistently, since female elites in Riau have also internalised such a strategy, they are voluntarily supporting the government. Thus, in regard to the policy of dress code in Riau, women's organisations act not only as supporters of government policy, but also as executors of that policy, though policy-making itself is still dominated by male elites.

Conclusion

Scholars of Malay culture are familiar with the strong connection between Islam and *adat*. However, the way *adat* and Islam are practised in Riau is also influenced by various factors. In this chapter I have underlined the significant influence of the Islamic resurgence movement and the Indonesian nation-state in reshaping and reconstructing Riau Malay identity.

The representation of Riau Malay identity is performed in various ways. Dress code is applied to create images and identity of ideal Riau Malay women represented as a symbol of ideal society. However, the style of Malay clothing is not fixed. As an important element of identity, style of clothing has its own dynamics. In Riau the redefinition and modification of Malay dress is influenced by the practice of wearing the *jilbab*, which has become popular since the 1990s. The *jilbab* is respected as 'making the Malay dress perfect' (perfecting *adat*). Thus women will be labelled as ideal if they wear a 'complete Malay dress' (*baju kurung* and *jilbab*).

Obviously, such a regulation has disregarded the fact that the population of Riau is heterogeneous and plural, composed of peoples from various religious and ethnic backgrounds. On the one hand, it may be respected as a reflection of democracy in Indonesia, because Muslims may express and practise their faith. On the other hand, it may be regarded as a challenge to democratisation, because Islamic principles are imposed on the community regardless of its heterogeneity.

Women are not merely the objects of cultural projects involving the reconstruction of Riau Malay identity. Some also actively contribute to the process of reconstruction, both as supporters and implementers. At the individual level, strategies of negotiation are applied. Women may contest the reconstruction of women's identity through the way they practise the dress code and interpret the compulsory *jilbab*. Ideally, wearing the *jilbab* is regarded as a representation of a good Muslim; therefore, users should ensure their behaviour and attitudes also conform to Islam. However, when the *jilbab* is compulsory, wearers have not voluntarily committed themselves to the ideals associated with it. Consequently, enforced veiling does not guarantee 'proper women'. This understanding allows those who disagree with the compulsion to veil to not fully practise it, without feeling guilty or opposing the dress code. Such women make compromises by wearing the *jilbab* only in certain contexts, such as in public places and at formal events, so as to respect others. In this way, they are able to negotiate the practices of the dress code.

Notes

1 *Anda memasuki wilayah berbusana Melayu.*

 Ciri busana Melayu:

 Baju kurung (dikurung oleh syariah dan adat)

 Menutupi aurat

 Tidak sempit/ketat

 Tidak transparan/jarang

 (Majelis Ulama Indonesia kota Pekanbaru)

 '*Baju kurung*' literally means a covering cloth. '*Kurung*' means cover or wrap. Thus, being covered according to *adat* and Islam symbolises the philosophy of '*baju kurung*', which is associated with Islam.

2 A *fatwa* (a religious edict) is an Islamic guidance given by those who are respected as religious experts (*ulama*) and is drafted by referring to the holy Qur'an and *hadits* (sayings of the Prophet) (Mudzhar 1993). Shehabuddin (2002:202) refers to *fatwa* as 'a clarification of an ambiguous judicial point or an opinion by a jurist trained in Islamic law'.

3 Literally, *adat* means custom or tradition. However, to provide a more comprehensive meaning of *adat*, I refer to Karim (1992:14), who defines *adat* as 'the total constellation of concepts, rules and codes of behaviour which are conceived as legitimate or right, appropriate or necessary'.

4 The data is based on Riau Statistics for 2000. At the time the census was carried out, Riau province covered the islands and the mainland. It consisted of 16 districts/municipalities. Since 1 July 2004, Riau islands have officially become an independent province. As a consequence, Riau province now covers only 11 districts/ municipalities (Pemerintah Provinsi Riau 2005). Accordingly, the data cited includes the population of Riau islands. However, the above figure reflects a similar figure for the present Riau province.

5 For example, the matrilineal variant of Malay culture obviously contradicts the majority of patrilineal principles of Islam.

6 The proverb '*Adat bersendi Syarak, Syarak bersendikan Kitabullah*' ('customs are based on *syariah*, *syariah* is based on the holy Qur'an') is common in this region regardless of ethnicity, whereas no such proverb is commonly found among ethnic groups in parts of Java.

7 *Apalah isi tunjuk ajar,*

 Syarak dan sunnah, ilmu yang benar.

 Apalah isi tunjuk ajar,

 Segala petunjuk ke jalan yang benar.

 Apalah isi tunjuk ajar Melayu

 Kepalanya syarak, tubuhnya ilmu.

8 In many parts of the coast and islands, there are Chinese communities that have lived in Riau for centuries. The ancestors of these communities came to Riau in the 15th century for trading (Yegar 1979:15). In these areas, intermarriage between Chinese and Malays is common.

9   The identification of '*menjadi Melayu*' or '*masuk Melayu*' for those who convert to Islam is apparently common among people in East Coast and West Coast Sumatra, as Kipp also indicates in her study about Karo identity (1993:29).

10   For a long time, however, these areas were well known as strongholds of the Islamic movement (such as Darul Islam—DI/TII) that fought for an Islamic state.

11   Effendy (2003) points to 'the recruitment of the new generation of Muslim political thinkers and activists into the executive-bureaucratic and legislative agencies of the state' and 'the enactment of religious court law (*Undang-Undang Peradilan Agama, UUPA*) in 1989 and the compilation of Islamic law in 1991 (*Kompilasi Hukum Islam, KHI*)' as illustrations of the state's way of supporting Islam in Indonesia.

12   All the names of informants are pseudonyms. Although most of my informants were willing to have their names used, I prefer to use pseudonyms to protect my informants who have given sensitive information, in accordance with research ethics convention.

13   *Yang disebut hutang laki kepada bini,*

   Hutang nafkah lahir dan batin,

   Hutang kasih dengan saying,

   Hutang tunjuk dengan ajar,

   Hutang petuah dengan amanah,

   Hutang rumah tempat berteduh,

   Hutang ladang tempat melenggang.

   Yang disebut hutang bini kepada laki,

   Hutang bela dengan pelihara,

   Hutang taat dengan setia,

   Hutang ingat mengingatkan,

   Hutang menjaga aib malu,

   Hutang hemat beserta cermat.

   Karena bini seperintah laki,

   Karena tuah sama berbagi,

   Berbagi membela anak,

   Berbagi senang dan susah.

14   The state established the association, and its membership was compulsory for civil servants' wives. Suryakusuma (1996:99) argues that through this association the Indonesian state had conceived a woman's role and status as a wife and mother.

15   *Pancasila* is the basic ideology of Indonesian nation-state. In the early period of independence, the formulation of *Pancasila*, particularly its first pillar, 'belief in God', was coloured by a conflict between Islamic and nationalist groups. As the Islamic group suggested adopting Islamic ideology as the basis of the nation-state, the supporters suggested wording the first pillar as 'belief in God with the obligation to carry out Islamic *sharia* for its adherence' (Effendy 2003:31). Nationalist followers preferred to formulate a more neutral phrasing, which is 'belief in One Supreme God' (ibid:30). Although, finally, the nationalists' suggestion was accepted, the debate about whether Indonesia should be based on an Islamic or secular state contributed

to the dynamic relationship between Islam and the state. To permanently suppress the idea of an Islamic state, in the 1980s the New Order government insisted that all parties and mass organisations accept the state ideology, *Pancasila*, as their own ideology. This posed a dilemma for some Islamic organisations that still hoped that Indonesia would become an Islamic state, since *Pancasila* explicitly accepts pluralism in religious matters. However, most organisations followed government policy, since it was the price of remaining legal.

16 Jamil et al 2001 say that previously *cadar* (face cover) were used among teenagers in Kampar and Siak.

17 There are various styles of veiling (including *jubah, jilbab, purdah* and *hijab*), but the most common style of veiling in Riau is the scarf pinned at the chin or drawn under the chin and pinned or tied at the back—popularly known as *jilbab*. *Jubah* or *purdah*, which hides the whole figure, is not popular among Muslim women in Riau. According to my observation during fieldwork, *jubah* is more commonly found among students in universities in Jakarta, rather than among students in universities in Riau. An informant who worked for a state university in Pekanbaru said that *jubah* is not popular because it is not suitable for Malay culture. She said it was more associated with Arabic culture. Moreover, according to her, the *jilbab* was more convenient and fashionable and matched Malay dress.

18 On 7 March 2005 the Municipal Government of Padang issued a decree, namely Instruksi No. 451.422/Binsos-III/2005, about compulsory veiling (*jilbab*) and Islamic dress for Muslim students (*pewajiban jilbab dan busana islami bagi siswa/siswi Islam*). This decree has raised a debate between those who agree and disagree with such a *syariah* law (http://islamlib.com/id/index.php?page=article&id=823).

19 The first implementation of flogging as a punishment was carried out in June 2005 in Bireun district. This was applied to a *penjudi* (gambler) (Liputan 6, 2005). The flogging punishment for gamblers is stated in Qanun (Nanggroe Aceh Darussalam Regulation/Perda No. 13/2003).

20 One informant told me that at the practical level, however, there are cases where the *jilbab* is also requisite wear for non-Muslim women, particularly for those who work in the district office. Although I had no opportunity to visit it, she named a district where the *bupati* applied the regulation of veiling to all his staff. She shared her story of visiting that district office, where her male friend who worked there asked her to veil to respect the rules.

chapter four

Kejawen Islam as gendered praxis in Javanese village religiosity

Bianca J Smith

This chapter argues that ordinary Javanese village women contribute to the (re)production of their village religiosity as *kejawen* Islamic through the framework of ritual and the wider village religious environment. The crucial role women play in the (re)production and constitution of village religiosity in Java has escaped the focus of anthropological scholarship on Javanese religion, perhaps because it is mostly male scholars who have interpreted men as the more important agents of Javanese religion, and women merely as subordinate actors who play less significant religious roles in village society. Indeed, the social construction of men as formal, public leaders and women as carers of the informal, private sphere plays a role in shaping how we interpret gendered religious roles in Muslim Indonesia. Further, the way in which we interpret 'religion' also contributes to how we understand the role of gender in religious societies and cultures. As we shall see, Western understandings of religion as 'belief' do not tell us much about cultures of gendered religious praxis. The dialectic relationship between gender and religion is thus key to understanding women's practices and contribution to gendered religious societies.

This chapter is based on anthropological fieldwork during 2001–02 in a south Central Javanese village, which I have given the pseudonym Nurgeni. This chapter demonstrates how women are not only essential to the ongoing religious life of village society through their ritual practice and dialogue with the spirit world, but that women contribute to the (re)production and maintenance of village religion through their practise of these rituals that embody a particular village cosmology. I demonstrate how women are significant practitioners and co-creators of their particular village Islamic religiosity through gendered praxis at popular village rituals, particularly *rewang* (women's rituals) for *slametan* and *syukuran* rituals (*slametan* rituals are held for death and anniversaries of death, and *syukuran* rituals are held for other life-crises and celebratory events. I will explain and discuss these rituals in more detail later in the chapter). In doing

so, I illustrate how women participate in a symbiotic field of practice, which
ensures the maintenance of the religious life of the village.

Religious fields, female specialists and cosmologies

Nurgeni is a small village located south of the city of Yogyakarta. Typical of
other villages on the city outskirts, it engages a mix of what villagers describe as
'traditional' and 'modern' modes of being. Although villagers distinguish between
the village as a place of 'tradition' and the city as 'modern', they perceive their
village as upholding *adat* (in the form of traditional practices) amidst change
and the modernisation of society. Particularly, these 'traditional' and 'modern'
modes of being are mapped onto the religious identities of Nurgeni villagers,
as they construct their Muslim identities through these social frames.

The majority of villagers were poor and worked in agricultural jobs, as
labourers and petty traders, or in markets and factories. Many of my female
informants were impoverished agricultural and market or factory workers aged
between 18 and 82 years. I lived in an agricultural quarter of the village, which
was dominated by a particular family whose women folk were known for their
specialist knowledge and execution of local ritual (especially *slametan* and
syukuran rituals). The materials presented in this chapter were gathered from
the life stories of these kin women: Par, 82 years of age, her daughter Siti, her
nieces Natha and Anisah, and their daughters and close female friends. Like
many others in Nurgeni, the women described themselves as practitioners
of *Islam Jawa*, which, to remain consistent with anthropological literature, I
interpret as *kejawen* Islam.

Kejawen consists of cultural practices that engage the spirit world, a
cosmology and sorcery that are distinctly Javanese. It also consists of a theology
and philosophy, which is practised as a mysticism, or spirituality, popularly
known as *kebatinan* (from the Arabic word *Batin*, 'inner world'). These
practices and belief systems existed in Java before they incorporated Hinduism–
Buddhism and Sufism into their spectrum, and still exist today in urban and
rural environments, where they manifest as part of a local Islamic religiosity.
Kejawen is an umbrella term to describe all things Javanese. The broader
kejawen milieu refers to the local practices found in court, urban and village
environments, commonly known as 'traditional' practices such as *slametan*
and *syukuran* communal feasts; use of *dukun* (traditional healers—sorcerers,
healers, mystics, spiritualists) and magic; veneration of the spirits of deceased
saints, spiritual leaders, ancestors and loved ones at their graves; interaction
with personal spirit guides; and worship of local spirits. *Kejawen* is 'rooted in
cults of the guardian and ancestral spirits' (Stange 1979:39). The *kejawen* and

kebatinan associated with the courts emphasise high-level self-induced mystical knowledge and practice, but in the villages *kejawen* manifests as local 'tradition' and practice, and usually implicates everyone as part of *adat*, whereas those interested in pursuing a mystical life do so on a personal basis.

The women with whom I lived in Nurgeni carry out their lives in an integrated religious environment that consists of different kinds of Muslim practitioners who practise Islam in specific ways within a common social structure. The village religious environment is dominated by *kejawen* Islam. *Kejawen* Islam contrasts with, but is not separate from, normative Islamic orthodoxies, and contributes to the diversity of Islamic practice. Orthodox Muslims, whose lived experience of Islam is strongly anchored by Qur'anic teachings, form a minority in the village, and are those who engage with Islamic doctrine rather than local oral practices that most particularly interact with ancestral spirit worlds.

The ways in which these two identifiable groups of Muslims practise their religiosities form a local and popular version of village Islam in Nurgeni. I note here that the groups I identify, and which villagers also identify, are fluid and integrated. Within these identifiable groups are variations of practice, interpretation and so on. There are those who are mystics, specialists, pious, not so pious, atheists affiliated with Islam because it is compulsory to have a religion as specified in the constitution, and those who practise their own versions in their own ways independently of scripture, custom or social grouping.

Indeed, religious practitioners in Nurgeni who describe themselves as *kejawen* Muslims understand Islam as a broad set of practices, which take place as part of a cosmos that is created by Allah. Village cosmology explains the existence of different dimensions in the cosmos, which spirits, Satan, guides and ancestors inhabit. For the women with whom I lived, the world is a rhythmic field of *cikal bakal* (ancestors), *danyang* (village guardian spirits), *sedulur papat* (personal guardian spirits), *setan* (Satan) and ghosts, deities and the afterlife, all of which are part of the greater cosmos, which gives life to everything in existence, otherwise known as Allah. My informants' understandings substantiate Koentjaraningrat's (1985:327) observations and descriptions of *Agami Jawi* (*kejawen* Muslims).[1]

It is important for me to note that Muslims in Nurgeni interrelate in a dialectic that shapes the wider plural cosmos with which they engage and (re)produce. This religious environment is often referred to as 'syncretism'. Anthropology has moved beyond the limitations of describing Javanese religion as syncretic because all religions are syncretic. What we are dealing with is an active cosmos with which agents interact and which they maintain through particular practices and belief systems. These practices and knowledge together constitute and maintain a particular plural cosmos that shapes the religious life of the village. The cosmos is 'a social, natural, physical order which involves not simply the physical environment but a metaphysical environment, which relates to the management of cosmic forces' (Miller & Branson 1989:95). I prefer to describe village religiosity as an integration and interrelation of differing wholes, practices, wisdoms and knowledge that have roots in various places and sources that are historically, politically and socially situated. Within this plural cosmos (of religious integration) is an interrelation that takes place between actors as part of a wider village religiosity, which maintains a common social structure and a fluid cosmos. Thus, agents within this structure have access to varying religious discourses with which they can choose to interact and from which they construct their identities as self-reflexive actors.

I use the notion of a plural cosmos to suggest that, in the case of Javanese religious culture, 'we are confronted with several landscapes of belief, some indigenous, others Muslim, transposed with their respective values from India and the Middle East' (Headley 2004:13). Beyond this, if we are to understand that there is a pluralistic cosmology in the village that this chapter examines, then we also have to understand that individuals are in constant engagement with this multifaceted cosmos, which is created, maintained and (re)produced by their ongoing strategic agency. Indeed, as anthropology has shifted from the idea of a singular culture to understand the notion of culture as a multifaceted plurality without boundaries, where 'the colours on our map are merging one to another' (Kahn 1995:130), which requires constant engagement and (re) production, then so too can we move to the understanding of the cosmos as a plurality, a symbiotic field with which strategists creatively engage to ensure its maintenance.

I note here the extensive range of literature on cosmology (in classical and contemporary forms) from the *kraton* (Javanese palace), as well as that of high-level *kebatinan* or Sufi mysticism and Islam with which religious specialists, mystics, *dukun* and the like may or may not engage. There is thus not one single Javanese Islamic cosmology, but, rather, as Koentjaraningrat (1985:332) asserts:

> There are several *Agami Jawi* myths of creation, [and] they all include Hindu–Javanese cosmological ideas and the Muslim belief in Adam as the first prophet on earth...The several Javanese concepts of creation, however, may be classified into three categories, namely, the myths with a dominant Hindu–Buddhist character, those with a syncretistic *Agami Jawi* Muslim character, and those with a magico-mystical character.

Yet here my concern is with a particular plural cosmology in Nurgeni, which is for the most part oral. This plural cosmos is constantly being strategically dealt with by villagers who (re)produce it because (re)production is an active process of creation.[2] My purpose is to describe the ways in which village women understand the world in which they live and their place in it as religious agents.

Women narrating village cosmology

Par and her female family members explained how they understand that Allah created everything in and of the universe. Because Allah created and creates everything, they understand that *semua diijinkan Allah* (Allah permits everything). Allah, they explained, is an energy that lives in everything in animate and inanimate ways. When I asked key informants Siti and her husband about God, they explained how Allah was in the chair in which I sat, the pen that I held and the paper upon which I wrote, and was urging me to write what they were telling me. Allah is a life force in the earth, sky, water, fire, wind and space, and humans emanate out of this force or energy to live in a physical world, which is part of a cosmos that also has unseen worlds where ancestors, different kinds of spirits, *setan* and deities dwell.

These women and their partners do not perceive Allah as gendered. They also understand that Allah is neither male nor female. Natha, her female friends and their husbands explained that human spirits also have no gender. Human bodies, however, are sexed and gendered in order for spirits to experience life on earth. It is not only humans that manifest as opposites in the form of male and female, but everything in the universe can be polarised: refined/unrefined, night/day, hot/cold, male/female spirits and so on. The women explained how these polarising forces form a whole that cannot exist without either part, just as they described male and female roles in popular *slametan* and *syukuran* rituals: male cannot exist without female and vice versa (more on this later in the chapter). The aim is to find a balance between the two.

Women understand that each physical formation has unique abilities as a mediator of Allah. Whether one is male, female, rich, poor, educated or famous is part of Allah's plan. Humans have specific roles to perform on earth as manifestations of Allah, yet they also embody personal destiny, which allows them opportunities to change their experiences and circumstances. These women described a sense of agency through their knowledge of the cosmos and their place in it as Muslims.

These *kejawen* Muslim women understand that different dimensions exist as part of Allah's universe. There are the souls of the dead, ancestors, deities, spirit guides, village guardian spirits and evil spirits known as *setan* and ghosts. People interact with these worlds for particular reasons, and at particular times, and this depends on one's personal history. In order to understand the religious worlds women in Nurgeni actively create through participation and the (re) production of ritual, it is necessary to contextualise the broader theoretical frames for interpreting religion in cultures of gendered religious practice.

The anthropology of religion: belief and practice

Anthropological understandings of religion are based on Western notions of reason and rationality and scientific discourse, which were stimulated by and grew out of the Protestant Reformation of the 15th and 16th centuries, to be consolidated in the British and French Enlightenment of the 17th and 18th centuries respectively. As modes of Western philosophical thought, these notions of reason and rationality guided the development of anthropology as it sought to interpret cultures and religions of non-Western peoples.

In some cultures the word 'belief' does not imply falsity, as it does in the English language. Rather, questions of belief simply do not arise because it is *known* that spirits, gods, magic and other forces exist: these are religions of practice, which emphasise an *orthopraxy*. Don Miller and Jan Branson (1989:97) elaborate:

> Religion is practised rather than thought; known rather than believed; efficacious or not rather than true or false. It does not mean that people are never sceptical or cynical or inquisitive. But positive, individual allegiance is often not involved and *religion is part of everyday experience*. It is not a discrete let alone privatised, phenomenon.

Despite the term religion not having a universal definition attributed to it,[3] many anthropologists still interpret religion as a category of 'belief' (as is seen, for example, by the question 'do you *believe* in God or spirits?').[4] To 'believe' in religion embodies notions of imagination, distance and uncertainty. The idea that people 'believe' in religion thus fails to explain how people *feel* and experience their religious worlds. Kenneth Morrison (2000:27) asserts that 'to say that people believe in such and such is, in effect to say nothing about how they constitute their world' (see also Needham 1972). I understand that how practitioners choose to know, feel and practise religion is always subjective and culturally situated—it is an orthopraxic way of life that is felt.

Early anthropological theories of religion and magic did not explore other-than-physical dimensions of religion and magic as such, but rather treated them as illegitimate modes of knowing and being. Suggestions that people 'believe' in religion and practise ritual based on those beliefs locks Western understandings of non-Western religious societies into an imagined reality. Susan Greenwood (2000:23–4) explains that:

> The problem is that anthropological theories that stem from the post-Enlightenment rationalistic tradition cannot explain magic in its own terms, and thus do not pay sufficient attention to the otherworld. Anthropology was the first social science to point out that reality is culturally constructed and that there are multiple ways of experiencing the world; but anthropology is itself a child of Western culture, and it has given little credence to informants' accounts that do not accord with some rationalistic worldview of Western science.

The Western focus on belief, coupled with a concern for rationality and logical understanding, has also contributed to the conceptual separation of religion from sorcery and mysticism. Analysing sorcery or mystical practices as categories different from 'real religion' is inappropriate for interpreting fluid and complex religious spheres of activity because these categories 'are at best intellectual constructs rather than descriptions of reality' (Bowie 2000:26).

Describing religion as 'belief', and magic, sorcery and mysticism as non-religious, implies the idea of a fragmented religious culture in which religious activities are performed devoid of interaction and integration with other practices that are based on false 'belief' on the one hand and efficacious practice on the other. In Javanese culture, where orthodox, scriptural Islam (as world religion) co-exists with *kejawen* practices (as indigenous religion), paradigms of 'belief' and practice as separate fail to explain religion as practice. I argue that religion in south Central Javanese society is an integration of *practice*, which men and women as gendered agents form as local religious expression. That is, in their gendered ways, men and women integrate village religion. My viewing all practices as part of an integration of wider religiosities gives me insight into the nature of religion as practised, known and experienced.

The notion of orthopraxy is key to understanding how women are absolutely significant to the village religious environment because it is religion that is practised rather than thought, it is part of everyday experience. For example, women 'practise' their *kejawen* Islamic religiosities rather than 'believing' in them or subscribing to doctrine—they arrive at their religious understandings through praxis. This orthopraxis engages the otherworld, which is alive and is known and felt. Its existence is not questioned. And it is through this praxis or action, this knowing and participating in the forces of the cosmos, that women keep alive or (re)produce the religious life of the village.

Indeed, it should now be clear that I am describing a culture of religious praxis rather than organised religion, and that because women not only participate in but also contribute to village culture through their daily life practices, they are therefore significant to its (re)production and (re)creation.

The intersection of *kejawen* Islam, gender and ethnography

In this chapter I am concerned with exposing the ways in which women not only maintain village religion as *kejawen* Islamic, but how they co-create it by constantly strategising with the forces of the cosmos through popular village practices (*slametan* and *syukuran*), which would not exist without their contribution. This is important because it is mostly male scholars who write ethnographies on Javanese religion and in doing so usually construct men as religious leaders or specialists, while ignoring women's fundamental contribution to religion. More particularly, these ethnographies ignore the role gender plays in the constitution of religious societies. Although male ethnographic accounts of Javanese religion do not omit women, as indeed women are present and visible in these ethnographies, they do, however, fail to examine women's strategic role in village religiosity. Beyond this, the village religion I write of is a particularised practice of Islam and women are crucial to its maintenance; therefore, we cannot understand the diversity of Islamic practice in Indonesia without examining how, at the level of praxis, women strategise with and (re) produce their local religion, which they describe as *kejawen* Islam.

Further, there is little research that focuses on '*kejawen* women' as a group of religious practitioners. Instead, I found that what I understand to be *kejawen* women are described in literature as 'nominal' Muslims—as 'traditional' Javanese women whose practices and belief systems are strongly animist and Hindu–Buddhist. It appears, then, that feminist ethnographers have more often than not separated 'Javanese tradition' from 'Islam' in their analyses of religious culture, and that Javanese tradition does not qualify as religion because it engages 'supernatural powers'. Indeed, Laura Cooley (1992:233) and Jutta Berninghausen and Birgit Kerstan (1992) contrast 'Islam' with 'Javanese beliefs' without examining the complex relationship between the two as different modes of Islam. They describe Javanese religion as syncretistic and they fail to identify village women's practices as religious when they write, 'various pre-Islamic customs have remained alive despite [the village] adherence to the Islamic religion' (Berninghausen and Birgit Kerstan 1992:67).

It is my understanding that descriptions and categorisations of these women as 'syncretistic', 'traditional' and 'nominal Muslims' come from Clifford Geertz's representation of Javanese Muslims as being either 'pure' or 'nominal'. Indeed, Saskia Wieringa (2002:vii) employs the term *abangan* to mean 'nominally Muslim, strongly influenced by Hindu–Buddhist and animist religious ideas'.

Similarly, Norma Sullivan (1994), who is responsible for disclosing women's important role in *rewang* for *slametan* rituals after decades of male scholarship that described it as a male ritual, describes these women as 'nominal' Muslims, those who fit Geertz's *abangan* group of the non-devout. My female informants, as *rewang* practitioners, however, do not describe themselves as non-devout Muslims (or nominal).

Western feminist anthropologists, in particular, have followed Geertz's lead by under-exploring the nexus between women and varieties of local Islam in Java (Newland 2000).[5] In their examinations of ordinary women's religious practices, they have not explicitly made the link between Sufism and *kejawen* as a local form of Islam, as other scholars have. Despite Islam being a major and pervasive element of Javanese culture for 500 years—and that the majority of Javanese describe themselves as Muslims—its diversity has traditionally been largely misrepresented in anthropological literature. This misrepresentation is something that William Roff (1985) and Mark Woodward (1989; 1996) describe as an anti-Islamic bias; a marginalisation that 'can be attributed to a complex combination of protestant understandings of the nature of religion, colonial policy, and the influence in recent decades of Weber's understanding of Islam as a religion of ethical prophecy' (Woodward 1996:14). These influences affect the interpretative processes involved in exploring religion and have framed the ways scholars interpret religion cross-culturally, particularly where they distinguish between 'real religion' on the one hand and sets of 'beliefs' on the other. The perceived separation between Islam as 'real religion' and 'traditional Javanese beliefs' as a category of 'the supernatural' taps into Western notions of belief and practice, which were discussed earlier in the chapter.

Slametan and *syukuran* rituals as gendered praxis

Through my examination of *kejawen* Muslim women's participation in village religion and their active (re)production of it, I argue that gender is integral to the village religious environment and its maintenance, a view that is significantly different from that of researchers of Javanese religion based on perceived male practices. Because this chapter examines women's contribution to village religion, I focus on popular village rituals to understand how women construct and (re)produce their religious identities through praxis. *Slametan* and *syukuran* rituals are popular gendered rituals that are central to the religious life of Nurgeni. I argue that they serve as frames for diverse religious integration. As men have mostly researched *slametan* as a male ritual, my chapter contributes to knowledge of women's religious role at the rituals, which, like men's, is complex.

Understanding how *kejawen* Muslim village women (re)produce their village religiosity entails analysing their community practices because they perform religion as gendered praxis as part of village society. Here I examine two popular rituals in village society, *slametan* and *syukuran*, because the rituals are central to village religious culture and practice and are meaningful expressions of religion for the women who practise them.

Slametan and *syukuran* in ethnography[6]

Andrew Beatty (1999:28) has rightly claimed that 'ever since the appearance of Clifford Geertz's book, *The Religion of Java* (1960), we have assumed we know what the *slametan* is about. As is often the case in anthropology, one well-wrought account freezes discussion for a generation.' This point could be no more relevant than in the case of the nexus between *slametan*, gender and the role of Islam in village religiosity.

Although Beatty's book *Varieties of Javanese religion* (1999) has redefined how we can interpret *slametan* as a ritual frame for integration where varying religious participants 'agree to differ', he has failed to examine the role of women in this integration, as have male scholars before him (see Geertz 1960; Hefner 1985; Jay 1969; Koentjaraningrat 1985; Woodward 1988; 1989). This means that the way we understand *slametan* is based on male religious practices. Yet, as Norma Sullivan (1987; 1994) revealed in her examination of the ritual, there is also a female aspect of *slametan* called *rewang*.

Male anthropologists overlook women's role in *rewang* because it is an all-female ritual at which women cook special *slametan* food and prepare *sajen* (offerings), which are transferred into the male ceremonial space, where they are blessed. If male anthropologists draw on Durkheim's notion of 'sacred and profane', then it is easy to understand why they perceive women's role in *slametan* as irreligious. Yet where male anthropologists have explicitly dealt with the question of religion and Islam in relation to the rituals, Sullivan has not. Rather, Sullivan's examination of *rewang* focused on its economic rather than religious aspects. I understand, then, that we are still lacking knowledge about what these rituals mean for village religious life if women's religious roles have not been explored. Before I turn to an examination of *rewang* in ethnography, I explain what the rituals are and how they have been represented as male religious practice.

Slametan and *syukuran* are communal feasts that bring communities, neighbours and families together to restore balance and harmony, or *slamet*, between the seen and unseen worlds and between individuals and society. The rituals' foods (which women cook) are blessed (by men) and distributed among the community. In Nurgeni in south Central Java, *slametan* rituals are performed at times of death and anniversaries of death; *syukuran* rituals are performed for other rites of passage (birth, circumcision, marriage, pregnancy) and for any other reason a host sees fit, for example, moving house, wishing success, farewelling a friend, clearing black magic or any celebratory desire—hence *syukur* (Arabic for 'to express thanks').

My interpretations differ from those of Beatty (1999), Geertz (1960) and Sullivan (1994), in whose field sites there was no distinction between *slametan* and *syukuran*. The majority of ethnographies on *slametan* to date are based in east Central Java or East Java, with the exception of Sullivan and Woodward's, which explore urban and court Central Javanese culture respectively. Even though Sullivan's field site is only 15 kilometres north of my field site, each site presents a different religious make-up, and the rituals are practised in specific ways in particular contexts. My field site presents an interrelation of varying expressions of Islamic identities and I represent how the rituals are practised in that particular location only.

Slametan as male communal ritual

Slametan is a central rite of Javanese religion: a ceremonial meal consisting of special symbolic food, a *sajen* offering, a formal speech by the host, and prayers to God and local spirits. It is a community event that symbolises mystical and social unity. The desired result of a *slametan* is a state of safety and well-being or *slamet*—to be free from trouble, impediment and imbalance. Geertz (1960:16) describes *slametan* as 'a kind of social universal joint, fitting the various aspects of social life and individual experience together in a way which minimises uncertainty, tension and conflict—or at least that is what it is supposed to do'. The rituals embody an awareness of the linkage between seen (physical, material) and unseen (metaphysical, spiritual) worlds, and facilitate communication between the two worlds.

For Javanese practitioners the rituals are integral life practices that embody significant meaning and purpose. Participants of *slametan* 'see it as integral to their lives as social beings and to their sense of themselves as Javanese; they regard it as the epitome of local tradition' (Beatty 1999:25). Yet these descriptions of *slametan* imply gender neutrality. When we analyse what takes place at these rituals, in male ethnographies we find descriptions of a male ceremony called *kenduren*.[7]

In ethnography, the male prayer and ceremonial meal at *slametan* is generally referred to as *kenduren* or *kenduri*. Indeed, Hefner (1985) claims that without *kenduren* the *slametan* cannot exist, and Geertz has equated *kenduren* with the *slametan* itself. *Kenduren* carries perceived importance because it is a formal religious ritual that establishes communication with God and spirits for the sake of seeking *slamet*. It involves male members of the community who gather at the host's house under the leadership of a religious official, in Nurgeni known as *Pak Kaum*. In Nurgeni *kenduren* is performed for *syukuran* rituals and consists of a brief prayer made to *cikal bakal*, the village *danyang* and Allah in the context of the reason for holding the event. By contrast, *tahlilan* (a verse (*tahlil*) chanted from the Qur'an) is performed for *slametan* death rites (although sometimes people perform both *kenduren* and *tahlilan* for one event) and lasts between one and one-and-a-half hours. At *tahlilan*, *Pak Kaum* prays to Allah and the deceased's soul, wishing it a safe journey in the afterlife. Rather than describing these male rituals, I want to focus here on the women who possess specialist knowledge and cook the special food that is fundamental to the functioning of the ritual, because their role has been grossly under-represented in ethnography, and, as we shall see, without women the ritual cannot exist.

Rewang and ritual food

Women in Nurgeni not only prepare special food at *rewang* for *slametan* and *syukuran* in the form of *besek* (food baskets) for blessing, but they are also responsible for preparing *sajen* offerings. Beyond this, certain women, whom I introduced earlier in the chapter, possess specialist knowledge about these rituals, without which the rituals could not exist. They are a group of *rewang* specialists who prepare *sajen* and perform an essential prayer to spirits as part of the wider religious life of the village. By participating in a dialogue with the unseen world, these women are contributing to the maintenance of village religiosity because ritual praxis embodies a cosmology that depends on a knowing of the otherworld.

Indeed, *rewang* is religious because at *kejawen* Muslim *rewang* specialists draw on Allah, the world of village guardian spirits and ancestors. Interactions with these spirits are seen as essential to the ongoing religiosity of the village: that is, women desire village harmony, and communication with spirits is vital to ensure this. By using *menyan* (a type of incense) and prayer, the women ask the spirits for peace, harmony and safety in the community, and other requests depending on the reason for holding the event. These women *know* the otherworld and know how to engage with it, which is essential to the success of a ritual that is based on an interaction with and knowing of the otherworld.

Beatty (1999), Geertz (1960) and Woodward (1988) have offered ethnographers and anthropologists significant insights into the complexities of male religious aspects of *slametan*. Their ethnographies show how the *slametan* functions as a communal ritual, where purpose lies in enshrining a social harmony—a harmony consolidated by males of differing religious perspectives whose intent is the same.

Although these ethnographers are aware of the important role of food in the rituals, they fail to examine the women who cook it. Villagers told me that the male ceremony cannot exist without *rewang* and vice versa, thus indicating that the two aspects integrate into a whole or, as Sullivan (1994:157) puts it, 'a synthesis of male and female parts in a communal whole'. She goes on to define *rewang* as 'the "all female" part of the *slametan* in which women work together on basic everyday food materials and through this collective labour turn them into "special" *slametan* food' (Sullivan 1994:157).

However, closer examination of Beatty, Geertz and Hefner's ethnographies reveals allusions to the spiritual importance of *slametan* food and offerings. For these anthropologists, food carries spiritual significance when blessed in male religious and spiritual spaces and not in female ones. Food is religiously important because, first, it is blessed and, second, invoked spirits eat its aroma.

Woodward (1988) suggests that *slametan* food is linked to other Muslim cultures and that it does carry religious significance. He asserts that *apem* (rice flour cakes) are almost always used in ritual food (*apem* are used in most *slametan* and *syukuran* food baskets) and are often used as offerings to the dead in Asian Muslim cultures (Woodward 1988:73). Unfortunately, his linking of religiously important *slametan* foods to other Muslim cultures does not stretch into women's *rewang* worlds in which such food is made. As I discuss later, *rewang* is just as spiritually and religiously important as *kenduren* or *tahlilan*.

Division of labour

Not until Sullivan's exploration of women's role in *rewang* had ethnography revealed in detail the gendered aspects of the ritual. Although male religiosity has dominated studies of *slametan*, feminist ethnographers still have work to do in their explorations of women's role in *rewang,* which I perceive to be just as controversial or religiously complex as the role of men. Sullivan's contribution to knowledge of *rewang* has mainly concerned women's economic role in the division of labour of the ritual. She asserts that *rewang* and *kenduren* function as separate rituals for the wider *slametan* event, which does not begin until women begin food preparations, sometimes several days before the male prayer, and 'within such a context the "all male" ceremony should be seen as the final, brief act in a drama which is played over several days' (Sullivan 1987:264–5).

Sullivan has linked women's role in *rewang* to their broader role in society as mothers and wives, who conduct their lives more often that not in informal spheres. Women's place in the kitchen at *slametan*, then, reflects wider gender discourses that ascribe women to informal family spheres, yet, as I show later in this chapter, women do not necessarily view their practices in this way.

Anne Stoler (1977) asserts that women's economic role in the *slametan*—as producers of special symbolic food—casts them as just as important, if not more so, as men as inter-family mediators in the village community. This is because women exercise control over *slametan* food and who receives it, which effectively locates them in powerful decision-making positions that form and perpetuate social relations. Sullivan (1987:275) elaborates:

> The main function of *rewang* is *economic*, and the main function of *kenduren* is *ceremonial*. *Rewang* relations and practices have important consequences for families and neighbourhoods. In *rewang*, labour and money are exchanged for ceremonial food…the economic contracts that women enter in rewang help redistribute scarce material resources throughout the community.

Indeed, the term *rewang* means 'to help' and, as Sullivan found in her field site, it also carries the specific meaning of women's cooking role at ritual, family or other community events.[8] Sullivan (1994) argues that because of women's place in the household, they are essentially constructed as unimportant in contrast to men, who perform the religiously important prayer role. She concludes her analysis of women and *slametan* by arguing that *slametan* guides women's subordination:

> Better than anything else, the *slametan* exemplifies the real but hidden subordination of women in kampung society, in the relationships between kampung men and women, and in the relations between their roles, functions and spheres of influence…The male masters of that world authorise women to manage the full ritual while they take over the starring roles in the short, highly visible, concluding ceremony (Sullivan 1994:171).

I do not follow Stoler and Sullivan by analysing women's economic roles here because I am concerned with examining women's religious roles at the rituals. As we shall see, my interpretation of women's roles is different to Sullivan's because it illustrates how women's religiosities contribute to village religious practice and its (re)production.

Sullivan (1987:266) argues that:

> *rewang* is conceived as a situation within which females and supernatural beings interrelate. But the women's labour is emphasised as the unifying principle (rather than their religious consensus). In contrast, at *kenduren* the stress is placed on the religious consensus of the male celebrants.

While I agree that women's labour unifies *rewang*, my exploration here concerns the religious aspect of *rewang*. As I have argued elsewhere (Smith 2005), there is no absolute religious consensus at *slametan* between males or females, but there is, rather, a sense of an integrated religious diversity. There is consensus, however, on the purposive aspects of the rituals, being the aim to restore harmony and need for celebration or to express thanks to God, and this concerns both men and women.[9]

In their attempts to understand Java's religious environment, male ethnographers have spent much time examining the religious complexities of *slametan* by asking to what extent it is Islamic. Indeed, *slametan* are not only performed in village and palace environments, but also in cities, *pesantren* and mosques. This point illustrates that different types of Muslims practise *slametan* and *syukuran* as part of their Islamic identities. Beatty (1999) deals with this issue of religious diversity and *slametan* most appropriately where he describes the religious interrelation at *slametan* as a site where practitioners 'agree to differ'. The women with whom I worked integrate in the same way, and thus Beatty's theory is applicable to my field site in the context of gender. I now turn to a discussion of *slametan* as a frame for religious integration in the context of female community practice—that is, how women integrate village religion through ritual praxis. Through this integration women actively (re)produce particularised aspects of *kejawen* Islam.

The religiosity of *rewang* in Nurgeni

Through *rewang* women contribute to the continuation of their village religion and the gendered roles at *slametan* and *syukuran* integrate to constitute the village religion as *kejawen* Islamic. As *rewang* specialists Par, Siti, Natha and Anisah claim, women do not formally recognise the same kind of Islam or set of spirits for worship during *rewang*. And as Sullivan points out, in her field site labour unifies women at *rewang* just as the religious prayer unifies men at *kenduren*. In Nurgeni, men's practice of *kenduren* or *tahlilan* substantiates Beatty's observations because men privately disagree over the rituals' theological meaning, although they do express formal unity by attending for purposes of social harmony. Just because Sullivan does not consider women's religiosities as germane to understanding *slametan* and *syukuran* rituals does not mean that *rewang* is devoid of religious diversity and complexity.

Par and Natha in particular articulated their religious identities in contrast to women who self-identified with religious qualities that were different to their own, and revealed that in Nurgeni conglomerations of religiously and spiritually compatible and incompatible women merge to perform *rewang* as part of the Islam of the village. Like men, women essentially perform *rewang* for community well-being and social harmony, as part of local discourses of *rukun* (social or personal harmony) and *gotong royong* (mutual help in the community or between neighbours). Because women know each other, they are aware of each other's religious orientations, an awareness that does not cause tension because they focus on the reason the event is being held for wider harmony in seen and unseen worlds. This reinforces Beatty's notion of 'agreeing to differ'.

The religiosity of the man or woman holding the *slametan* or *syukuran* ultimately determines the religious particularities of the event—in both male and female spheres. Religious particularities that separate orthodox Muslims from *kejawen* Muslims in female spheres concern interaction with spirits and *sajen* offerings. Sullivan's ethnography notes the presence of spirits at *rewang*, although she does not note which spirits or their significance to women or the event at large. Women of *kejawen* Islamic devotion with whom I lived elucidated that spirits are always present at *slametan* and *syukuran*. First, the deceased's spirit embeds itself in the ritual upon being called to attend. Second, local village *danyang* and ancestral spirits are omnipresent: they do not make a special appearance, unless called upon, because they are part of village ethereality. Allah, the Creator, is always present, because Allah is everywhere and in everything.

These beliefs and knowledges belong to a particular group of *kejawen* Muslim practitioners. This is their religion of *rewang*. They perform *rewang* based on their perspectives of the universe for a community event. *Kejawen* Muslim women are aware of how *rewang* fits into the cosmos and how metaphysical notions of energy transference from women to food, food to spirit and spirit to cosmos power it. The women have an inherent understanding that prayer imbues food with power in its symbology of the cosmos.

Although *kejawen* Muslim women work alongside orthodox Muslim women at *rewang* for the same reasons, subjectively they hold differing views on how it fits into theology. Indeed, different women emphasise different religious and spiritual dimensions of *rewang*. The distinction between orthodox Muslim and *kejawen* Muslim women is particularly marked where *sajen* offerings are concerned. *Kejawen* Muslim women celebrate the use of *sajen* and orthodox Muslim women usually shun it because it engages the spirit world through prayer.

My argument that *rewang* serves as a frame for religious integration, and that women strategically construct their Islamic identities through a distinction between modes of Islam, implies that *rewang* hinges on cosmologies, which reveal emic (insider) and etic (outsider) divisions between orthodox Islam and everyday village *kejawen* Islamic religiosity. My descriptions of their *rewang* practices has shown that, for *kejawen* Muslim women, reality consists of different dimensions with which they interact or are exposed to at *rewang*, which makes particular women essential to the ongoing religious life of the village. Here I want to elaborate on these worlds to illustrate how particular women's practices (as orthopraxic) embody the ways in which they understand the world and their place in it.

Managing the cosmos: specialist women

Village agriculturalists including Par, Siti, Natha, Anisah and their daughters attended almost all *slametan* and *syukuran* in Nurgeni because they know how to make special foods, *sajen* and create ongoing dialogue with spirits. I refer to them as *rewang* specialists. They are a group of kinswomen headed by Par, the grandmother, who knows special prayers to invoke relevant spirits for *sajen* at *rewang*. *Sajen* cannot be handed over to *Pak Kaum* for male prayers before Par prays over them. Siti, Natha and Anisah also possess specialist knowledge about *rewang*, which other women lack. Despite the women's lack of formal religious education, their knowledge of local ritual generates for them a status in the religious life of the village, which is crucial to its maintenance. These are particular women who know how to communicate with forces in the otherworld, and villagers understand that without their knowledge of ritual practice, *slametan* and *syukuran* would not be successful.

This means that village religion, as popularly expressed through *slametan* and *syukuran* rituals, cannot continue without women's contribution. Women, then, are crucial to its (re)production. Yet these women's religious importance extends beyond *rewang* and into local practices more broadly as essential to the (re)production of the life of the village. Indeed, *rewang* for *slametan* and *syukuran* is just one aspect of women's *kejawen* Islamic identities, and women are not just playing vital roles in village religiosity through *rewang* and other rituals; these roles embody a particular cosmology, which is core to village life. Therefore, women are not only participating in culture and cosmology, but they are creating it through constant strategising that employs a kind of knowing through praxis; it is not 'belief' because it is known, experienced and felt as part of an active process of creation and (re)production.

I use the example of a *mitoni syukuran* ritual to further demonstrate how individual women are not only crucial to village religion, but how they contribute to its (re)production because their execution of ritual embodies a particular village cosmology. *Mitoni syukuran* or *tingkeban* is a ritual held for the seventh month of pregnancy (for a woman's first child only) to prepare the baby's soul for a safe and healthy entrance into the world free from possession by evil lurking spirits (*setan*), as passing from womb to earth is dangerous for mother and baby. In Nurgeni *mitoni* is a *syukuran* and, as with other *syukuran*, it has male and female aspects, which are crucial to the functioning of the ritual. For the female aspect, a female spiritual specialist called a *dukun bayi* (or traditional birth attendant) is called in to perform the ritual and to make it successful. Particular *dukun bayi* specialise in specific matters related to pregnancy, childbirth and the processes that follow. *Kejawen* Muslim *dukun bayi*, such as the one I describe here, possess high-level *kejawen* knowledge of mantras, spells, prayers and so on, and know the world of magic. They can repel lurking evil forces in the cosmos at *mitoni* by calling Allah, as by speaking Allah's name brings protection and safety. This knowledge of the otherworld and communicative praxis generates a status for such women in the village, and although *dukun bayi* are generally low class and elderly, they have a level of respect in the community because their expertise is essential to village religiosity.

The first *mitoni* I attended was that of Sulastri, my 21-year-old neighbour. Both Sulastri's family and her husband's family were *kejawen* Muslims, and it was essential as part of their Muslim identities for Sulastri's *mitoni* to be performed by a highly sought-after *dukun bayi* from a neighbouring hamlet. The *dukun bayi* was known for her high-level spiritual powers and knowledge and, because of this, families had to book her services in advance.

Sulastri's *mitoni*

Female neighbours knew of Sulastri's *mitoni* at least three weeks in advance and began *rewang* three days beforehand. The lively occasion was fuelled by upbeat, modern Islamic music that streamed from music speakers that Sulastri's husband had installed throughout the house, ensuring the event reached into the far corners of the neighbourhood. Many young and old men joined in the festivities from the sidelines, eating *rewang* foods. *Rewang* finished at 2 pm, just before the *dukun bayi* arrived at 3 pm when female kin prepared the house for the ceremony.

The *dukun bayi* was an old woman from a neighbouring village, and I refer to her as *Mbah dukun* (as did village women. *Mbah* is from *Simbah*, which is a Javanese title for an elderly person). Par, as the most skilled *rewang* specialist, was not skilled in *mitoni* ritual practices and was thus unable to perform the ceremony. When *Mbah dukun* arrived at Sulastri's house, Sulastri's mother escorted her to the back room that was set up especially for the *mitoni sajen* preparations. She had with her a bag full with foods for the *sajen*, along with *menyan* incense, a razor blade, eggs, flower petals, seven sarongs and two coconuts.

Mbah dukun made the *sajen* offering on a table in the room from ingredients she brought with her to the ceremony. The *sajen* was a food doll (approximately 35 centimetres by 20 centimetres), which represented a baby. Its body was made from sticky rice. *Mbah dukun* made the torso, head and limbs separately and then joined them together. She decorated and coloured the body with other foodstuffs and flowers, and finally attached a penis made from rice because Sulastri's *rasa* (intuition) informed her that the child was male (and Sulastri did give birth to a boy). After completing the *sajen*, *Mbah dukun* prayed to the baby's spirit and asked it to have a safe and healthy journey from womb to earth and asked Allah to protect it from *setan*.

Pak Kaum collected the *sajen* and took it to the front room of the house where *kenduren* would take place. At *kenduren* men also prayed to Allah, ancestors and village guardian spirits for the safe and healthy delivery of the child, free from disturbance. As *kenduren* began, Sulastri's kinswomen, close female friends and *rewang* specialists gathered at the wash area at the back of the house. The female aspect of *mitoni* was about to begin.[10]

Sulastri, her mother, mother-in-law, sister, close female friends, *rewang* specialists and *Mbah dukun* were present. First, *Mbah dukun* lit some *menyan* incense and placed it on the floor, as incense creates a line of communication to the spirit world, where Allah and the baby's spirit could be contacted. *Mbah dukun* prepared for communication by grounding herself with the help of the *menyan*, and lightly whispered mantras to invoke a connection with Allah. Simply by uttering Allah's name immerses one in Allah's presence and repels evil spirits that may seek to possess Sulastri as a pregnant woman.[11]

Once connection with Allah and the baby's spirit was established, *Mbah dukun* began the first part of the *mitoni* called *mandiin* (bathing), which involves the use of seven sarongs and blessed water, which is specially prepared with petals from seven flowers. Before blessing Sulastri with sacred flower water, *Mbah dukun* wrapped a sarong around Sulastri's naked body. She then pulled the sarong down and wrapped another one around her, repeating this action seven times, during which she simultaneously poured the special water over Sulastri's head while blessing her. When she had finished, *Mbah dukun* smashed an egg on the ground beside the *menyan*, still uttering invocations. Sulastri then stepped out of the wash area and the *dukun* wrapped another sarong loosely around her breasts. She then dropped two baby coconuts, one after the other, through the loose sarong. As the coconuts fell through the sarong, Sulastri's mother-in-law caught them in another sarong she was holding.

Next, *Mbah dukun* took a razor blade and cut a piece of Sulastri's hair from above her ear. She threw the hair into the *menyan* to burn. *Mbah dukun* accidentally cut Sulastri's face and caused bleeding. The women found this funny, but *Mbah dukun* continued her utterances and maintained her concentration while giving Sulastri's face a quick wipe. The ritual was over at this point. Sulastri quickly disappeared into her house to look for clothes, relieved the whole process was over. Meanwhile, the men had finished *kenduren* and were making their way home. Sulastri and her husband sat down to eat *rewang* food with their families. *Mbah dukun* joined them, was paid and then left the village.

Sulastri and her female kin did not know the symbolism of the seven washes, the flowers, the egg or the hair cutting. They did know, however, that dropping the coconuts through the sarong symbolised a smooth and easy birth, and that it was important for them to continue the way of the ancestors by practising particular rituals. Even more importantly, the women understood that by partaking in this particular ritual with *Mbah dukun*, a spiritual expert, they would have done all they could to secure a safe delivery of the child from the mother's cave (womb) into the physical world.

The fact that low-class families are willing to invest large amounts of money in the services of a spiritually powerful woman suggests that women religious specialists significantly contribute to the (re)production of village religiosity through their knowledge of ritual execution, magic and spirit worlds, which affords them a particular status not only in their natal villages but also further beyond. Ordinary women contribute to the maintenance of the *dukun*'s status by employing her services and in doing so actively (re)create a particularised practice of *kejawen* Islam for their village. The rituals and practices embody a cosmology, which women strategically interact with and give meaning to. In this way women's participation in the daily religious life of the village as *rewang* specialists, *dukun bayi* or ordinary participants significantly contributes to the (re)production of Nurgeni's religiosity.

Conclusion

This chapter has argued that the traditional Western focus on rational and scientific modes of interpreting religion as 'belief' has led to a conceptual separation of modes of practice in religious societies, which in turn has created the notion of a 'real' religion. This focus on religion as 'belief' has led to the (rational) invalidation of 'the otherworld' as false because it cannot be empirically proven. The notion of religion as 'belief' contrasts with the idea of 'practice' or 'praxis', which emphasises knowingness or direct experience of 'the otherworld'. By understanding that 'the otherworld' is real for my female informants, I am better able to interpret the roles they perform as gendered agents at particular rituals that rely on contact with spirits in these unseen worlds.

As explained, Geertz's ethnography in particular paved the way for a more general approach to understanding Javanese Islam as being either 'pure' or 'nominal'. Yet by demonstrating how Islam is a set of discursive practices, this chapter has shown that Javanese Islam is diverse in practice and thought, and has asserted that at the level of religious praxis there are distinct differences between different kinds of practising orthodox Muslims and *kejawen* Muslims as representatives of two major modes of Javanese Islam.

The chapter has also demonstrated how *slametan* and *syukuran* rituals are key to *kejawen* Muslim religious praxis in Nurgeni, and that women's role at *rewang* is integral because without it the rituals could not exist. My observations contribute to understandings of village religion that have traditionally been based on male accounts of perceived male practices. Not only has this chapter demonstrated the importance of women at the rituals, because their cooking of sacred food and assembly of *sajen* is essential to establish contact with the spirit world, but it has shown how women's knowledge and religiosities also contribute to the religious identity of the rituals.

The rituals serve as frames for religious integration in male and female spaces as part of the Islam of the village, because varying Muslim practitioners come together to perform the rituals as part of village social life. They do so with the same intent of seeking *slamet* for the reason the event is being held or to express *syukur*, and participate in wider *gotong royong* and *rukun* discourses by doing so. Indeed, my informants interpret the rituals as Islamic and their varying understandings of Islam reflect the nature of Islam in Java more broadly, where a difference in opinion and practice confirms varieties of Muslim practitioners. Yet this chapter has illustrated how these rituals integrate these practitioners, and that gender is significant to this integration.

Beyond this, *rewang* is core to women's contribution to the religious constitution of the village and its (re)production because they perceive it as an integral religious activity in community life. Their notions of womanhood are also constructed through *rewang* praxis: women understand their roles are important because they cook religiously powerful food for the wider village. My descriptions bring a different perspective to *rewang* compared with those of Sullivan, who argues that labour unites women at *rewang* but *slametan* essentially guides their subordination. The women with whom I lived understand that their role at *rewang* is religious because they are cooking special foods that not only have contact with the spirit world, but also implicate the entire village in an essential performance that contributes to the life of the village. Both *dukun bayi* and *rewang* specialists perform vital roles for village religion and these roles indeed embody the cosmology of the village because, as cosmology explains the existence of different forces in the cosmos, these women perform rituals that deal specifically with these forces and in doing so (re)produce them as a mode of *kejawen* Islam.

Notes

1 Koentjaraningrat (1985:324) describes the *kejawen* Islamic belief system as consisting of 'beliefs, concepts, views, and values. These are, for example, the belief in Allah, in Muhammad the prophet, in other prophets, in saints, the cosmological concept of creation, and the cosmological view of nature and the world, eschatology, the belief in deities, the concept of death and the afterlife, in ancestor spirits, in guardian spirits, in ghosts, spooks, and giants, and the concept of magical power.'

2 For more on cosmology see Stephen Headley (2004).

3 Ranges of meanings given to the term religion exist and are still debated today in the anthropology of religion. See for example Geertz (1966); Klass (1999). Durkheim viewed religion as a collective organisation like a church and its surrounding religious community, and saw magic as self–motivated practice (Tambiah 1990). Malinowski, however, defined religion by 'function, primarily psychological and secondarily sociological, and in terms of a means (instrumental) and ends (ultimate) distinction'. Malinowski also separated magic from religion: 'religious action was not like magic a means to an end, it was an end in itself and it celebrated ultimate values' (Tambiah 1990:69).

4 Early anthropologist Edward Tylor (1871) generated the idea that religion was the belief in spiritual beings (Barfield 1997).

5 Two major volumes about women in Indonesia (Errington 1990; Sears 1996) do not explicitly address the nexus between women and Islam.

6 I note here that the ethnographies I analyse do not refer to *syukuran* rituals because in those field sites the term *slametan* covered all rites of passage as well as other celebratory events that in Nurgeni were referred to as *syukuran*. Although I examine the differences later in the chapter, during my analysis of ethnography I refer to *slametan* only.

7 In Nurgeni *kenduren* is performed for *syukuran*, and *tahlilan* is performed for *slametan*. I examine these later in the chapter. I note here that villagers also refer to *tahlilan* as *tahlil*.

8 Berninghausen and Kerstan (1992) also note that in their Central Javanese field location *rewang* was the term used to describe women's process in *slametan*.

9 Although *kejawen* Muslims are the dominant practitioners of *slametan* and *syukuran* rituals in Nurgeni, Muhammadiyah Muslims and *kejawen* Muslims with different religious interpretations often participate in the rituals together.

10 'Traditionally' the female aspect of *mitoni* was performed at the front of the house (with one's husband also joining in the bathing ceremony) before all present guests, male and female. Sulastri felt uncomfortable with this practice and instead chose to experience it in a female-only environment. No-one objected. See Geertz (1960) for more on this.

11 Newland (2001) points out that in different parts of Java *setan* has different meanings. Usually *setan* is seen as evil spirits in contrast to 'dead souls'. In her field site *setan* referred to spirits of deceased who sought to trouble the living.

chapter five

Negotiating public space: three *nyai* generations in a Jombang *pesantren*[1]

Eka Srimulyani

In this chapter I argue that the construction of gender relations is a continuing process. Through the study of *pesantren* (Islamic boarding schools), I examine how female figures from a *pesantren* background have negotiated gender positions imposed on them by society or by institutions such as a *pesantren*. I argue that it is more than a simplistic dichotomy of public and private spheres in which men are associated with public space, power and authority and women with the private sphere and a subordinate position. Rather, the negotiation takes place not just in relation to the men in their lives, but also in relation to the changing position of education for women in Islamic schools in Indonesia, and to the global influence wherein a range of feminisms continue to debate women's place in the workforce and in the domestic sphere. The public/ private spheres dichotomy has been the predominant discourse in the West in the discussion of Muslim women's lives in Middle Eastern and other Muslim societies. Nevertheless, some scholars argue that research on Muslim women based on a strict division of public and private is 'superficial and conditioned by Western presupposition' (Smith 1998:90). In fact, women's private and public lives have been gradually changed by globalisation and social changes in various Muslim countries, such as better access to education and employment for women. According to Afsaruddin (1999:6), 'social class, economic status, and educational attainment are variables that profoundly dilute the traditional dichotomy between the public and private spheres'. Kandiyoti (1988:275) promoted the idea of 'patriarchal bargains', which she said are 'not timeless or immutable entities, but are susceptible to historical transformations that open up new areas of struggle and renegotiation of the relations between genders'. Similarly, Nazareh Tohidi, as quoted by Moghadam (2002:26–7), challenged the assumption that women are powerless and repressed: instead, she recognised the spirit of empowerment and resistance among Iranian women, arguing that women can 'renegotiate gender roles and codes and find a path of compromise and creative synthesis'.

Studies in different regions have found that Muslim women's lives are not marked by a strict dichotomy of public and private, including in religious life. Evers-Rosander (1998:172) recorded female religious participation in organisations such as a Senegalese Muslim sufistic group. She began the study with the assumption that it was a male-dominated society, but paid particular attention to pious women within the group, observing that they are 'able to partly overcome their ideological, culturally constructed "handicap" in religious life and in the society at large'. Coloun (1988), in her article 'Women, Islam and Baraka', about an African Muslim society, focused on the high-profile female figure Sokhnas Magot Diop, who inherited the leadership of the *tariqa* (sufistic group) from her father, and thus his power and influence of *baraka* (a bounty of grace). She had considerable political power in the region in which she lived because of her disciples' loyalty and her many influential connections.

Studies of the Indonesian experience suggest a similar phenomenon. A book on Indonesian female *ulama* (Burhanuddin 2002) compiled cases of Muslim women who have influential public roles or activities of a religious, social, educational and political kind. Some of them come from a *pesantren* background. Earlier, Horikoshi (1982:27) also documented a prominent female figure who was an *ulama* of considerable authority.

The *pesantren* tradition itself has some influential female figures who deserve to be studied for their ability and contribution to society. However, the presence of those female figures is not well represented in most studies on *pesantren*. Husein Muhammad (2002:68), the director of NGO Rahima, who comes from a *pesantren* background as a *kiai* (male religious leader) of a *pesantren* in West Java, said, 'Women in *pesantren* remains a topic which many observers of *pesantren* tend to overlook'. Dhofier's (1982) study, which became a central reference for the study of *pesantren,* presented five elements of *pesantren*: *Pondok* (dormitory), *Masjid* (mosque), *Pengajaran kitab-Kitab Islam Klasik* (the teaching of Islamic classical texts), *Santri* (male students) and *Kiai*. As the central figure of the *pesantren,* the *kiai* is almost always the central figure of research on *pesantren*.

The issue of women and *pesantren* tends to be problematic. Although *pesantren* institutions have existed since the 18th century, it was in the 20th century that *pesantren* education become widely accessible to female students, beginning with Pesantren Denanyar Jombang in 1930 (Masyhuri nd:37–8).[2] Moreover, *pesantren* traditions have been understood to apply some limitations on women, such as the preference for a son of a *kiai* to be the successor of the *pesantren* leadership instead of a daughter. If a *kiai* has only a daughter, and no son, then his son-in-law will be given preference as future leader of the *pesantren*.

Female instructors, both *nyai* (wives or daughters of *kiai*) and *ustazah*s (female teachers), are generally not allowed to teach the *santri* (male students). In student organisations, a *santri* will also be preferred for high-ranking positions such as a chairperson, whereas a *santriwati* (female student) will be given roles that are assumed to suit her nature as a woman, such as secretary or treasurer (Muhammad 2002:71). In terms of the curriculum, some material in the *kitab kuning* (Islamic classical literature) has been criticised as promoting concepts of inegalitarian gender relations (Mas'udi 1993).

The case study of Pesantren Salafiyah Seblak

This article is based on a case study from a *pesantren* in the Jombang area of East Java, which is widely known as a *kota santri* (town of *pesantren* students). In terms of female leadership, Pesantren Salafiyah Seblak is unique: it has had a dominant female leadership for several generations, beginning with Nyai Khoiriyah (in the first generation), followed by Nyai Abidah and Nyai Djamilah (in the second generation) and Nyai Djamilah's daughter and daughter-in-law in the third generation. According to Haidlor (2004), the dominance of female leadership in the Pesantren Salafiyah Seblak is due to incidental factors such as the fact that Kiai Maksum Ali, the founding father of the *pesantren*, had no son from his marriage to Nyai Khoiriyah. This argument can be challenged: why, then, was his son-in-law not appointed as the director of the *pesantren*, rather than his wife (Nyai Khoiriyah) or his daughter (Nyai Djamilah)? Generally, most *kiai* will pass the leadership of the *pesantren* to a son-in-law if he does not have a son of his own. Regardless of whether it is accidental, I argue that the ability of those *nyai* earned them both their positions as educational leaders and their public appointments.

Pesantren, as institutions existing in a patriarchal (Javanese) society, maintain those patriarchal values. To some extent, this is compounded by the patriarchal religious interpretation of Islamic texts, sourced from the *kitab kuning* and usually taught in the *pesantren* curriculum. My study aimed to observe how such gender dynamics play out in an institution such as a *pesantren*. In this case, the women from *pesantren* (the *nyai* figures, the wives or daughters of *kiai*) could 'negotiate' their place in the public sphere.

In this chapter I focus on three generations of Pesantren Salafiyah Seblak *nyai*, starting with the late Nyai Khoiriyah, wife of the founding father of the *pesantren*. The other two female figures are Nyai Khoiriyah's daughter (Nyai Abidah) and Nyai Khoiriyah's granddaughter-in-law (Nyai Mahshuna). These three women represent three generations in the *pesantren* and are considered influential figures in the leadership and the management of the *pesantren*.

Diagram 1 shows the kinship relations between the different *pesantren* leaders. This chapter discusses their educational leadership and their public participation in different fields, within and outside the *pesantren*. It also examines the kind of bargaining chips they wielded to take part in public life and the challenge of occupying an in-between position between the public and private spheres.

Diagram 1: Kinship in the leadership of Pesantren Salafiyah Seblak (Salafiyah al-Machfudz and Salafiyah Syafiiyah) (family tree)

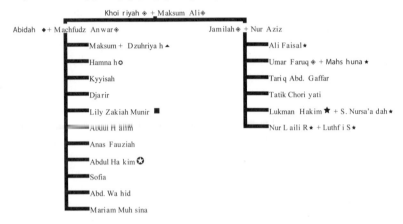

◈= former leader of the Pesantren Salafiyah Seblak (both Salafiyah al-Machfudz and Salafiyah Syafiiyah)
◆= current leader of Pesantren Salafiyah al-Machfudz
▲ = current member of structural leadership of Pesantren Salafiyah al-Machfudz
★= committee members of Khoiriyah Hasyim foundation (Salafiyah Syafiiyah)
✪= former temporary leaders of Pesantren Salafiyah al-Machfudz
■ = director of Centre for Pesantren and Democracy Studies

The history of Pesantren Salafiyah Seblak

The Pesantren Salafiyah Seblak was founded by Kiai Maksum Ali in 1921. Like other *pesantren*, in its early history Pesantren Salafiyah Seblak only had *santri* (at least, no female students were recorded during that time). When Kiai Maksum Ali passed away in 1933, the leadership of the *pesantren* was taken over by his wife, Nyai Khoiriyah. When Nyai Khoiriyah married an *ulama* who lived in Mecca, she left Java to join her new husband, and the leadership of the *pesantren* was managed by her son-in-law, Kiai Machfudz Anwar, and her daughter Nyai Abidah. During this period, the *pesantren* began to accommodate female students. The quarters of the *pesantren putra* (male students) and *pesantren putri* (female students) were segregated by a wall and a small road. Nyai Khoiriyah returned from Mecca in 1956 and resumed the leadership of the *pesantren* in 1957, while Nyai Abidah and her husband moved to Jombang to manage the Nahdlatul Ulama Islamic teacher-training college there. In 1970 Nyai Khoiriyah's health began to deteriorate. One of her daughters, Nyai Djamilah, who lived in Malang, decided to return to Seblak. She became the director of Pesantren Salafiyah Seblak in 1969. As the daughter of Kiai Maksum Ali, Djamilah inherited land within the *pesantren* campus and so the *pesantren* grounds were expanded. In 1979 the *pesantren* registered a *yayasan* (foundation) as the umbrella organisation, naming the foundation after Nyai Khoiriyah.

The periods of Pesantren Salafiyah Seblak leadership

Pesantren Salafiyah Seblak has experienced several periods of leadership, as listed below. All the leaders after Kiai Maksum Ali's period have come from his family, including his wife, his daughters and his son-in-law.

Kiai Maksum Ali (1921–33)

Nyai Khoiriyah (1933–37)

Kiai Machfudz Anwar and Nyai Abidah (1937–57)

Nyai Khoiriyah (1957–69)

Nyai Djamilah (1969–88)

After Nyai Djamilah's leadership, the *pesantren* split into two sections with separate leaderships: Pesantren Salafiyah al-Machfudz and Pesantren Salafiyah Syafiiyah. Pesantren Salafiyah al-Machfudz was a section of the *pesantren* at the original location of the Pesantren Salafiyah Seblak. It was here that the mosque was built during Kiai Maksum Ali's period. Kiai Machfudz Anwar and Nyai Abidah were joint directors of Pesantren Salafiyah al-Machfudz. When Kiai Machfudz Anwar passed away in 1989, Nyai Abidah took over the leadership of the *pesantren.* She was assisted by her sons and daughters. A brief note on Pesantren Salafiyah Seblak, based on statements from Kiai Machfudz Anwar and Nyai Abidah, mentions that their son and daughter Kikin A Hakim Machfudz and Hamnah Machfudz were being prepared for the future leadership of the *pesantren.* Despite this, Nyai Abidah has remained the director. Nyai Abidah's daughter Lily Zakiah Munir also played important roles in the *pesantren.* She established the NGO Centre for Pesantren and Democracy Studies within Pesantren Salafiyah Seblak. Meanwhile, Nyai Djamilah's sons and daughter managed another part of the *pesantren,* an extension known as Pesantren Salafiyah Syafiiyah. Nyai Djamilah's son Umar Faruq (Nyai Mahshuna's husband) was appointed as the director of the *pesantren* after Nyai Djamilah's period. When Umar Faruq passed away in 2003, Nyai Djamilah's sons and daughters-in-law succeeded him at Pesantren Salafiyah Syafiiyah in a collective leadership. In the current structure of Pesantren Salafiyah al-Machfudz, Nyai Abidah holds the position of a director of the *pesantren*. Nyai Mahshuna is the vice chairperson of the Yayasan Khoiriyah, collectively managing the *pesantren* with her brothers and sisters-in-law.

The *nyai* mentioned above have taken part in the management of the *pesantren*. Interestingly their public roles are not just limited to their public positions in *pesantren* affairs, but have extended to public appointments and activities in the community at large. Despite the *pesantren* tradition of teaching concepts of inegalitarian gender relations derived from *kitab kuning* such as *Uqud al-Lujain*,[3] and also despite the patriarchal tradition of *pesantren* leadership, these *nyai* engaged in a process that I would call 'negotiation' in order to allow their public participation.

Biographical sketches of the *nyai*

This section provides biographical data on the three *nyai* of Pesantren Salafiyah Seblak, beginning with Nyai Khoiriyah. These biographical sketches specifically focus on their private lives and their engagements in different public roles and activities within and outside the *pesantren*.

Nyai Khoiriyah (Mbah Khoiriyah)

Nyai Khoiriyah was born in 1906, the second child of Kiai Hasyim Asy'ary[4] and his wife Nyai Nafiqoh. Being born into a *kiai* family gave her the opportunity to learn from her father, for the majority of women in her time were not formally educated. Since the *pesantren* did not accommodate female students at the time, Kiai Hasyim did not allow his daughter to sit in his class. Instead, Khoiriyah followed her father's instruction from behind a curtain to avoid mixing with her male counterparts.

When she was about 13 years old, she was married to Maksum Ali, a learned student of her father. From this marriage the couple had nine children: Hamnah, Abdul Jabar, Abidah, Ali, Djamilah, Mahmud, Karimah, Abdul Aziz and Azizah. All of them died in infancy except Abidah and Djamilah. After her marriage to Kiai Maksum Ali, her father offered to establish a new *pesantren*. This idea was warmly accepted, and Pesantren Salafiyah Seblak was founded in 1921, about 200 metres from Pesantren Tebuireng. Kiai Maksum Ali was the first director of the *pesantren*. Nyai Khoiriyah took over the leadership of the *pesantren* in 1933 when Kiai Maksum Ali passed away. Khoiriyah remained a widow for several years until Kiai Muhaimin, an Indonesian *ulama* who lived in Mecca, asked for her hand in marriage.

In 1938 Khoiriyah and her younger brother, Abdul Karim, left for Mecca, where she joined her husband, who was involved in educational activities in Mecca with other *ulama*s from the archipelago. Khoiriyah lived in Mecca for 19 years. Her husband was one of the leaders of Madrasah Darul Ulum in Mecca. Living in the centre of Islamic learning, Khoiriyah took the opportunity to learn the Islamic sciences. This was common among the other *ulama Jawi*, the people from the archipelago who made the pilgrimage and then remained in Mecca to learn Islamic sciences from masters, most of whom also came from the Indonesian archipelago. Syaikh Nawawi al-Bantani, Yusuf al-Banjary and Machfudz Al-Tremasi were among the most prominent of these masters. There are no records detailing how Nyai Khoiriyah learned in Mecca. Did she participate in the *halaqah* (Islamic learning circle) held in the Masjid al-Haram with her male counterparts? Or did she join an Islamic women's circle in Mecca, where the segregation of men and women was strictly applied? Her adopted son said in an interview, 'It was clear that *Ibu* (Nyai Khoiriyah) was also learning in Mecca, but technically how—whether she attended *halaqah* with other male attendants or not—I have no idea' (interview with Muchsin Zuhdy, 25 September 2003).

All my interviewees believed that Nyai Khoiriyah pioneered the establishment of a school for girls in Mecca, namely Madrasah Banat. They also believed that this was the first girls' school in Mecca, but its history stretches back as far as 1927, when Sayid Muchsin Musana from Palembang founded Madrasah Darul Ulum in Mecca. Some people from the archipelago who lived in Mecca objected to Sayid Muchsin Musana, so the leadership of the school was passed on to Syeikh Yasin al-Fadany. After Syeikh Yasin's period, the director of the *madrasah* was Kiai Muhaimin (Nyai Khoiriyah's husband). There had been discussions about establishing a school for girls since the early years of Madrasah Darul Ulum, but it was not until 1942 that Nyai Khoiriyah actually opened one. It was supported by Syeikh Yasin al-Fadany himself. Structurally, the Madrasah Banat was part of the Madrasah Darul Ulum.

Kiai Muhaimin passed away in Mecca in 1956 and Nyai Khoiriyah returned to Indonesia in 1957. This was partly on the suggestion of Sukarno, the first Indonesian president, who she met in Mecca. There, he invited her to return to Indonesia to make a contribution to the newly independent country (Zuhdy 1986:44). Regardless of how she studied, the fact is that, upon her return to Indonesia, her ability in Islamic sciences was comparable to other well-known *ulama* of her time. Yusuf Hasyim, the director of Pesantren Tebuireng and the youngest brother of Nyai Khoiriyah, admitted that Nyai Khoiriyah had an outstanding capability: 'She is a *kiai putri* [female *kiai*]' (interview with Kiai Yusuf Hasyim, 25 September 2003). In his description of Kiai Hasyim Asy'ary's family, Aboebakar (1957:105) described Nyai Khoiriyah as 'a female *ulama* with outstanding capabilities in Islamic learning'. As the daughter of a celebrated *ulama*, it seems she inherited her father's ability in the Islamic sciences. In her time, Nyai Khoiriyah's understanding of the different branches of Islamic sciences was exceptional and she mastered a great number of *kitab kuning*. Sinta Nuriyah, the director of PUAN Amal Hayati (an NGO working on the issue of *pesantren* for women's empowerment), said, 'As far as I know, the real female *ulama* is Mbah Khoiriyah from Seblak, Mas Rahman's auntie' (interview with Sinta Nuriyah, 12 February 2003).

Nyai Khoiriyah's capability was extraordinary for a woman of her time. But even today, it is still uncommon to find a female *ulama* with such mastery of classical Islamic literature who is recognised fairly by her male counterparts. One student who accompanied her in various activities noted that Nyai Khoiriyah was brave enough to express her opinion, even an opposing opinion, in a *bahsul masail*[5] attended by well-known *kiai* or *ulama*:

> Who dares to oppose the opinions of the *kiai sepuh* [senior *kiai*] in *bahsul masail*? But Mbah Khoiriyah was brave enough to do that. She referred to the classical *kitab kuning* to support her opinion, having equal mastery of the *kitab kuning* as those *kiai* did (interview with Machtumah, 11 October 2003).

In Nyai Khoiriyah's case, it is almost impossible to maintain that the label of *ulama* is exclusively attached to male scholars. Evidently, some women earned the title as well.

A staff member who worked during Nyai Khoiriyah's leadership of Pesantren Salafiyah Seblak said, 'Nyai Khoiriyah tested some male teachers on their fluency in reciting the Qur'an to determine if they were eligible to be the *imam* of the communal prayers' (interview with 'Khadijah', 23 September 2003). One of her students also said, 'I still remember when Mbah Khoiriyah examined the recitation of *sura al-Fatihah*. Several male teachers of Pesantren Salafiyah Seblak were tested, but only a few of them passed this examination' (interview with 'Aminah', 14 October 2003).

For the local people, Nyai Khoiriyah was an active public figure. She was invited to a great number of local *majelis taklim* (Islamic learning councils). One of her students at Pesantren Salafiyah Seblak said:

> Mbah Khoiriyah was a smart, disciplined and active woman. Every Friday, she had several socio-religious activities and was invited to the *majelis taklim*. Sometimes she was invited to five different *majelis taklim* at the same time.

When this happened, she would go to one *majelis taklim* and direct her students to go to the others. All of those students had a *becak* [pedicab] prepared by Mbah Khoiriyah for their transportation, should this occur' (interview with 'Khadijah', 14 October 2003).

For health reasons, Nyai Khoiriyah retired to Surabaya in 1970. She remained active in public life, involving herself in the committee of Yayasan Pendidikan Khatijah, which organised an Islamic school for different educational levels. Between 1972 and 1979 she also established a *majelis taklim*, namely YASMARA (Yayasan Masjid Rahmah), where she regularly lectured on Islamic classical literature. During her life, Nyai Khoiriyah also published several articles; one that I can trace is on the Islamic school and its tolerance (Khoiriyah 1962). In July 1983, Nyai Khoiriyah passed away and was buried in the Pesantren Tebuireng graveyard.

Nyai Abidah (Bu Abidah)

Nyai Abidah was born in 1924, a daughter of Nyai Khoiriyah and Kiai Maksum Ali. Like her mother, Abidah was an active female figure; one of the interviewees told me she seemed to be like '*ibu Kartini dari Jombang*' (Kartini from Jombang) (interview with Umam, 20 September 2003).[6] Abidah had no formal education; instead she learned from her mother, grandfather (Kiai Hasyim Asy'ary) and her uncle (Kiai Abdul Wahid Hasyim), all of whom were celebrated figures in the *pesantren* world. During her time, few women were literate and most obtained no education. On this issue, Nyai Abidah said:

[T]here were still some people who had a fanatical view on the issue of education for women. To them, women were not allowed to learn, it was *haram* (prohibited). Mbah Khoiriyah said, 'It is useless to have children if we cannot benefit from them. If you don't believe me that women should also be supported to pursue education, come and ask Mbah Hasyim about it' (interview with Nyai Abidah, 18 September 2003).

According to Nyai Abidah, her mother expected her to have an education to continue her dream of serving the *pesantren* and the community. Nyai Abidah married into another *kiai* family: her husband was Machfudz Anwar,[7] a son of Kiai Anwar of Pesantren Pacul Gowang. He had studied in several *pesantren*, and was also an instructor at Pesantren Tebuireng and Pesantren Tebu Ireng.

During my fieldwork research in 2003, Nyai Abidah was the oldest *nyai* I interviewed. Nevertheless, she retained her clear voice and strong spirit. According to Nyai Abidah, her mother handed her the responsibility of participating in managing the *pesantren*, as 'you are my oldest daughter'. Nyai Abidah said she was fortunate to have a husband like Kiai Machfudz Anwar, who assisted her in her duties as the female instructor for the *pesantren*. Lessons in the *pesantren* were usually written in the Arabic script, which Nyai Abidah could not write:

> I said to my husband, '*Bapak,* could you please help me? After breakfast, before you go out to teach in Pesantren Tebuireng, could you please write something on the blackboard for me?' 'What should I write?' Kiai Machfudz asked me. 'Please write what I would like to teach for today' (interview with Nyai Abidah, 27 September 2003).

Her husband would prepare three written blackboards for her, and she would change from one to another for each session to suit the material of her instruction. Apart from her husband, Nyai Abidah also learned from her uncle, Wahid Hasyim. Wahid Hasyim invited her to his house to accompany his wife, Nyai Solihah, who was also trying to learn the Arabic script.[8] For Nyai Abidah, Wahid Hasyim was a great teacher, and encouraged her to teach the female students in Pesantren Salafiyah Seblak and in the Pendidikan Guru Agama (PGA, Islamic teacher training college) at Jombang.

The first cohort of girl students of Pesantren Salafiyah Seblak was far bigger than predicted. A great number of girls from different ages turned up at the *pesantren* to learn. Nyai Abidah had to consult with Wahid Hasyim to work out how and what should be taught. The PGA in Jombang was also part of Wahid Hasyim's efforts to establish a public school for girls in the area. Once again, Nyai Abidah was his choice to manage the school. The PGA prepared the teachers for the elementary and secondary levels of Islamic schools. Nyai Abidah said, 'To teach the PGA students is more difficult, so I asked Pak Wahid what I should do. Pak Wahid said, "You have to teach, this is *wajib* [obligatory]"' (interview with Nyai Abidah, 27 September 2003). It seems that Nyai Abidah was a person who was trusted by Wahid Hasyim[9] to support his idea of expanding formal education for women.

During her experiences as an instructor at the *pesantren*, Nyai Abidah not only taught the female students, but also was known to give instruction to classes of male students. One student said, 'I attended a class taught by Nyai Abidah on Islamic theology, using *kitab Jawahir al-Kalamiyah*[10] as a text. The students were both male and female' (interview with 'Ahmad', 13 October 2003). This is unusual: it is a tradition among the majority of *pesantren* that a woman does not teach male students. During my fieldwork, I discovered that very few *nyai* instructed classes of male students; the majority exclusively teach *santriwati*.

Nyai Abidah's public activities developed more broadly when she was selected to be a member of the national Constituent Assembly and the DPRD. At this stage, her focus was not necessarily *pesantren* or even education. She was also appointed as a judge at the Jombang religious court for the periods

1960–64 and 1965–68. Like her mother, she was actively involved in *majelis taklim*, the Islamic learning council for women at her *pesantren*. As well as her public activities within and outside the *pesantren*, she was a mother of 11 children. According to one of her daughters, Lily Zakiah Munir, Nyai Abidah represented the presence of Muslim women in public space:

> Nyai Abidah was actively involved in Muslimat Nahdlatul Ulama organisation. She was also a member of the local House of Representatives in Jombang in 1951. I just want to say, the stereotype that Muslim women are merely attached to the domestic sphere is not completely correct. I was a baby at that time, during which time my mother would…travel the eight kilometres from Seblak to Jombang. If there was a meeting, she still took me with her, because there was no baby formula at that time. She would take me to *ibu rodho'*, a wet nurse, and I was breastfed there. This was part of her struggle (interview with Lily Zakiah Munir, 15 July 2003).

Currently, among other *nyai* in the area, Nyai Abidah is known as *nyai sepuh*, which literally means an elderly *nyai*. In the NU community the *kiai* and *nyai sepuh* are more respected because their age indicates knowledge, maturity, wisdom and experience. Armed with these qualities, Nyai Abidah is regarded with the utmost respect by the *pesantren* and local society.

Nyai Mahshuna (Bu Sun)

Nyai Mahshuna was born in Jombang on 29 December 1952, into the *kiai* kinship of Pesantren Darul Ulum Rejoso, one of four well-known *pesantren* in Jombang. She attended primary and senior secondary school in the complex of Pesantren Darul Ulum. Aside from her formal education, she also gained an informal *pesantren* education between 1964 and 1970. As a woman she had to struggle to get her father's consent to pursue higher education and was eventually allowed to study at the IAIN Sunan Kalijaga in Yogyakarta province.

Nyai Mahshuna said that it was in Yogyakarta that she first knew a world outside the *pesantren*. 'I read the newspaper and magazines from the first moment I began studying in Yogya. From reading, I began to realise there is a lot that I needed to know' (interview with Nyai Mahshuna, 1 October 2003). During her time in Yogyakarta, she was also actively engaged in organisations such as Pergerakan Mahasiswa Islam Indonesia (Islamic Students Movement of Indonesia) and Ikatan Pemuda Pelajar Nahdlatul Ulama (NU Students Network). She held the position of chairperson of the latter organisation from 1974 until 1976. After completing her tertiary education, she married Umar Faruq, the son of Nyai Djamilah. He was the director of Pesantren Salafiyah Seblak from Nyai Djamilah's death in 1988 until 2003.

Nyai Mahshuna's involvement in social and political organisations continued after she completed her tertiary education. Between 1989 and 1992 she was the chairperson of Fatayat NU (young woman's branch of NU) in Jombang. In 1999 she became the vice-chairperson of the political party Partai Persatuan Pembangunan for the Jombang region. Eventually, she became a member of the DPRD of Jombang. She was the vice-chairperson of its committee on development issues from 1997 to 1998, and of its committee on governance issues between 1998 and 1999. In 1999 she was appointed the vice-chairperson of DPRD Jombang itself, a position she held until 2004, and she was elected a member of the Dewan Pendidikan (education board)[11] of Jombang in 2004. Regarding her involvement in the DPRD, Nyai Mahshuna said:

> I just want to prove that, as women, we are capable of being progressive...
> because in the past women have been the victims of subordination. I used to tell
> my *santriwati* that, as women, you should be progressive, especially in terms
> of education, because it will give you your proper position in society (interview
> with Nyai Mahshuna, 8 October 2003).

Nyai Mahshuna collectively manages Pesantren Salafiyah Syafiiyah with her sisters and brothers-in-law. She makes the *pesantren* a priority above her public activities. She still leads the prayers, especially for *Subuh* (early morning) prayer, and lectures after *Subuh* prayer. Once a month, she lectures at a *majelis taklim* for local women, which is held in the *pesantren*. Nyai Mahshuna said that her involvement in the leadership and the management of the *pesantren* gave her significant experience in dealing with people from different backgrounds, which was invaluable for her roles in the political party and local DPRD (interview with Nyai Mahshuna, 8 October 2003).

Between public and domestic spaces

It is commonly assumed that *pesantren* maintain strict segregation of the sexes, shielding women from public life. However, the participation of *pesantren* women in public roles and activities is not a new phenomenon. Nyai Abidah has been actively involved in the political field since the 1950s. Nyai Solihah, a *nyai* from Pesantren Denanyar who married Kiai Abdul Wahid Hasyim, was a member of Dewan Perwakilan Rakyat Gotong Royong (the name given to the national parliament during the Sukarno era). However, it was only during its 1999 *Musyawarah Nasional* (congress) in Lombok that the NU organisation recommended women's political participation. Most *pesantren* affiliated to NU then officially also endorsed the participation of Muslim women in the political field.

It has become problematic for *pesantren* to maintain patriarchal traditions and preserve the inegalitarian gender relations derived from the teachings of *kitab kuning* dominated by *fiqh* perspectives. According to Dzuhayatin (2003:66), the *fiqh* literature does not reflect the reality of women working outside the home. The *pesantren* textbooks on women's issues usually stress the significance of being a good wife and mother. Emphasis is placed on the relationship between husband and wife, urging a woman to serve her husband well. Husein Muhammad (2002:71) said that *kiai* or *ulama* used to quote that men and women are God's creations and have equal positions before Him, with similar obligations in pursuing knowledge and performing the *amr ma'ruf nahy mungkar* (enjoining good and forbidding evil acts). But the concept of gender equality is absent when it comes to practical matters such as the leadership of *pesantren*, where sons are prioritised over daughters.

In fact, all the *nyai* discussed above attained significant positions in the educational leadership of a *pesantren*. Moreover, they expanded their participation in wider public roles and activities outside the *pesantren*. Nyai Khoiriyah became the director of the *pesantren* in two different periods before and after her journey to Mecca. Nyai Abidah was a *pesantren* director, especially after her husband passed away, when she became its sole director. Nyai Mahshuna is involved in the leadership of the *pesantren*, especially in dealing with the *pesantren putri*. In addition these women participated in the instructional process—even, in the case of Nyai Abidah, instructing male students. Nyai Mahshuna also did so when the *pesantren* had *kelas persiapan* (preparation class).[12]

As the *nyai* of the *pesantren*, these women were responsible for leading the female students in communal prayers. They were the leaders or managers of the *pesantren*, resolving any issues or problems relating to the *pesantren* or the students. Some of them had regular programs giving advice, mainly to female students, on top of their instructional duties. Nyai Mahshuna said:

> I tried to be in touch with the students all the time. Apart from my political activities, I make time to be with the students, be an *imam* for their communal prayer and give the *kuliah subuh* [a brief sermon after the early morning prayer] for them every day, or encourage them to study seriously (interview with Nyai Mahshuna, 20 October 2003).

Outside the *pesantren*, Nyai Khoiriyah, Nyai Abidah and Nyai Mahshuna were involved in socio-religious organisations such as Muslimat or Fatayat NU, and held significant positions in these organisations. Although it is not well documented what specific position Nyai Khoiriyah or Nyai Abidah held on the committee of Muslimat NU, the fact is they were well known as Muslimat NU figures and worked together in social and educational activities. Nyai Khoiriyah and other Muslimat NU members pioneered the establishment of the health centre in Tebuireng under the co-ordination of Dr Sudioto (Zuhdy 1986:45). Nyai Abidah and her husband founded the PGA NU *putri*, the NU Religious Teacher Training College for girls, in Jombang. They participated in socio-religious activities to serve the local people and meet their demands for attaining Islamic knowledge. Nyai Khoiriyah was invited to lecture in different *majelis taklim*. Nyai Khoiriyah also founded YASMARA, the learning circle that studied the *kitab kuning*, where she regularly gave lectures. Nyai Abidah had a *majelis taklim* in Majelis Seblak, but is currently not teaching because of health problems. She delegated the duty to her son-in-law, Kiai Taufiqurrahman, but still attends the monthly gathering in the mosque of Pesantren Salafiyah Seblak. Nyai Mahshuna holds a monthly *majelis taklim* in the Pesantren Salafiyah, where she usually prepares a meal and a lecture for a gathering of local women students

Nyai Khoiriyah tended to concentrate on her educational duties, steering clear of political roles outside the *pesantren*, but Nyai Abidah and Nyai Mahshuna extended their public roles into the political arena, becoming members of the House of Representatives. Nyai Abidah was a member of the Constituent Assembly during the 1950s and was involved in the judicial system as a religious judge, despite the fact that, in Islamic jurisprudence discourse, it is still debated whether a woman should be allowed to be a judge at all. Nyai Mahshuna was active in her chosen political party, eventually becoming a member of the local House of Representatives in Jombang. Nyai Abidah and Nyai Mahshuna had limited political experience before becoming members of the House of Representatives but their appointments as leaders in their political party suggests that their broader qualifications were recognised.

Despite all this, most Indonesian Muslim communities, including traditional Javanese society, still maintain that a woman's space is the domestic space. It is thought to be in a woman's nature to be a good wife and mother. It seems that the *nyai* discussed were aware of these expectations. They realised that both their public and domestic duties were significant, and had to work out how to balance their public and domestic roles. To some extent, a well-managed domestic sphere is a starting point for a move into public life. Nyai Abidah said:

> I'll try to go out for other activities after I am sure that I have done my duties at home. Therefore, I prefer not to have outside activities in the early morning, because at that time I still have to deal with my duties at home (interview with Nyai Abidah, 18 September 2003).

Similarly, Nyai Mahshuna commented:

Regardless of my public activities, I still set aside time to manage the household, to make sure that everything is under control, to be with my children as much as I can and give directions to the maids who are in charge of preparing meals. I also make a commitment to attend only those ceremonies for which my presence is really needed, where no-one can replace me. But if my presence is not essential and my duties can be performed by others, I prefer not to go (interview with Nyai Mahshuna, 20 October 2003).

A well-managed domestic sphere provides a woman with the 'legitimacy' to negotiate access to public life with the significant males in her household. As such, women with religious, cultural and educational capital can aim to inhabit the public and private spheres at the same time.

The obvious question is: do they shoulder a double burden? The *kiai* household resembles an aristocratic family: almost all *kiai* households have several assistants (either students or local people) for different jobs. So these women are more like managers of the *kiai* household rather than workers in it. Mansurnoor's (1991) research on the *kiai* in Madura portrayed the *nyai* as a manager in the *kiai* household, having several people to assist her with domestic duties. For lower-class women, their involvement in economic activities in the public sphere did not necessarily mean egalitarian gender relations: however, middle-class women who were involved in the public sector had fairer relations with their male counterparts. This is because they were involved in public life for *aktualisasi diri* (self-actualisation), not because of urgent economic needs. Also, middle-class women are more likely to have servants to carry out the domestic chores. This theory also tends to be relevant to the experiences of the *nyai* discussed above.

Negotiation and bargaining positions

There are several factors determining whether it is possible for *nyai* to have an active public life. The *pesantren* has a central figure, a *kiai*. Some respondents have compared the *pesantren* and the *kiai* to a *kraton* (Javanese kingdom) and a king. Dhofier (1982) places the *kiai* as one of the key elements of the *pesantren*. The female figures in the *pesantren* are mainly the wives or daughters of the *kiai*. As the central figure, the *kiai* has a great deal of power in determining the ethos of the *pesantren*. If he is flexible, this provides the scope for women from the *pesantren* to have access to the public sphere. In Nyai Khoiriyah's case, her father, Kiai Hasyim Asy'ary, allowed her to participate in his class at Pesantren Tebuireng. Kiai Hasyim Asy'ary was also the person who recommended the establishment of a female *pesantren* within Pesantren Salafiyah Seblak: 'Mbah Hasyim supported us in establishing the female *pesantren* in Seblak. Without his support, we would not have dared to do so because at that time women were prohibited from obtaining an education' (interview with Nyai Abidah, 18 September 2003).

In the case of Nyai Abidah, her husband, Kiai Machfudz Anwar, also had an influential role in creating her path for public participation. Lily Zakiah Munir, Nyai Abidah's daughter, described how her father voluntarily offered to look after the children when Nyai Abidah felt reluctant to take up time-consuming positions because she had several small children. Lily Zakiah Munir noted how her father supported her mother's activity and showed willingness to share the responsibility of child-rearing:

> When my mother became a member of the Constituent Assembly in 1959, her children were very young. My mother had 11 children with two- or three-year intervals between them. Regarding her status as a member of DPRD and the Constituent Assembly, she wanted to say that her children were very young, but then her husband Pak Kiai Machfudz Anwar said, 'Just leave the children with me, why can't you trust that I am also able to look after them?' (interview with Lily Zakiah Munir, 15 July 2003).

However, it is unfair to conclude that the opportunity for these women to attain public positions is simply due to the blessing of the respective *kiai*. Their qualifications and capabilities are also an important factor. These qualities become bargaining positions in negotiating their goals, not only with their male counterparts but also with people from the *pesantren* and local community who hold patriarchal views. When Nyai Mahshuna asked for her father's consent to pursue tertiary education, she showed strong motivation in arguing with him. This motivation was also revealed when she decided to join the local House of Representatives, showing that there are women who can be progressive. Their capabilities and qualifications were factors determining their involvement in public activities. When Nyai Khoiriyah performed several public roles in Madrasah Banat, Pesantren Salafiyah Seblak or in different *majelis taklim* activities, she was not challenged by the *pesantren* and local community because she was adequately equipped to undertake these public roles. As Afsaruddin (1999:6) has stated, 'For women of means and education in Islamic societies, the exercise of power, formal or informal, and negotiation of public space have frequently been less of an ordeal than for women who do not enjoy the same advantages.'

Another bargaining position was their familiarity with the instructional and leadership framework of a *pesantren*. Some *nyai* had a *pesantren* education. It is part of *pesantren* tradition for *kiai* families to practice endogamous marriage, in which one *kiai* family will have an interrelationship with other *kiai*. This was widely practiced in several *pesantren* in Jombang, especially during Kiai Hasyim

Asy'ary's generation. It is still practiced, although less commonly among current generations. Endogamous marriage plays a role in preparing the succession of the *pesantren,* as a *kiai* will deliver the leadership of the *pesantren* to his son-in-law if he has no son to inherit, or a *nyai* will be given the role of co-ordinating the *pesantren putri* in her husband's *pesantren* family. The familiarity of these *nyai* with the leadership of the *pesantren* gave them an advantage in that they had a basic knowledge of how it worked. There were also sociological factors, as the society has certain expectations of the *kiai* family. In the case of Nyai Abidah, the fact that many women in her time were uneducated and that she was born into a *kiai* family 'forced' her to fill the position as the main player in girls' schooling in her family's *pesantren.*

Finally, the notion of maintaining honour and modesty is also a crucial issue in public activities of *nyai.* To some extent, it becomes a sort of prerequisite for entry into the public space. According to Afsaruddin (1999:19), 'Women were not required to retreat altogether from public entertainment, but rather had to prove that in spite of their heightened public presence, they still subscribed to traditional norms of moral behaviour and respectability'. A woman is allowed to work in a public space as long as she can maintain the Islamic ethical and moral values (Shihab 1999:88). The women from *pesantren* who appeared in public maintained the norms or values of respectability, meeting the standard and fixed values either from the Islamic community or from their society. This was one of the prerequisites for them to negotiate a possible path into the public spheres. They accommodated those values, while still being active in public.

The issue of veiling or dress code seemed not to be a controversial one among these *nyai.* While for some women activists the struggle for empowerment also includes the freedom to choose whether to wear the veil or not, for the *pesantren* women there is no compromise at all; they feel it is an obligation, and it is rare to hear an opposing opinion on the issue among them. All of them appear in public in 'Islamic' dress. (See Chapter two by Rachmah Ida in this volume for a discussion of Islamic dress.) While emphasising an Islamic dress code, these women were also careful about personal relationships, and avoided close relationships with the men from non-*mahram*[13] categories. Nyai Mahshuna told me: 'I prefer a female assistant to help me with my duties. I also try to work seriously and then leave the office if I feel the work has been completed, instead of hanging around and chatting about unnecessary issues' (interview with Nyai Mahshuna, 20 Spetmeber 2003). Most of her colleagues are male; there are only three women in the DPRD Jombang. It seems that Nyai Mahshuna intends to keep a distance between herself and her male colleagues, since it is widely believed that to have a close relationship with non-*mahram* categories indicates an improper attitude.

In Nyai Abidah's case, in a workshop held by the Centre for Pesantren and Democracy Studies on the topic of *pesantren*, terrorism and radicalism on 16 October 2003, there were local, national and international speakers. A lecturer from a United States university, an NGO activist from Australian Volunteers International and a Christian leader from Italy took part as speakers in the workshop. Nyai Abidah began the workshop with an opening address, speaking to a mixed male and female audience. With a clear voice and without a prepared speech, she talked confidently in front of the public, including the foreign speakers. At the end of workshop, she was invited to give a gift to each of the speakers. She gave the gifts to the male and female speakers, but she did not shake the men's hands; she believed a Muslim woman should not shake hands with men except those who fit the *mahram* categories. It seems that, for her, she came into the public space as a Muslim woman determined to uphold 'Islamic' values, traditions and etiquette.

Conclusion

The real experience of women's lives shows a more dynamic gender relationship than a simplistic dichotomy of public and private spheres, based on an assumption that a woman is attached to the domestic sphere and is subordinated by a patriarchal culture. Such a dynamic gender relationship also plays out in an institution like a *pesantren*, in which women's access to public participation is made possible by some significant factors. These include the flexibility of the *kiai* and the women's bargaining power in 'negotiating' their public space. The notion of maintaining honour and modesty based on the 'Islamic' precepts and *pesantren* values is well preserved by those women, and also becomes a kind of 'justification' for their access in public activities. Although the social change wrought by these women may not appear significant in a Western context, in the context of the *pesantren* world of Java, the negotiated move to the public sphere is significant and provides an important role model for future generations.

Notes

1   I would like to thank Dr Barbara Leigh and Dr Maja Mikula for helpful comments and feedback on this article.

2   An informal class for female students had begun since 1919 in the backyard of Kiai Bisri's residence at Pesantren Denanyar, but it was not until 1930 that a formal *pesantren* for girls was established.

3   This *kitab kuning*, written by Syaikh Nawawi al-Bantany, is the most popular *kitab kuning* on marital relationships. It is also a recommended subject for female students in the vast majority of *pesantren*.

4   Hasyim Asy'ary was the founding father of Pesantren Tebuireng in Jombang, and of the Nahdlatul Ulama organisation.

5   A discussion of religious matters attended by *kiai* or *ulama* to produce a religious legal interpretation and a recommendation from the Islamic perspective on particular issues.

6   The allusion is to Kartini, the well-known Javanese feminist and promoter of women's education at the turn of the 20th century.

7   From this marriage, they had 11 children: Maksum (born in 1938) Hamna (1942), Kyisah (1945), Jarir (1947), Lily Zakiyah (1950), Abdul Halim (1953), Anas Fauziah (1956), Abdul Hakim (1958), Sofia (1962), Abd Wahid (1965) and Mariam Muhsinna (1968).

8   A short biography on Nyai Solihah mentions that Abidah was chosen to accompany Solihah from Pesantren Denanyar as 'a new comer' into the Pesantren Tebuireng family when she was newly married to Wahid Hasyim (Dahlan 2002:117).

9   At the time Wahid Hasyim was the Minister of Religious Affairs. The establishment and the arrangement of religious schools in Indonesia are co-ordinated by the Ministry of Religious Affairs.

10   One of the textbooks on Islamic theology taught in *pesantren*.

11   An organisation concerned with developing the quality of education.

12   This was a one-year preparation course, before junior or senior secondary schools, at the *pesantren*. This program is no longer conducted in the *pesantren*.

13   *Mahram* is the group of men a woman may not marry because of marital or blood relationships.

chapter six

Women negotiating feminism and Islamism in Indonesia: the experiences of Nasyiatul Aisyiyah, 1985–2005[1]

Siti Syamsiyatun

The rise of feminist activism and scholarship in Indonesia in the mid-1980s provided analytical tools for women to launch systematic challenges to the New Order state's discourse of ideal womanhood, which was submissive and apolitical. In order to implement their feminist ideas, many young women established independent associations known in Indonesia as Lembaga Swadaya Masyarakat or NGOs (Mukhtar 1999:1–2). Their feminist assertions, however, were not generally accepted; in fact, state and religious authorities had major roles in refuting their ideas. Entering the 1990s, the debates on feminism intensified as religion became involved in the discourse. Islam in this context was used as an alternative perspective in looking at gender issues, as well as being a subject of feminist scrutiny. After the fall of the New Order government in 1998, various non-government actors, from women activists to religious clerics, had more scope to promote their ideologies about womanhood. It is within such a context that I locate my examination of the role of young Muslim women as active agents in the making of religious feminist discourse in contemporary Indonesia.

This chapter selects the experiences of Nasyiatul Aisyiyah (henceforth shortened as Nasyiah), the young women's wing within Muhammadiyah, for a number of reasons. Despite its long history of catering for young Muslim women and its nationwide network, little research has been done on Nasyiah. Discussions of feminism in Indonesia have focused on women's associations and NGOs, which mostly channelled their struggles for gender justice through political and legal means (Blackburn 2004; Mukhtar 1999). However, this does not mean that the 'quieter' organisations, like Nasyiah, have contributed nothing to shape the discourse. On the contrary, as argued in this chapter, Nasyiah's preference for adopting cultural transformation as a way of mainstreaming gender perspectives within the organisation and the big family of Muhammadiyah has shown positive results, without disturbing social harmony or creating lengthy controversies.

Founded in 1931 in Yogyakarta, Nasyiah is a long-established women's organisation, a rare phenomenon amongst contemporary women's NGOs. Throughout its history, Nasyiah has experienced organisational changes in terms of visions, structure, leadership and membership. From 1931 to 1965 Nasyiah was a section within Aisyiyah, the Muhammadiyah women's wing, and it catered for school-age girls. After gaining autonomy in 1965, Nasyiah became independent from Aisyiyah, and began to have rights to make its own organisational decisions, including determining its target membership, and developing and prioritising its programs. In its current statutes, Nasyiah identifies itself with the Muhammadiyah women's movement, and focuses its programs in the fields of *bidang keperempuanan* (women's issues) and social and religious affairs for Indonesian women aged between 12 and 40 years of age. Nasyiah has branches in 32 provinces, and claims a membership of about four million women.[2]

Being a part of the Indonesian women's movement and committed to improving the conditions of young women's lives, Nasyiah, since the mid-1980s, has shown new approaches to women's issues. While feminism was not known in Nasyiah circles prior to the 1980s, it is no longer a foreign term for Nasyiah members. Nasyiah organisationally has no objection to adopting gender theories to make its case for women's issues more understandable and justifiable.

Nasyiah's triple loyalty to the causes of Islam, young women and Indonesian nationalism has become a noticeable factor distinguishing Nasyiah from other women's NGOs. In this chapter I examine how Nasyiah has adapted feminist theories while at the same time reconfirming its allegiance to Islam to advance its ideology of religious womanhood in the contemporary Indonesian context. Nasyiah's endeavour in this regard could be seen as its contribution to the development of religious feminist discourse in Indonesia.

In presenting my arguments, I begin by discussing how Islamic education, previously regarded with scant respect, has become a source of authority for women to enter religious debates on women's issues. Young women graduating from Islamic higher education have utilised their expertise to confront misogynist interpretations of Islamic texts circulated widely in society. The second section investigates Nasyiah's efforts to develop a counter-discourse on religious feminism as an alternative to those offered by some streams of 'Western-generated' feminism penetrating Indonesia. Section three elaborates the main strategies applied by Nasyiah to promote and secure its vision of Islamic young womanhood by incorporating women's issues as significant agenda items in Muhammadiyah's Council of Religious Opinion and Development of Islamic Thought.

Islamic higher education and the rise of women *ulama*

The translation into Indonesian of several English books by feminist Muslims such as Fatima Mernissi, Rifaat Hassan, Amina Wadud and Asghar Ali Engineer, as well as their presence in person to address Indonesian intellectuals and activists interested in gender issues from religious perspectives, signified the beginning of the development of religious feminism in Indonesia.[3] The initiative was warmly welcomed by new graduates of modernised Islamic higher education, especially graduates of IAINs.[4] Many changes have occurred in Islamic education during the last two decades, particularly in terms of concepts, course content and images, which have made it possible for students to view Islam with critical eyes (see Aryani 2004; Hidayat 2000; Jabali & Jamhari 2002). Plenty of significant factors contribute to this transformation of Islamic education in contemporary Indonesia. In this section, however, I highlight only a few of them, as my focus is on the contribution of women pursuing Islamic higher education and the emergence of authoritative voices of women in religion, thus opening the door for women to participate actively in the debates on Islam and women's issues.

Until recently, Islamic educational institutions such as *pesantren, madrasah* and IAINs have received much less financial support from the government compared to 'secular' schools.[5] As a consequence, facilities and human resources in these Islamic educational institutions have been relatively inferior in terms of quality and quantity; and, in turn, they look less attractive for most school-age children (Jabali & Jamhari 2002:126–7). Despite the government's lack of financial assistance, Muslim communities have striven to keep their schools operating and have even built more, as they believe religious education is important for their children. Accordingly, almost all *pesantren* have been self-reliant in funding, and the number of private *madrasah* has been higher than state-owned *madrasah* (Jabali & Jamhari 2002:68–9). While these Islamic schools, especially *madrasah*, were not a favoured choice for pupils, they absorbed more girls than boys as shown in the following table.

Table 1: Percentage of male and female students enrolled in state-owned and private madrasah *(primary and secondary) 1995–2000*[6]

Type	Male	%	Female	%	Total
State-owned	2,325,686	46.3	2,695,452	53.7	5,021,138
Private	11,221,599	47.9	12,219,827	52.1	23,441,426

The statistical data above can be interpreted in different ways. One might argue that the reason females have a higher degree of participation in *madrasah* than males is because Muslim parents prefer their daughters to receive a religious education rather than a secular one. However, taking into consideration the fact that *madrasah* in general are of lower quality than secular schools, it can be asserted that more girls have been sent to second-class educational institutions than boys.

Most graduates of *madrasah* and *pesantren* have seen IAINs as their main destination when seeking higher degrees.[7] The higher percentage of female students found in *madrasah* is, however, not found in IAINs, particularly at the postgraduate level. That means only a small proportion of *madrasah* female students continue their education to the postgraduate level in IAINs. Postgraduate programs at IAINs in Yogyakarta and Jakarta are the oldest and have been considered the best; therefore, lecturers from IAINs all over Indonesia have been sent to postgraduate programs in both these cities to advance their academic training (Jabali & Jamhari 2002:47–8). The percentage of women attending postgraduate studies at IAINs in Yogyakarta and Jakarta has increased since the late 1980s, as shown in the following tables

Table 2: *Number and percentage of students enrolled at the Faculty of Postgraduate Studies, IAIN Sunan Kalijaga, Yogyakarta, 1987/8, 1992/3 and 1997/8*[8]

Academic year	Male	%	Female	%
1987/1988	37	92.5	3	7.5
1992/1993	58	87.88	8	12.12
1997/1998	110	84.62	20	15.38

Table 3: *Number and percentage of students enrolled at the Faculty of Postgraduate Studies, IAIN Syarif Hidayatullah, Jakarta 1987/8, 1993/4 and 1996/7*[9]

Academic year	Male	%	Female	%
1987/1988	180	90	20	10
1993/1994	330	84.6	60	15.4
1996/1997	700	87.5	100	12.5

Muslim women who have gained their masters and doctoral degrees in Islamic studies from IAINs have earned legitimacy and authority to speak publicly in their own right about religion, as well as to teach Islamic studies in IAINs or other universities. Female staff and gender issues in general began to gain more serious attention at managerial and academic levels in IAINs when, through assistance from the Ministry of Religious Affairs, they accelerated modernisation and staff up-grading by establishing various joint projects with other universities abroad in the late 1980s. The most important of such links have been those with Leiden University in the Netherlands, McGill University in

Canada and Al-Azhar University in Egypt, all of which offer advanced studies on Islam from different perspectives.[10] Since then, female lecturers have had better opportunities to undertake masters or doctoral degrees in various universities abroad.[11] Recently, many more IAIN female lecturers and graduates have also succeeded in gaining scholarships to pursue their graduate degrees abroad: in Australia, Europe, the Middle East and North America.

The lecturers who graduated from overseas introduced to IAIN circles new and critical approaches in Islamic studies (Jabali & Jamhari 2002:147). One of the most important results from this new academic development in IAINs has been the recognition of the importance of approaching Islamic teachings from feminist perspectives and vice versa—linking gender issues to a religious perspective (Aryani 2004; Dzuhayatin 2000). While academically some of these women scholars have acquired religious expertise and authority, socially many of them have been immersing themselves in gender issues at community levels by participating in some Muslim women's organisations. They have been activists in Nasyiah, Fatayat NU, Aisyiyah, Muslimat NU and Pemudi Persis, as well as in NGOs engaging with women's issues, such as Yayasan Annisa Swasti (shortened as Yasanti), Rifka Annisa Women's Crisis Centre, Rahima and PUAN Amal Hayati.

Several IAIN graduates have made an enormous contribution to the growth of Islamic feminism in academia and social activism. Siti Ruhaini Dzuhayatin is an outstanding example of a woman scholar who has manifested her concern over Islam and gender issues through a combined engagement in both academia and social activism. While teaching at the Faculty of Islamic Law and heading the Centre for Women's Studies at IAIN Yogyakarta, Ruhaini is also one of the founders of Rifka Annisa Women's Crisis Centre and a member of Muhammadiyah's Council for Religious Opinion and the Development of Islamic Thought. Her role in steering the discussions about contemporary women's issues and Islam in Nasyiah's circles was noticeable when she was a member of Nasyiah's Research Centre in 1995–2000. There were other proponents who brought a gender perspective to review Nasyiah's strategic plans in the 1990s, such as Siti Noordjannah Djohantini and Lathifah Iskandar (both were also involved in establishing Yasanti and Rifka Annisa Women's Crisis Centre in Yogyakarta).

Many other IAIN graduates have also made considerable contributions to the discussion of women's issues in other Muslim women's organisations and various NGOs. Masruchah, for example, was an activist in Fatayat NU and director of Fatayat Welfare Foundation in Yogyakarta before being appointed as the general secretary of the Indonesian Women's Coalition in 2004. For some years Farha Ciciek has been a director at the Rahima Centre for Training and Information on Islam and Women's Rights Issues in Jakarta. Sinta Nuriyah and Badriyah Fayumi have contributed greatly in the recent development of Islamic feminism in Indonesia through their engagement in Muslimat NU and Fatayat NU respectively, as well as in NGOs like PUAN Amal Hayati in Jakarta. Siti Musdah Mulia has directed the Institute for Religious and Gender Studies to carry out a gender-mainstreaming program within the Department of Religious Affairs.

From the discussion it is clear that IAIN, as the highest level of Islamic formal training in Indonesia and which has been a destination for Muslim women graduating from *madrasah* and *pesantren,* has become a major source for women's religious empowerment. The institution that was once seen as second class in relation to the secular educational bodies has now provided the necessary academic tools for women to engage in debates on Islamic issues at the highest levels in any religious institution or organisation. With IAIN degrees in hand, women have entered many public arenas such as Islamic universities, courts, organisations and religious councils. Women have used their knowledge of Islam and their formal qualifications to advance their gender interests through various means. How this process is taking place in Nasyiah is discussed further in the next sections.

Facing issues raised by secular feminists and Islamist clergy

The 1980s was a significant decade for Nasyiah's shifting approaches to religion and feminism. Both the rise of the women's movement and Islamic resurgence revitalised Nasyiah's energies to claim spaces and voices different from the official ones dictated by the New Order regime (Anwar 1995; Hassan 1982). Being part of the Indonesian women's and Islamic movements, Nasyiah was influenced and energised by the emergence of such new social-religious dynamics. Unlike most women's NGOs established during the 1980s and 1990s, which used developmental and secular feminist approaches to challenge the scripts on development and gender composed by the New Order regime (Mukhtar 1999), Nasyiah has consistently put religion at the forefront.

Nasyiah's *Muktamar* (national congress) of 1985 gave a mandate of national leadership to Cholifah; this event could be regarded as an input of fresh blood after Sulistyowati had led the organisation for about 14 years since 1971. Herself a graduate of IAIN Yogyakarta, Cholifah recruited young women, mostly university graduates and students, to assume posts in Nasyiah headquarters. Unlike her predecessor, who applied an inward-looking policy, Cholifah felt it was time for Nasyiah to engage in broader issues faced by young Muslim women.

There was an immediate need for Nasyiah to improve its understanding of women's issues from different perspectives, as ideas of womanhood in Indonesia were being contested by various social actor groups, ranging from the state to women's NGOs and religious clerics (see Blackburn 2004).

Cholifah considered it important that Nasyiah should be able to respond appropriately to the challenges posed by some secular feminist activists who regarded Islam as the source of women's degrading position in society and by religious clerics who argued that since women were the root of *fitna* (social chaos), they should be controlled, veiled and kept at home (Shehadeh 2003:93–4). To face these challenges, Cholifah made the formation of intellectual discussion groups in Nasyiah (as distinct from its regular *pengajian* or religious learning groups) a priority of the action plan during her leadership term from 1985 to 1990 (interview with Cholifah, 5 August 2003).

The women's religious issues that Nasyiah was concerned to address included veiling, the institution of marriage, and the morality of pre- and extra-marital sexual engagement, as there were conflicting views on these matters. On the one hand, according to Cholifah, several feminists in Indonesia considered that veiling was a real sign of how Islam has devalued women. On the other hand, some Islamic clerics regarded women as a source of social chaos, a site of evil attraction and incapable of handling public affairs (Kazemzadeh 2002; Doumato 2003; Shehadeh 2003).[12] In Cholifah's view, it was necessary for Nasyiah, as an organisation of Muslim women, to clarify these issues one after the other, beginning with veiling. She explains:

> I think the idea of associating veiling with backwardness of women has been spread around since long ago. I was ridiculed for wearing a headscarf when I was a young girl in the 1960s. But in the late 1980s the tone of accusation was rather different, more systematic and *ilmiah* [scientific], so I thought Nasyiah should respond in the same way. Nasyiah always encouraged its members to wear *kerudung* [head-covering], and it did not carry any negative meaning for us. It did not restrict us from doing what we want to do. Their accusations about the veil were not true, and Nasyiah wanted to respond to that properly, but then I realised we were not well trained in serious intellectual debates. Nasyiah lacked that capability. Partly for that reason I recruited many university students and graduates to sit in Nasyiah's national executive board, and initiated the establishment of a discussion group (interview with Cholifah, 5 August 2003).

Nasyiah has always held in high esteem the practice of women covering their bodies and hair. The main reason asserted by Nasyiah is that Islam encourages women to do so, as mentioned in Qur'anic verses 24:31 and 33:59. Qur'anic verse 24:31 says: 'And say to the believing women that they should lower their gaze and guard their modesty; that they should not display their beauty and ornaments except what [must ordinarily] appear thereof; that they should draw their veils over their bosoms...' Verse 30 advises believing men to lower their gaze and guard their modesty, which will make for greater purity for them. So, explicitly, the request for maintaining self-purity is not only for women but also for men. Verse 33:59 says: 'O Prophet! Tell thy wives and daughters, and the believing women, they should cast their outer garments over their persons [when abroad]; that is most convenient, that they should be known [as such] and not molested. And God is Oft-Forgiving, Most Merciful.'

Despite the assertion, there has been no kind of organisational discipline applied to members who do not wear headscarves, which is very different from practices adopted by fundamentalist Muslims in other parts of the world. For example, under Khomeini's regime, a harsh disciplinary device to control Iranian women's dress code was adopted.[13] Nasyiah has relied on individual judgment and willingness rather than organisational sanction concerning the dress code of members.

Regardless of Nasyiah's persuasion on religious grounds, at the practical and day-to-day level there have been various motives expressed by its members as to why they wear head coverings: to show religious devotion, to adjust to the social environment, to please their parents and peers, and to gain employment in Muhammadiyah or Islamic institutions (interviews with a number of Nasyiah members). My observation and research into pictures of Nasyiah's activities shows that the styles of the outfits and headscarves worn by Nasyiah women have varied over time from one place to another.

Cholifah's initiative to encourage intellectual pursuits in Nasyiah circles was developed further by her successors. In 1990, as soon as Siti Noordjannah Djohantini was elected as the chief executive, she shared her experiences of managing an NGO, Yasanti, with her colleagues in Nasyiah. As a graduate of a management department, she also introduced fresh approaches in organisational structures and administration. Knowing the atmosphere within Nasyiah and the conditions of members at the grassroots level, and noting the immediate need of Nasyiah to develop intellectual engagement to respond to contemporary challenges, she proposed the foundation of a semi-independent institution in which Nasyiah might discuss important issues critically without being worried about the reactions of the ordinary members (interview with Diah Siti Nuraini, 19 August 2003).

While discussing technical aspects of establishing a semi-independent foundation within Nasyiah, Djohantini initiated the formation of a 'Discussion and Dialogue Group', where several members of Nasyiah with various academic backgrounds, some of them directors of the Women's Studies Centres in IAINs, Indonesian Islamic University, Muhammadiyah University and Sarjana Wiyata

University, would critically discuss gender issues in Islam. This group held intensive discussions and invited experts from outside Nasyiah. Through the discussion group, Nasyiah was exposed to feminist thought from academicians in systematic ways. Occasionally important figures from Muhammadiyah, such as M Syafi'i Ma'arif, M Amin Abdullah and Chamim Ilyas, were invited to speak and to hear recent concerns of Nasyiah on gender discourse (Pimpinan Pusat Nasyiatul Aisyiyah 1992c). Through these informal communications, Nasyiah's commitment to review women's issues from an Islamic perspective and Islamic issues from a woman's perspective was conveyed to Muhammadiyah. Some members of the Muhammadiyah leadership responded positively to Nasyiah's gesture. Thus, when M Amin Abdullah was appointed to lead Muhammadiyah's Religious Council in 1995, he included gender issues in the agenda items and invited Nasyiah's Siti Ruhaini Dzuhayatin to be a member of the council.

Djohantini's proposal for establishing a Research Centre was approved in the 1995 *Muktamar* of Nasyiah held in Banda Aceh, where Diah Siti Nuraini was elected as the new chairwoman. Djohantini was appointed director of the centre, and she led Nasyiah in embarking on a new mental endeavour. Through this Research Centre, Nasyiah started reflecting more seriously on certain practices performed by the organisation: the what, why and how questions were critically raised on such issues as dress code, women's leadership, political participation, women's rights in marriage, and contemporary moves by secular feminists. Later, in 2000, Trias Setiawati, in her capacity as the chief executive, instructed all Nasyiah's leadership offices in provincial and municipal levels to establish their own research centres.

These research centres have in many cases served as think tanks for Nasyiah boards in their respective levels, particularly in terms of introducing feminist ideas. In 2001 the Research Centre collaborated with the Yogyakarta IAIN's Centre for Women's Studies and Alifah Foundation in inviting several outstanding Muslims feminists from overseas (Asghar Ali Engineer of Mumbai, India,[14] and Zainah Anwar of Malaysia[15]) to give lectures on Islam and women's issues and to have discussions with young Muslims in Yogyakarta. Thus Nasyiah has initiated direct contacts with other Muslim feminists abroad. Other esteemed Muslim scholars from Indonesia who campaigned for feminist perspectives, like Siti Ruhaini Dzuhayatin, Nasaruddin Umar and Chamim Ilyas, all IAIN lecturers, had given lectures in the centre and had dialogue with Nasyiah members (interview with Dewi A Suryani, 5 August 2003).

On issues of marriage and personal morality or adultery, Nasyiah has not followed the path taken by some feminists of social and radical persuasions who consider that heterosexual-based marriages are fertile sites for women's oppression (Evans 1995:69, 73). Nasyiah has consistently held *akhlaqul karimah* (religious-based piety and fine character) in the highest regard. Accordingly, the organisation has opposed assertions that women, just like men, should be freed from any moral and social stigma to engage in illegitimate sexual activities as they wish. Instead, Nasyiah has emphasised the importance of heterosexual-based marriage and made efforts so that this institution should function properly. Nasyiah is aware that there have been plenty of cases of women being treated badly in families during their marital lives. However, abandoning marriage is not the favoured solution. Persons involved in the arrangements of a marriage according to Islamic law—bride, groom, guardian and witnesses—should perform their duties and exercise their rights as prescribed in the Qur'an and the Prophet's examples. Instead of abandoning dysfunctional institutions, Nasyiah would rather rectify them (Pimpinan Pusat Nasyiatul Aisyiyah 1992b; 1996; 2003).

Polygamy has been an uneasy tenet for Muslims, and its practice in Indonesia has been contested since the colonial period (Blackburn 2004; White 2004; Hooker 2003; Nasution 2002; see also the chapter by Nina Nurmila in this volume). Nasyiah's standpoint on this issue has not changed much since the 1960s and 1970s—monogamy is the ideal practice and the norm of Islam, and polygamy should be discouraged. Nasyiah prefers to rely on cultural evolution to change people's perceptions of polygamous marriage in Islam rather than ban it outright through immediate legal reform, as previously demanded by the secular women's organisation Perwari and other nationalist associations and politicians. Rahmawati, former Nasyiah general secretary (2000–04), explains Nasyiah's argument as follows:

> Nasyiah has always been a *dakwah* organisation, although it has embarked on women's gender issues more intensely in recent years. Nasyiah is aware of the need to handle carefully religious issues with wide social impacts. Nasyiah has to consider and juggle between encouraging the fulfilment of individual human's rights and maintaining the social unity, solidarity and harmony of Indonesian communities. We cannot enjoy our rights if we live in a chaotic environment; and when we talk about our rights we also talk about someone else's rights and, of course, our duties, too. There must be a balanced consideration. Some women's NGOs emphasise the advancement of individual rights and give less consideration to social harmony.

> With regard to the issue of polygamy, Nasyiah considers it is important for us to promote cultural transformation and change of perceptions regarding the issue. In order to do so, we give attention to providing mass education and raising consciousness about abuses, fatalities and unjust treatments in marriages, not only in polygamous ones, and how to prevent and overcome those problems. Enforcing legal prohibition totally and at once will not be effective, and it will create waves of prolonged mass controversy, which sometimes become counter-productive to achieving our goals (interview with Rahmawati, 9 March 2005).

Other contemporary Muslim feminists in Indonesia have striven to adopt political and legal approaches to eliminate the practice of polygamous marriages. The case of some feminist scholars affiliated with the Working Group for Gender Mainstreaming (chaired by Siti Musdah Mulia) within the Department of Religious Affairs is a most recent example. As also discussed by Nina Nurmila in this volume, the working group has attempted to provide a Counter Legal Draft revising the views expressed in the KHI of 1991, particularly on marriage issues, in anticipation of the Compilation becoming a positive law. The Counter Legal Draft proposed new arrangements on several crucial marital issues: total prohibition of polygamy, the possibility for a woman to marry without her guardian's consent or presence, marriage based on temporary contract and interfaith marriage. However, in 2004, before being examined intensively and extensively by the larger public, two important Islamic bodies, namely the Ministry of Religious Affairs and the Council of Indonesian Ulama, rejected the proposal (*Kompas* 2004; 2005; *Sinar Harapan* 2005a; 2005b).

Responding to the government's intention to legalise the KHI and to the Counter Legal Draft, Nasyiah demanded that the government should invite elements of Muslim communities and Muslim organisations to participate in making the decision, and that a gender perspective should be employed in the process of revising the KHI document (Pimpinan Pusat Nasyiatul Aisyiyah 2004a). Furthermore, Rahmawati says:

> Nasyiah, in spite of its disagreement over some items proposed by the team, was disappointed to see the immediate rejection of the [Counter Legal Draft] by the Minister of Religious Affairs. The team is in fact from the Ministry, so there must be some sort of lack of communications within the department. I suspect the reason why this draft was instantly rejected was because it had not been discussed with other influential Muslim leaders, scholars or organisations. But I think it is important that before we make a judgment we must read carefully first what the KHI is saying, then compare its content with that of the [Counter Legal Draft], and study why the [Counter Legal Draft] wants some revisions, and what their arguments are. The [Counter Legal Draft] demanded that temporary marriages should be legalised, because according to the team's research there have been a lot [of] temporary marriages done 'under hand' [*sirri*—secretly] and women have... suffered disadvantages from such practices: they lost their rights over *mahar*, *nafkah* (financial and spiritual maintenance), and their children's right to *waris* (inheritance) has been ignored (interview with Rahmawati, 9 March 2005).

Nasyiah's preference for the cultural evolutionary approach appeared again in addressing the question of whether women can marry without their guardians' consent and presence. Instead of promoting legalisation of the practice as recommended by the working group, Nasyiah demanded that a guardian should perform his role properly to make sure that a woman under his guardianship is safe and protected from any abuses in embarking on her marriage and the life beyond. A guardian must not abuse his authority by forcing a woman to marry a man she does not want to or by preventing a woman from marrying a man she likes without valid reasons.

In the case of *perzinaan* (pre- and extra-marital sex), the solution was not to remove the stigma of immorality from women, but to apply the same condemnation to men: men who commit adultery are disgraceful and sinful and should not be tolerated. In Nasyiah's view, illicit sensuality was the work of *hawa nafsu* (forces of wild instinct) and it should be controlled. Such issues were highlighted by Nasyiah in its 1992 national congress and documented in the Decisions of Nasyiah's National Congress I:

> Lack of internalisation of Islamic teachings and *akhlak* [ethics of conduct] amongst Muslims has resulted in their practising unlawful behaviours, such as adultery, prostitution, violence, rape, disrespect of the institution of marriage, violation towards many other religious norms in their daily lives as an individual, as a member of family, as well as a member of a larger community...
>
> Life styles echoing individualism, materialism and hedonism have threatened the religious and spiritual life of the community...
>
> The rise of *fanatisme sempit* [narrow fanaticism] in understanding and practising religious teachings has caused disharmony and disturbed sisterhood...
>
> The promotion of *mut'a[h]*, *sirri* and polygamous marriages by certain Muslim groups is seen by Nasyiah as a challenge and should be responded to carefully (Pimpinan Pusat Nasyiatul Aisyiyah 1992a:12–13).

While on the one hand Nasyiah faced challenges posed by secular feminists, on the other hand it confronted ideas propagated by some Muslim groups that claimed to be following a *salafi* (that which pertains to ancestry) way of life.[16] These Muslim groups have encouraged the practise of *mut'ah, sirri* (secret marriage, without proper civil administration) and polygamous marriages among their members and society at large.[17] Nasyiah has disagreed with their conduct and, as expressed in the above document, has concluded that certain actions should be taken to prevent Nasyiah members from adopting extremes according to either secular or those particular *salafi* views. From the recommendation passed in the congress, it is clear that Nasyiah opposes the view of feminists who, it considers, denigrate the institution of heterosexual-based marriage, nor does it see that *mut'ah, sirri* and polygamous marriages are good customs for its members to adopt. Accordingly, the congress gave a mandate to Nasyiah's central executive board, then led by Djohantini, to develop training manuals for the preparation of building *Sakinah* (happy, harmonious and peaceful) Families (Pimpinan Pusat Nasyiatul Aisyiyah 1992a:14).[18]

As one of the preparatory steps to developing a training manual for building *Sakinah* Families, a pamphlet called 'Pembinaan akhlak dalam keluarga' ('Character building within the family') was produced by Nasyiah in 1992, shortly after the congress. The book contains Nasyiah's views on some issues in marriage, such as women's rights and duties and sexual orientation, as well as guidance towards acquiring good personal traits and a happy, peaceful and harmonious family. Marriage between a man and a woman is seen by Nasyiah as a social and sacred covenant fulfilling God's command to seal their *ma'ruf* (good, proper) relationship as husband and wife based on *mawaddah* (love) and *rahmah* (mercy) as stipulated by Qur'anic verses 30:21 and 4:19. Verse 30:21 says:

> And among His Signs is this, that He created for you mates from among yourselves, that ye may dwell in tranquillity with them, and He has put love and mercy between your (hearts), verily in that are Signs for those who reflect.

Verse 4:19 reads:

> O ye who believe! Ye are forbidden to inherit women against their will. Nor should ye treat them with harshness, that ye may take away part of the dower ye have given them—except where they have been guilty of open lewdness; on the contrary live with them on a footing of kindness and equity. If ye take a dislike to them it may be that ye dislike a thing and God brings about through it a great deal of good.

It is within such a religiously endorsed marital institution that couples should enjoy the pleasure of sexual engagement and may have children to raise to become good Muslims. The following are some of the traits derived from Qur'anic values emphasised by Nasyiah to be adopted by all members of a family so that happiness, harmony and peace will be achieved:

1 Performing Islamic devotional rituals, including reciting the Qur'an.

2 Applying deliberation in making decisions such as in matters related to having children, spending money, division of tasks and education.

3 Parents should become good role models for their children, and treat them with dignity, love, justice and respect. Children are seen as both *amanat* [trust] and *cobaan* [test] from God for parents.

4 Children must pay respect to and love their parents, siblings and other relatives; and a mother has three times more right in this matter than the father.

5 All family members should maintain their honour, and refrain from any engagement that is unlawful religiously and socially, such as illicit

sex, criminal acts, and living off unlawful income, for instance through corruption, gambling, theft, and fraudulent businesses.

6   They should be generous, honest, trustworthy, polite, responsible, patient, avoid excessive anger, and be persistent, full of devotion, disciplined, and hard working.

7   They should avoid arrogance, hypocrisy, *riya* [showing off], jealousy and greed (Pimpinan Pusat Nasyiatul Aisyiyah 1992b).

Sakinah Family training was designed by Nasyiah's Department of Social and Economic Affairs to address young unmarried women and men. The training manual covers various subjects such as marriage according to Islam, psychological issues in adulthood and marriage, communications, sex education and reproductive health, as well as home economy and management (Pimpinan Pusat Nasyiatul Aisyiyah 1996b:5–6; 2003:17–18). Training for building *Sakinah* Families began to be implemented nationwide after Nasyiah's *Muktamar* in 1995. It is one of the pro-active initiatives taken by Nasyiah to respond to what are seen as the currently escalating problems of family and women. By involving young men in Nasyiah's training, it was expected that women's voices and concerns would reach men's ears and hearts. Despite its lack of interest in taking up such issues at an organisational level, Pemuda Muhammadiyah (Male Youth) nevertheless supported its 'sister's' programs by sending its members to participate in Nasyiah's training sessions.[19]

Unlike earlier periods when Nasyiah mostly relied on the opinions of Muhammadiyah's Religious Council on religious and women's issues, since the early 1990s Nasyiah has tried to interpret them independently within its own organisation. However, it was found that the voice of Nasyiah as a women's organisation was not yet as influential and acceptable among ordinary Indonesian Muslims as that of its paternal organisation, Muhammadiyah. Therefore it was necessary for Nasyiah to convince Muhammadiyah to make it a close ally in mainstreaming gender perspective in religious edicts. A significant fruit of Nasyiah's investment in communicating its concern over gender issues in Islam was harvested in 1995 when Muhammadiyah agreed to rename its Religious Council from Majlis Tarjih to Majlis Tarjih dan Pengembangan Pemikiran Islam (Council for Religious Opinion and Development of Islamic Thought). Since then Muhammadiyah has appointed a few Nasyiah women (Siti Ruhaini Dzuhayatin, Isti'anah and Evi Sofia Inayati) to posts on the council board.

Claiming space and gender mainstreaming in Muhammadiyah

Nasyiah was delighted to have representatives in Muhammadiyah's Religious Council. Having women representing its organisational voice in Muhammadiyah was one of Nasyiah's strategic achievements, since this would open doors to wider organisational involvement. It was a sign that Nasyiah's concern about the gender interests of young women would reach a larger audience and be considered formally within organisations of the Muhammadiyah family.

The Religious Council has occupied a special position within Muhammadiyah as an Islamic organisation.[20] Muhammadiyah's standpoints on religious issues ranging from prayers, marriage and women's political leadership to in-vitro fertilisation are decided by the council. Although the council has repeatedly declared that its *fatwa* do not bind Muslims to strictly adopt them, most Muhammadiyah members and sympathisers make an effort to follow the council's opinion. Any *fatwa* issued by Muhammadiyah will have a nationwide impact. In previous decades, its women's wings, Aisyiyah and particularly Nasyiah, always referred to the council's *fatwa* in any religious problems simply because 'we did not have yet sufficient religious knowledge and capacity to make our own decisions, so we just followed what the council had to say about the issues we were concerned with' (interview with Sulistyowati, 6 August 2003).

The Religious Council was established in 1927 in response to the demand of the Muslim community, which needed religious opinions with greater certainty. As an Islamic reformist movement in the early 20th century, Muhammadiyah often expressed different opinions from those held by traditionalist Muslims on many religious practices, such as where to conduct congregational prayers of *Ieds*, how to perform night prayers during Ramadan, to whom *zakat* (alms) and cattle sacrifices should be distributed, and whether Muslims may use dead saints and *ulama* as mediators for their prayers to God.[21] Differing opinions and practices on religious matters were taken seriously by lay Muslims at the grassroots level to the extent that they threatened Muslims' unity. One group of Muslims accused another group of being infidels because they had held different opinions on certain issues (Noer 1978:227–34). Social conflict like this was mentioned in the document on the background of the establishment of Muhammadiyah Religious Council in 1927:

> The committee was aware that the Muslim world longed for unity, therefore all Islamic organisations, even all Muslim individuals, had to increase and improve their religious knowledge so that mutual understanding and unity amongst Muslim community could be achieved and maintained. The disease of narrow mindedness and the habit of accusing other fellow Muslims should be cured and removed from Muslims' lives, because both were the enemy of unity; and Islamic teachings did not approve such actions.

Muhammadiyah, as the oldest Islamic organisation in the Dutch East Indies, was called to cure such social diseases down to their deepest roots. The establishment of Majlis Tarjih [Religious Council], in which religious issues should be carefully discussed and examined, would serve as the first step to reach that goal. The Council should follow a procedure in making any decisions on religious problems so that the result would be the closest to the *Haq* [truth]. While making its own decisions, the Council should not reduce its trust, loyalty and love towards its brothers who had showed different opinions. They should be respected and embraced as brothers in Islam who shared with us the same God, faith and *kiblat* [direction when performing prayers] (Mulkhan 1990b:244).

Members of the council board have consisted of respected *ulama* and scholars who have various academic backgrounds: from Islamic studies, medicine and economics to astronomy and political science in different eras. The council has produced a large number of religious *fatwa*, considerations and admonitions on various issues, which have been published through mass media: books, question–answer formats in newspapers and magazines, leaflets and journals (Hooker 2003; Abdullah 1997; Abdurrahman 2003; Majlis Tarjih 1972; Majlis Tarjih 1980; Djamil 1994). It was not until 1995, when the council underwent a transformation in terms of the name of the institution, mandates and methodology applied, that women of Nasyiah were invited to become full members of the council board.

The 1995 *Muktamar* in Banda Aceh that approved the renaming of the council decided that M Amin Abdullah, a professor in Islamic philosophy and theology, should head the council. Under his leadership the council conducted self-criticism and evaluation of opinions and laws produced by the institution. Discussions on the methodology of *ijtihad* (individual interpretation) have been intensively conducted (Abdurrahman 2003). In Abdullah's view Muhammadiyah had to take advantage of the vast development of any sciences and knowledge to enrich its perspectives and broaden its horizons in examining problems faced by modern Muslim society. It was impossible that Muhammadiyah could ignore the growth of intellectual debates and social activism generated by different streams of feminism. As vice-rector of an IAIN at that time, Abdullah had been exposed to feminist scholarship, mainly through his patronage of the Centre for Women's Studies. Moreover, he believed that the council was strategically the most suitable institution to introduce feminist ideas and gender analysis to *ulama* and scholars in Muhammadiyah circles, because the council had earned considerable respect and obedience from members and the Muslim community at large. Had the gender issues been handled by other councils in Muhammadiyah, the response would have been very different (interview with M Amin Abdullah, 15 July 2003). Abdullah's assessment turned out to be correct: once the Religious Council put gender issues onto its agenda, the strong resistance from Muhammadiyah *ulama* to deal with the issues weakened steadily.

From the discussion above it is obvious that the methods of gender mainstreaming taken by Nasyiah were different from those adopted by some Western feminists. Unlike radical feminists, Nasyiah did not jeopardise its relationships with its 'male relatives', Muhammadiyah and Pemuda Muhammadiyah, in making its voice and concerns over gender issues heard, nor did it accuse them of being culpable of gender injustice. Rather, Nasyiah regarded them as partners and supporters with whom together they would learn further about gender relations in Islam by way of constant persuasion and dialogue. Nasyiah consistently used religious teachings and language in reminding its male counterparts to address gender issues. Several Qur'anic verses, in addition to the *al-Fatihah* (The Opening Chapter), have been selected by Nasyiah to show the basic norms of its triple loyalties as stipulated in the preamble of its constitution. The profession of faith and the Qur'anic verse in 3:104 clearly show Nasyiah's allegiance to Islam. Verse 3:104 says, 'Let there arise out of you a band of people inviting to all that is good, enjoining what is right, and forbidding what is wrong; they are the ones to attain felicity'. Its religious view of gender ideology and relations is based on Qur'anic verse 9:71:

> The believers, men and women, are protectors one of another; they enjoin what is just, and forbid what is evil: they observe regular prayers, practice regular charity, and obey God and His Apostle. On them God pour His mercy, for God Is Exalted in power, Wise.

A transcendent view of a prosperous Indonesian community is inspired by verse 34:15, which refers to 'a territory fair and happy, and a Lord Oft-Forgiving'.

Nasyiah had invested time and energy so as to make effective its strategy to campaign for its gender interests in Muhammadiyah circles; it used any means of communications available, formal and informal, to talk about the issues with its male counterparts as mentioned previously. Such an approach might be regarded as slow and conventional by some observers (Marcoes-Natsir 2002; Doorn-Harder 1999); however, so far the result has been fruitful.

In 1999, at a national conference of the Muhammadiyah Religious Council held in Malang, women officially delivered their speeches regarding the question of women and religion before representatives from all over Indonesia. At the conference Siti Ruhaini and Siti Chamamah, representatives of Nasyiah and Aisyiyah respectively, explained the detailed revision of the manual about *Sakinah* Families in which a gender perspective was adopted. Their proposal for revision as contained in the 'Supplement to *Sakinah* Families' was approved;

among the revised items was one about the morality of the *Sakinah* Family. It is stated that the *Sakinah* Family is built on five principles, namely *orientasi Ilahiyah* (divine/transcendent oriented), *pola keluarga besar* (extended family), *pola hubungan kesedarajatan dan dialogis* (equal and mutual relationships), *perekat mawaddah wa rahmah* (cementing love, compassion and mercy) and fulfilment for a better life in this world and the world to come (Pimpinan Pusat Aisyiyah 2000).

Sita (pseudonym), a Nasyiah local leader in Yogyakarta, explained how these principles of the *Sakinah* Family have been spread among Nasyiah members through *pengajian* and training sessions to strengthen women's position in marriage:

> The concept of *Sakinah* Families promoted in Nasyiah is actually protecting women from polygamy or other mistreatment; and it also calls on human beings to be aware of *godaan syetan* (satanic temptation). The first principle is to prevent women and men from marrying only because of wealth, beauty or other factors which are not permanent and will change. We prefer extended families, because they will protect women. Suppose the father or husband of a woman is dead, she will always have a family to rely on and maintain her. So there will be no reason for a man to take her as a co-wife on the grounds that he wants to take care of her. As for the fulfilment of happiness and goodness in this world and the hereafter, Nasyiah really wants marriage to be a happy journey for both men and women. You know, often women are forced to accept polygamy and endure suffering and anguish throughout their lives with promises that they will be rewarded with heaven in the world after. We want *fiddunya hasanah, filakhiroti hasanah* (a good life in this world and the world after) just as the Qur'an clearly says (interview with Sita, 15 May 2005).

Another issue of the 1999 meeting concerned women assuming the highest national leadership. Nasyiah has articulated its standpoint that a woman may be a president, a prime minister or a leader of a political party, a view expressed by the Religious Council since 1972 (women may assume the highest rank of government offices, courts and other important political posts (Majlis Tarjih 1972:55–8)). However, probably due to certain political calculations, some Muhammadiyah leaders did not like to recognise, let alone emphasise, such an opinion during the late 1990s. In the political context of that time, many Muhammadiyah leaders wanted to support M Amien Rais, a former Muhammadiyah chief executive, then National Mandate Party leader, in his competition with Megawati Sukarnoputri, who led the Indonesian Democratic Party of Struggle, and others during the general election.

Nasyiah was not in an easy position at that time: it was torn between loyalty to its paternal organisation and loyalty to the women's cause. In such a situation, however, Nasyiah was willing to make its gender interest clear at the expense of its cultural solidarity. Rufaida (pseudonym), a member of Central Board, explained Nasyiah's experience in dealing with the situation as follows:

In the 1999 election Nasyiah experienced a difficult and odd situation. Before the election, Nasyiah in collaboration with the Asia Foundation conducted nationwide political education. We organised *pengajian politik* (political teaching) to promote and encourage women's active participation in politics. Nasyiah organisationally did not support any political party, but understandably most, although not all, of Nasyiah members would favour Pak Amien Rais and his [National Mandate Party]. Apparently our message of emphasising women's participation in politics that we delivered in *pengajian politik*, which were attended by tens of thousands of women in total (not all were Nasyiah members), was understood by our audience as support for Megawati. They thought we were asking them to vote for Megawati. This is because she was the only woman to lead a political party contesting in the general election at that time. Really Megawati gained a lot of advantages from our 'free' campaign. In fact Megawati was not the ideal president candidate from Nasyiah's point of view, but we could not say that in our meeting, as we were neutral. We only mentioned characteristics or requirements of president candidates, but still people thought Nasyiah supported Megawati. Well, at least a woman can be a president in Indonesia. We must find a better way to convey our message next time (interview with Rufaida, 15 September 2003).

Muhammadiyah local Religious Councils at the provincial levels had also appointed a number of women as board members, most of whom were IAIN students and graduates. Syamsul Anwar, who succeeded Abdullah in 2000 in chairing the council, has strengthened its concern over women's issues. Thus in 2003 the council held a national conference on 'Islamic laws on women's issues: Muhammadiyah perspectives'. Two outstanding feminists from Muslimat NU and Fatayat NU, Siti Musdah Mulia and Badriyah Fayumi, were invited to share their ideas and concerns as speakers in the conference. Isti'anah and Evi Sofia from Nasyiah were actively involved in planning the occasion, in the steering committee and in chairing the sessions.

Following the Muhammadiyah congress held in Makassar in 2003, other major changes in Muhammadiyah's constitution, which accommodated the demands of Nasyiah, were approved. One was that women would have the same rights as men to be elected as executives in all levels of Muhammadiyah leadership (from hamlet to national levels). The previous Muhammadiyah constitution designated men as leaders. However, there was a suspicion that the amendment of Muhammadiyah's constitution on leadership had not been well understood or wholeheartedly received by its members, because at the congress held the following year in Mataram, only 15 out of 32 Muhammadiyah provincial executive boards had women representatives. Further confirmation of the inclusion of women in Muhammadiyah executive bodies was approved at the 2004 Tanwir (the highest national congress after Muktamar): if women were not elected to assume posts in Muhammadiyah executive boards at each level after its 45th *Muktamar* in July 2005 in Malang, an affirmative action to include women would be adopted. There should be at least one woman on Muhammadiyah boards at every level (interview with Rahmawati, 9 March 2005).

Nasyiah has also been involved actively in several working groups formed by Muhammadiyah, such as in the working groups for corruption elimination, for developing the agenda of Muhammadiyah *Muktamar* 2005 (Pimpinan Pusat Nasyiatul Aisyiyah 2004a:6) and for organising social relief for tsunami victims in Nangro Aceh Darussalam. Rahmawati, a Nasyiah representative, has been entrusted to lead Muhammadiyah relief missions in Aceh since the middle of January 2005. Many more Nasyiah members from the surrounding regions have been heavily involved in the relief mission (interview with Rahmawati, 9 March 2005).

Muhammadiyah leads the other large Islamic organisation, NU, in accepting women at its highest levels. Official recognition and inclusion of women in the 'father' organisation's Central Board and its most 'sacred' Religious Council is not yet enjoyed by Fatayat and Muslimat women of NU, as stated by Badriyah Fayumi, a leader of Fatayat NU:

> I don't know when the *Syuriah* (legislative/consultative board) of NU will have women as its members; it seems very difficult for NU women to be seated in that board. This is because culturally the members of *Syuriah* Board are from *pesantren*, and most [of] them deal with male *santri*. With regard to women's gender issues, the aspirations of Fatayat have on many occasions been blocked by NU. For instance, when we proposed that the NU Board of Bahtsul Masail (Council for Religious Affairs) should discuss further about alternative options on abortion, the Board just dismissed our request and outlawed abortion (interview with Badriyah Fayumi, 31 July 2003).

Aisyah Baidlowi, a distinguished leader of Muslimat NU, also expressed her disappointment that NU has not approved women to sit on its *tanfidziyah* (executive) and *syuriah* boards (*Kompas* 2005). Despite this structural, organisational obstacle, the Fatayat and Muslimat NU women have been very progressive in handling contemporary gender issues within the context of internal organisation and the women's movement in Indonesia in general (Marcoes-Natsir 2002; Doorn-Harder 1999).

Highlighting some of Nasyiah's achievements in utilising its autonomy to enhance its gender interests within Muhammadiyah does not mean that Nasyiah women did not encounter resistance from their male counterparts in the organisation. In fact, the resistance shown by Muhammadiyah members in the 45th *Muktamar* in 2005 was so strong that they did not obey a request from the Central Board. Muhammadiyah's Central Board had asked Muhammadiyah leaders at district level to send at least one woman representative per district, but the leaders at district level did not fulfil the request. For instance, only eight of the 35 Muhammadiyah district offices in Central Java sent women as members of their teams of representatives to the *Muktamar*. Many Muhammadiyah members attending the *Muktamar* were also reported to have shown disrespectful attitudes and behaviour towards women representatives by constantly disparaging and interrupting their speeches (interview with Sita (pseudonym), 10 September 2005).

There is still a large gap of understanding and acceptance within the organisation with regard to gender policy emanating from the Muhammadiyah Central Board. While the Central Board has approved gradual strategic steps to lessen gender gaps and biases as discussed earlier, the majority of Muhammadiyah local representatives attending the 2005 *Muktamar* failed to understand why there should be women representatives in Muhammadiyah's executive boards at all levels. Rahmawati recalled a bitter comment from a Muhammadiyah representative:

> A *bapak* from a Muhammadiyah branch in Yogyakarta said in the meeting something like, 'Hi, you women, you already have Aisyiyah and Nasyiah, now why should you interfere in Muhammadiyah's affairs? Aren't Aisyiyah and Nasyiah enough for you?' I was really disappointed with his comment, so I retorted, '*Bapak*, please don't misunder[stand]. We do not want to take over Muhammadiyah or to rule Muhammadiyah. What we want is to have women representatives to convey our concerns directly to Muhammadiyah leadership. Look, Muhammadiyah has a lot of hospitals, universities, schools and other enterprises. Many women are employed in those institutions, but until now no women are sitting in Muhammadiyah's executive boards. These boards have indeed had important role[s] in the process of making decisions in these institutions at their respective levels.' Apparently many Muhammadiyah men still misunderstood what we want (interview with Rahmawati, 10 September 2005).

In the 2005 Muhammadiyah *Muktamar* there were 11 women candidates from Aisyiyah and Nasyiah contesting Muhammadiyah Central Executive Board membership. The procedure of election in Muhammadiyah consists of several steps. As a first step, a special committee verifies whether executive candidates have met all the conditions requested. In 2005, 126 candidates (from 204 names nominated by members) had met the requirements. Those 126 names of candidates, including 11 women, were presented and verified in the Tanwir meeting for further approval before they were announced in the *Muktamar*. Next, members of *Muktamar* voted in the first round to choose 39 candidates: these 39 candidates competed in the second round for the 13 positions of permanent members of Muhammadiyah Central Executive Board.

None of the women candidates succeeded in reaching the second round, although Siti Chamamah was only one vote away from the 39th position.[22] Consequently, all 13 elected leaders of the Central Executive Board of Muhammadiyah for the period 2005–10 are men.

There are various explanations as to why women failed to gain enough votes. The reluctance of Muhammadiyah members to have women in strategic positions on the Central Executive Board may be caused by the strong legacy of patriarchal resistance amongst Muhammadiyah members toward women's empowerment in general, or because there was not enough time and opportunity to disseminate and promote Muhammadiyah's decision on the inclusion of women taken in the Tanwir meeting of 2003.

From the perspective of internal strategy developed by Nasyiah and Aisyiyah women, there are advantages and disadvantages in having many women candidates competing for election in the *Muktamar*. The advantages of having more women candidates include showing Muhammadiyah men that many women members have fulfilled the same requirements as men to run for leadership election. Aisyiyah and Nasyiah women indeed have the capacity to sit on the Muhammadiyah executive board. Further, having many female candidates serves to eliminate gender stereotypes of women's passivity and to encourage acknowledgment of women's active subjectivity. It also demonstrates that Muhammadiyah women are ready to compete fairly with their male counterparts.

The disadvantage of having a number of women candidates is that the few votes given to women were distributed amongst many women. In 2005 this meant that no woman achieved the necessary 39th rank of votes to go to the second round of the election. The opportunity presented to these women to be elected was low indeed; women representatives in the Muhammadiyah *Muktamar* were the minority, about 15% (interview with Sita (pseudonym), 4 December 2005), and only a few Muhammadiyah (male) members gave their votes to women candidates. If the number of women candidates had been fewer, one or two of them might have been among the 39 candidates in the second round.

Indeed, the obstacles faced by young Nasyiah members to mainstream a gender perspective are greater following Muhammadiyah's latest *Muktamar* in July 2005. This is partly because some Muhammadiyah leaders who have been most supportive of Nasyiah's gender cause are no longer in strategic positions within the Muhammadiyah central executive structure. Syafi'ie Ma'arif, for instance, refused to contest the election for Muhammadiyah leadership for 2005–10, and M Amin Abdullah and Abdul Munir Mulkhan failed to be amongst the 13 people elected to the Muhammadiyah Central Executive Board for the 2005–10 leadership term.

Conclusion

Indonesian governments and some religious authorities have failed to recognise women as independent agents; rather, they have envisioned them in their functional relations to male relatives and have paid little attention to the needs and interests of unmarried, young women. Consequently, these young women since the 1980s have fiercely challenged the state's ideology of submissive womanhood. They founded independent organisations to articulate their feminist ideas in relation to public policies on women's issues. Others who had already joined long-established mass organisations like Nasyiah promoted changes within their organisations by adopting a gender perspective.

As an organisation with a nationwide network and strong loyalty to the cause of Islam, Nasyiah faces specific problems, which require different strategies from those encountered by other women's NGOs. Nasyiah considers itself to have a duty to respond to two opposing schools of thought with growing influence in Indonesia: secular feminist thought, which has denigrated Islamic values, and Islamist groups, which have propagated ideas of restricting women to their reproductive roles. To do this, Nasyiah has juggled to maintain the balance between its loyalties to the causes of Islam, young women's gender interests and society when it deals with women's issues that have strong religious sanctions.

An important step was taken when Nasyiah developed its intellectual capacity and ability by recruiting university graduates and students to assume posts on Nasyiah's board. Higher degrees in Islamic studies held by young women from IAINs, which in past decades had been seen as secondary to those earned from secular universities, have now become a necessary tool for women to enter the debates on women's issues in Islam. Muslim women have made use of their formal qualifications to enhance women's agency in decision-making, including in determining which ideas to articulate, through which channels and by using what methods.

Unlike some feminist NGOs or Islamist groups which preferred to employ political means and legal methods to propagate their gender causes, Nasyiah adopted cultural transformation and psychological approaches, as seen in relation to the issues of women's rights in marriage, polygamy and illicit sexual engagement. On the one hand, some Indonesian feminists emphasised women's individual rights by demanding that women be able to marry without their guardians' consent and presence, that polygamy be totally banned and that women should be given freedom in expressing their sensuality. On the other hand, some Muslim groups, including those allegedly promoting a *salafi* way of life, demanded that women should be kept at home and that polygamy should be practised. Nasyiah's standpoint is to foster awareness among women about unjust treatment, abuse and violence that may happen in marital and familial life. Nasyiah conducts mass education on these issues and urges women to confront them wisely. So it could be said that Nasyiah promotes a gradual, peaceful transformation from within. It may appear that Nasyiah has held conventional, mainstream views on gender issues, but in fact it has advocated new methods in approaching problems. Nasyiah has systematically empowered women by providing them with necessary tools, mainly in the form of religious knowledge and a gender perspective, to safeguard their rights without disturbing social harmony.

Unlike secular feminists who represent the relationship between women and men as antagonistic, Nasyiah does not regard men as culprits in advancing its gender discourse in Islamic perspective; rather, it treats them as partners. The results have benefited Nasyiah; slowly but surely Nasyiah has successfully made its paternal organisation, Muhammadiyah, recognise the importance of women's representation in the organisation. Thus from 1995 Nasyiah women have held posts in Muhammadiyah's Religious Council and since 2003 women have had the same rights as men to be members and leaders of Muhammadiyah. Nevertheless, Nasyiah's struggle to implement gender equity within the Muhammadiyah family organisation is still far from being accomplished, as many local Muhammadiyah leaders have shown strong resistance to the inclusion of women in their Central Board, as exemplified in their behaviour during the *Muktamar* of July 2005.

Notes

1   My thanks to my supervisor, Associate Professor Susan Blackburn, for her thoughtful comments on this chapter and her continual support during its preparation.

2   The four million members claimed by Nasyiah are 'casual members'. Most of them do not have membership cards, but they often participate in Nasyiah's *pengajian* or other programs. Nasyiah does not require that these young women be official members with an organisational identification card; it prefers active participation from them instead. Identification-card membership is highly encouraged only for young women who are holding particular executive positions within the organisation (interview with Umi (pseudonym), 13 December 2005).

3   The following are some translated works by feminist Muslims abroad that have received wide readership in Indonesia: Engineer (2004; 2000), Mernissi (1999; 1997; 1995; 1994), Wadud (1994), Hassan (1995; 1994; 1990) and Ahmed (2000).

4   IAINs in Yogyakarta and Jakarta were transformed in the early 2000s to become UIN, which offer more subjects in the sciences.

5   For more detailed explanation on the differences between *madrasah* and *pesantren*, refer to Abdullah (1986); Jabali and Jamhari (2002); Soebardi (1976); Steenbrink (1974) and Boland (1971).

6   The data is adapted from that of Jabali and Jamhari (2002:131).

7   There are several books revealing useful historical accounts of a number of IAINs in early and contemporary periods: IAIN Sunan Ampel (1970); IAIN Sunan Kalidjaga (1968); Jabali and Jamhari (2002).

8   Sources for the table are Jabali and Jamhari (2002:29–30) and author's personal investigation.

9   Sources for the table are Jabali and Jamhari (2002:29–30) and author's personal investigation.

10 The process of modernising IAINs in particular and the Department of Religious Affairs in general began when Prof Dr HA Mukti Ali was appointed as the Minister of Religious Affairs (1971–78). But it was not until the 1990s that IAIN female lecturers were included in the project. Mukti Ali, himself a graduate of the Institute of Islamic Studies, McGill University, Canada, in 1957, sent nine staff (all male) of the Ministry to pursue higher degrees in the same university. Upon their return they assumed strategic positions in the Ministry and their policy transformed IAINs in subsequent years. The Ministry's collaboration with the Institute of Islamic Studies at McGill in the 1970s was resumed in the 1990s when Dr Munawir Sadzali became the Minister of Religious Affairs. He officially established a new memorandum of understanding with McGill University following which a number of Indonesian women have been sent to study there (Jabali & Jamhari 2002).

11 The two phases of the IAINs–McGill University Project funded by the Canadian International Development Agency from 1990 to 2000 alone have produced at least 12 doctors (eight male, four female), 82 masters (58 male, 24 female) and 75 librarians (49 male, 26 female); the new Social Equity Project between IAINs Yogyakarta–Jakarta and McGill University involves more female staff (Jabali & Jamhari 2002:25–7).

12 Issues of veiling or wearing head-covering for Muslim women have long been
debated. However, the intensity and arguments put for and against the issue have
varied over time. In Indonesia the controversy about the issues began in the 20th
century, when Muslim reformists began to promote the practice of hair-covering to
the public; see White (2004) and Vreede-De Stuers (1960). See also the chapter by
Rachmah Ida in this volume.

13 In March 1979 Khomeini issued a directive requiring women to wear the veil:
'[S]hops, restaurants, cinemas, and all other public areas, including offices, were
instructed not to receive or serve unveiled women. The open defiance of this directive
was to be immediately punishable by seventy-four lashes without court action, the
offence being self evident' (Shehadeh 2003:88).

14 His books on women's rights in Islam (2004; 2000) have been translated into
Indonesian and have become amongst the most widely read books on the issue.

15 She is the director of a Muslim feminist NGO, Sisters in Islam, based in Kuala
Lumpur, Malaysia (Foley 2001).

16 *Salafi* or *salafiyah* is an Arabic term referring to the time of the Prophet and his
faithful companions during the seventh century. Usually the label *salafi* movement
is also used to designate the fundamentalist Islamic movement; however, the
movement itself is not monolithic. Two distinct Islamic fundamentalist movements
are popular in today's Muslim world. One attempts to reproduce the social system
of the Prophet's time. It is believed that the era represents a genuine model of how
Muslims of all ages should live their lives in all aspects, including in conducting
their marriages. Another type of fundamentalism, in Esposito's statement as cited
in Shehadeh (2003:2), refers to those who 'do not seek to reproduce the past, but
to reconstruct society through a process of Islamic reform in which principles of
Islam are applied to contemporary needs'. The *salafi* being discussed here is that
of the first type.

17 *Mut'ah* is a temporary marriage in which the longevity is defined based on certain
terms and conditions stipulated by a man and a woman. It was believed that during
his lifetime the Prophet had allowed the practice of *mut'ah* during the period of
wars in which men were on duty far from their wives, sometimes for a prolonged
period. Most Sunni Muslims consider it as unlawful, but most Shiites believe that
mut'ah is lawful (Shehadeh 2003:85–6). As for *sirri* marriage, it is a marriage done in
secrecy that only fulfils the minimum religious requirements, and it is not conducted
according to the procedure stipulated by national law. *Sirri* marriage was common
practise among Muslims in Indonesia when, for various reasons, parents wanted to
marry off their children early but holding a proper ritual was not yet possible for
other reasons. For more discussion of this issue, see Blackburn and Bessell (1997)
and Nasution (2002).

18 The concept of *Sakinah* Family itself was proposed by Aisyiyah at its *Muktamar*
in 1985, and a manuscript called *Tuntunan menuju Keluarga Sakinah* (*A guide
to Sakinah Family*) was produced and presented at the national conference of
the Muhammadiyah Religious Council in 1989. After a series of revisions and
improvements, the program of building *Sakinah* Families based on the revised
concept was approved as a national program for all Muhammadiyah family
organisations, including Nasyiah. In this respect, Nasyiah was in accord with

Aisyiyah (Pimpinan Pusat Aisyiyah 1994:i–ii, vii; Pimpinan Pusat Aisyiyah 2000). See also Jennifer Bright's research on this issue (1999).

19 Interviews with Nasyiah members and author's observation.

20 In Nahdlatul Ulama the religious council is called Bahtsul Masail.

21 For more accounts on the differences between Muhammadiyah and Muslim 'traditionalists', see Geertz (1976), Noer (1978), Nakamura (1983), Jainuri (1981; 2002), Djamil (1994), Fananie and Sabardila (2000), Ka'bah (1999) and Damami (2000).

22 The following are the names of the women candidates and the votes they gained in the first round of the election: Siti Chamamah (61), Rahmawati (55), Isnawati (40), Diah Siti Nuraini (32), Masyitoh Chusnan (32), Shoimah (29), Siti Hadiroh (29), Siti Wardanah (25), Trias Setiawati (22), Siti Karimah (18) and Nurpati (18) (Pikiran Rakyat 7 July 2005; interview with Sita (pseudonym), 10 September 2005). In the second round of the election each participant of Muhammadiyah Muktamar selected 13 names from amongst the 39 most-voted candidates. The 13 people with the most votes elected to lead Muhammadiyah for the next five years were: Din Syamsuddin, Haedar Nashir, Muhammad Muqaddas, Malik Fajar, Yunahar Ilyas, Rosyad Sholeh, Dahlan Rais, Goodwill Zubair, Zamroni, Mukhlas Abror, Bambang Sudibyo, Fasichul Lisan and Sudibyo Markus.

chapter seven

Women, Islam and philanthropy in contemporary Indonesia

Amelia Fauzia

Philanthropic practices are closely associated with caring, and in Indonesia, as in many other cultures, caring tends to be done mainly by women. Caring is often thought of as the 'female mandate', which is unfortunately 'invisible' and therefore is poorly paid (Baines, Evans & Neysmith 1991). Women's involvement in caring and social work starts in the home with their function as wives, daughters or mothers. Home, in philanthropic studies, is regarded as the foundation of philanthropic education (McCarthy 1990; 2001), while the work of 'Lady Bountiful' has been recorded in many places and times. Moreover, while caring could be considered as work mostly for the family, philanthropy—which has its roots within the family—is devoted to the public good, where giving and volunteering are done beyond the home and private circles.

Women's role as carer even at home is not insignificant. Philanthropy starts with home and family—which in the Indonesian context is the extended family and sometimes encompasses villages and clans. Recent surveys conducted in the United States have identified the 'intergenerational transmission of generosity' (Wilhelm et al 2004; Steinberg & Wilhelm 2003) from parents to their children. Parents' generosity is strongly correlated with their children's generosity in religious giving, although less so in secular giving.

In this chapter, the term philanthropy is defined as 'voluntary private giving for public purpose' (Martin 1994) and includes beneficent activities such as giving, caring and volunteering. The terms charity and philanthropy are used interchangeably, as they are almost the same. The difference between the two is the approach: charity is short-term assistance, while philanthropy is long-term, sustainable assistance aimed at eradicating social problems such as poverty and lack of education.

This chapter seeks to explore Indonesian Muslim women's philanthropic practices and their role in the public sphere, in line with Kathleen D McCarthy's findings that philanthropy has a pervasive role in shaping NGOs, civil society and women's political culture in many parts of the world (McCarthy 2001). The chapter focuses on philanthropy and religious institutions, due to the findings of a survey that has demonstrated that giving to religious organisations occurs at a much higher rate than giving to secular organisations (*Faith and Philanthropy* 1995).

The chapter further considers the roles of Indonesian women in Islamic philanthropic organisations. It argues that there are differences between male and female practices of charity and volunteering; that issues of gender and women's empowerment are not mainstream among philanthropic organisations; and that private Islamic philanthropic organisations are more gender-sensitive due to more professional management.

Data and methods

This chapter utilises three main resources: interviews; data from selected Islamic philanthropic organisations; and quantitative databases on Islamic philanthropy for social justice, derived from two national surveys (public and institutional) on the practice of Islamic philanthropy in Indonesia carried out by Pusat Bahasa dan Budaya (Centre for Languages and Culture, Universitas Islam Negeri, Jakarta) in 2003/2004, where I was involved as one of the researchers.[1]

The last resource, the quantitative databases, is based on a public survey where 1,501 Muslims (70% male and 30% female)[2] were surveyed in ten provinces, namely West Sumatra, South Sumatra, Jambi, DKI Jakarta, West Java, Central Java, East Java, South Kalimantan, South Sulawesi and Nusa Tenggara Barat. This survey recorded the socio-economic and religious backgrounds of the respondents interviewed, their practices of both religious and non-religious philanthropy, and their attitudes towards and motivation for such philanthropic practices. This survey, however, could not sufficiently depict the differences between male and female practices of philanthropy, since the responses provided mainly represented families, not individuals.

The other survey data is from an organisational survey that interviewed 297 philanthropic organisations in the ten provinces listed above.[3] The organisations were selected through purposive technique sampling based on three different types of institutions: mosques, state-based organisations and private organisations. This survey represents the social, political and religious affiliation of the organisations, their members and staff, and their philanthropic practices.

The second source is data from selected Islamic philanthropic organisations that have considerable resources on their websites. I selected three organisations, Dompet Dhuafa Republika, Portal Infaq and Pos Keadilan Peduli Ummat (PKPU), and collected data from their websites mainly in the months of May and June 2005. The data consists of financial reports, details of donors, beneficiaries, program activities and the profiles of organisations.

Finally I conducted a number of interviews with such personalities as advocates of philanthropy, female philanthropists and leaders of philanthropic organisations in Indonesia. The interviews were conducted face-to-face, by email or by telephone.

I selected relevant data from both public and institution surveys in the framework of three philanthropic components: donors (givers/volunteers), philanthropic (intermediary) organisations and beneficiaries. I analysed the data using SPSS software[4] in which gender aspects and women's issues are well accounted for. I also used some quantitative data and analysis for the background of the chapter. Islamic teachings and observations of philanthropic organisations are extensively used to enrich the data analysis.

Islamic teachings of philanthropy

In Islam there are many forms of philanthropy mentioned in the Qur'an and *hadis* (Prophet's tradition), but the most highly recommended are *zakat* (almsgiving), *sedekah* (voluntary giving) and *wakaf* (religious endowment). *Zakat* constitutes an obligation for well-to-do Muslims, requiring them to pay a specific amount, at a specified time and for specific beneficiaries. There are two kinds of *zakat*: *zakat fitrah,* which is money or basic food given at the end of Ramadan to the poorer members of the community,[5] and *zakat mal,* which is a percentage of a Muslim's total wealth obligatory for those whose wealth has reached a certain level. *Zakat* is actually a moral obligation, as the teachings of Islam suggest, not one based on law. In practice *zakat* is voluntary giving in which there is no legal obligation or punishment imposed by the state. While *sedekah* can comprise any kind of donation without limitation of amount, time and beneficiaries,[6] *wakaf* usually constitutes a donation of property for religious or community use, usually for establishing mosques, religious schools and public buildings.

Philanthropy is a profound concept in Islamic teachings. There are three primary notions of Islamic philanthropy found in the Qur'an and *hadis*, the first of which is the notion of religious piety and morality; the second, religious obligation; and the last, social justice. Numerous Qur'anic verses and *hadis* assert that charity, or philanthropy, is a sign of piety and virtue, the right of the poor and a religious obligation, which Muslims should obey.[7] The Qur'an contains 82 verses that mention both the obligation to pay *zakat* and the obligation of *shalat* (prayers) together, hence underlining the supreme importance of *zakat* in Islam (Fauzia 2003). Furthermore, the Qur'an clearly emphasises the importance of charitable giving from both men and women:

> The Believers, *men and women*, are protectors one of another: they enjoin what is just and forbid what is evil: they observe regular prayers, *practise regular charity* [pay *zakat*], and obey Allah and His Messenger. On them will Allah pour His mercy: for Allah is exalted in power, wise (Qu'ranic verse 9:71) (author's emphasis).

> *Whoever works righteousness, man or woman*, and has faith, verily, to him will We give a new Life, a life that is good and pure and We will bestow on such their reward according to the best of their actions (Qu'ranic verse 16:97) (author's emphasis).

Given the importance of philanthropic teachings in Islam, Indonesian Muslims have practiced *zakat, sedekah* and *wakaf* since the 13th century (Fauzia & Hermawan 2002), when Islam was strongly institutionalised in the Indonesian archipelago (Ricklefs 2001). The school of law followed by Indonesians in implementing practices pertaining to *zakat, sedekah* and *wakaf* is the Shafii School, the rules of which are written in many well-known *fiqh* books distributed throughout the country. Over the centuries philanthropic practices have adapted to changing circumstances; however, the practice remains traditional in the sense that donations are made from one individual to another, not through institutions, and the majority of donations consist of consumable goods given to meet the immediate needs of the recipients and not for economic or social empowerment, which would involve a process of increasing the community's capacities to eradicate social problems such as poverty. An emphasis on long-term philanthropy programs is significant, alongside the short-term charity programs.

Philanthropic practices

In the Indonesian Muslim context, philanthropic practices can be divided into in-kind donations, non-material donations and volunteering. In-kind donations are usually made in the form of money, food, clothes, books and buildings. *Zakat fitrah* and many different categories of *zakat mal* (for example, *zakat* on property, on trades, husbandry and on crops) are considered in-kind donations. On the other hand, many types of *sedekah* can be considered as examples of giving non-material services, such as giving shelter, accommodation and—according to a well-known *hadis*—even a smile. Volunteering in the Indonesian language is called *kesukarelawanan*. The concept of 'non-material' donations is better known to Indonesians than volunteering, as volunteering is usually only used for unpaid work. Such a perception is also heavily influenced by several well-known *hadis*, which define *sedekah* as including such good deeds as smiling, prayers, removing thorns from the street, unpaid teaching at schools and *gotong royong* (working together) for public facilities.

Almost all Muslims in Indonesia, including poor Muslims, give donations, with only 0.7% not giving. Those who do not donate usually come from small trader and casual labour families with an average monthly income of Rp416,363 (AU$59.50). These people are, in fact, also the recipients of *zakat fitrah* and other forms of charity.

According to the survey findings, 98.5% of Muslims give *zakat fitrah*, 34.7% give *zakat mal*, 93.6% give *sedekah* and 22.8% give *wakaf*. *Zakat fitrah* is the most widely practised form of giving in the Muslim community of Indonesia, since it is an obligation for those Muslims who have enough food to eat at the end of Ramadan. *Sedekah* is the second most practised form of philanthropy, since there are no regulations surrounding what or how much is to be donated. In rural communities, for instance, the Rp1,000 note (15 Australian cents) tends to be the amount most commonly donated, the one that fills the charity boxes. *Zakat mal* is the second least commonly practised form, with only about one third of Muslims paying it, due to the ruling that it is obligatory only for well-to-do Muslims. Consequently, one of the most common reasons that respondents do not pay *zakat mal* is because they think they are not obliged to. The last, *wakaf*, is not a popular type of Islamic philanthropy. The main reason for this is the common perception that *wakaf* is given in the form of land (cemeteries, for example), mosques, schools and the like. This is in line with the Shafii School of law, where *wakaf* consists of non-movable and durable properties. Therefore, it is assumed that only rich people can give *wakaf*, which is not correct according to Islamic law: cash *wakaf* (with no limit to the amount of money given) and book *wakaf* are also permissible. In Indonesia women are rarely involved in *wakaf*-making and *wakaf* management, although there is no gender restriction about it according to Islamic law. In the history of the Ottoman Empire there were many Ladies Bountiful who made significant *wakaf* (Singer 2002). During that period, *wakaf* also served to give women better inheritance, escaping the discrimination inherent in the strict implementation of Islamic law (Singer 2002). Although intended to implement religious obligation and contribute to the community, *wakaf* legally could function as a protection of personal wealth for the founder's family, and for distributing inheritance (Singer 2002:26).

The reasons for philanthropy in Muslim communities in Indonesia can be divided into individual and religious motives. Muslims are motivated strongly by religion, namely by the desire to observe religious teachings (50%) and get 'close' to God (26%) in making their donations (see Table 1). In addition, the majority of Muslims (79%) prefer to maintain the secrecy of their donations, as recommended in the Qur'an verse 2:271[8] and a *hadis:* '...who gives charitable gifts so secretly that his left hand does not know what his *right hand* has given'.[9] Many respondents answered that giving secretly is better to avoid self-promotion.

Table 1: Motivation for donating (according to gender)

Motivation for donating* (first choice of three**)	Responses (%)	
	Male	Female
Tradition of the community	15	10
Observing religious teachings	49	51
To be 'close' to God	24	27
To reduce the poverty level	5	4
Redistribution is the right of the poor	5	6

* There were nine choices; only those nominated by more than 5% of respondents are cited here. Other choices were for social status reasons, to continue the family tradition, for self-satisfaction, and to help the government increase people's welfare.

** Respondents were asked to choose three answers for the first choice, second choice and the third choice. This is the percentage of the first choice answer.

To whom Indonesian Muslims pay their *zakat* is more often than not a political decision. During the New Order period, the residents of some rural communities in East Java—which were led by NU *kiai*—did not want to pay *zakat* to the committees created by the local governments, but rather gave their *zakat* money to local NU *kiai* and NU *pesantren*. Since the fall of Suharto, Muslims have freely paid their *zakat* through any of the *zakat* collection bodies. As a result, the existence of private philanthropic organisations has risen significantly.

Women and philanthropic organisations

The proportion of Indonesian Muslims who make donations to organisations, mainly to religious associations, neighbourhood associations, religious gatherings and schools, is 80%. Women's associations are not major targets of donations because the motive for charity is mostly religious causes. Statistics show that only 16% of the Muslims who give to organisations donate to women's associations, and 41% make their donations through charitable or philanthropic organisations. Women's Islamic organisations such as Aisyiyah and *pengajian ibu-ibu* (women's religious gatherings) can easily get donations because of their religious character. Women's religious gatherings, which actually provide informal religious education for married and old women, are very popular not only among rural Muslim communities but also among urban ones, and among youth. At the *pengajian*, members collect regular donations for *pengajian* expenses and social causes, mainly to be distributed before *Idul Fitri* (end of Ramadan) to widows and orphans.

As yet, no philanthropic organisations focus exclusively on women's affairs, such as women's empowerment, although the number of Islamic philanthropic organisations has increased significantly since the fall of the New Order in 1998. However, there is one organisation that closely fits the bill. The Muhammadiyah women's organisation called Aisyiyah functions as a philanthropic organisation. It has offices in every province in Indonesia. The organisation collects funds and community resources and then supports such activities as building orphanages, hospitals and schools. Aisyiyah has micro-economic and advocacy programs to improve women's social, economic and political position. Muhammadiyah and Aisyiyah are pioneers in changing the practice of 'individual' giving into institutional giving. Furthermore, there has been a recent tendency for new philanthropic organisations (mostly the private ones) to be gender-focused.

Indonesian philanthropic organisations, in a modern sense, were established early in the 20th century, during the Dutch colonial period. *Wakaf* foundations, however, have existed since the Islamic Kingdom period in the 13th century. The New Order government supported the establishment of Islamic philanthropic organisations under its provincial administration. The number of private Islamic philanthropic organisations has increased slowly since the end of the New Order period and rose rapidly in the *Reformasi* era. The change of political conditions has had a significant impact on NGOs and non-profit organisations.

The absence of women's philanthropic organisations is due to the short history of private philanthropic organisations. However, current social conditions indicate the possible advent of women's philanthropic organisations in Indonesia in the future. This is because there is now more acceptance and support from Muslim communities for these organisations, while the more open political and social conditions have provided women with energy to change their situation. As mentioned earlier, an exception to the absence of women's philanthropic organisations is Aisyiyah, a women's organisation established on 19 May 1917 that has strong charitable functions. Although it is not specifically a philanthropic organisation, Aisyiyah has a greater focus on Islamic charitable activities than Muhammadiyah, its father organisation. Aisyiyah members support their organisation's programs by donations, fundraising drives and volunteering. It seems that in the future women's philanthropic organisations may be created and supported by either advocates of philanthropy or by women's movements.

The fast-increasing number of Islamic philanthropic organisations today suggests that the socio-political atmosphere is supportive and civil society is strong, with the door for social activities wide open. Philanthropic organisations are more independent, self-confident, assertive, proactive and communicative. They have good management, so many of them gain trust from international aid agencies. This is contrary to the situation that was prevalent during the New Order regime, when financial reports were a sensitive subject; today philanthropic organisations compete to publish their financial reports, not only for their donors but for the public also.

The state has recognised private philanthropic organisations by law through the Zakat Constitution issued in 1999. Since then the Ministry of Religious Affairs has appointed managers of a Badan Amil Zakat Nasional (National Zakat Collection Body) from private philanthropic organisations. The current government, led by President Susilo Bambang Yudhoyono, has recognised the positive work of private philanthropic organisations, as demonstrated by their response to the tsunami that hit Aceh and North Sumatra, alongside the efforts of international aid agencies and the government. Democratisation has created more opportunities for Indonesian citizens, including women, to be more involved in different activities of philanthropic organisations.

Based on the observation of their characteristics, management and form, philanthropic organisations can be categorised into four different types (see Table 2): mosque-based organisations, state-based organisations (Badan Amil Zakat or BAZ), private organisations (Lembaga Amil Zakat or LAZ) and micro-finance institutions (Baitul Mal wa Tamwil or BMT). In this chapter, BMT is included under LAZ, since the number of BMT is small and its charitable function is less significant than its primary function. Therefore, according to the survey, the Islamic philanthropy organisations are divided as follows: mosque-based (62%), state-based (19%) and private (19%).

Table 2: Categories of Islamic philanthropic organisations

Type	Characteristic	Management	Form	Basis
Mosque-based ZIS*	Temporary/ non-permanent	Committees	Non-government	Neighbourhood and mosques
BAZ	Permanent	Semi-professional. Government administration	Government	State
LAZ	Permanent (*yayasan*)	Professional	Non-government	Private
BMT	Permanent	Micro-finance/ economy	Non-government	Private

* Zakat Infak and Sedekah

State-based organisations have a formal structure and are established in each *kecamatan* (sub-district) under the Kantor Urusan Agama (Office of Religious Affairs). In villages BAZ, commonly called Bazis (Badan Amil Zakat Infak dan Sedekah), has a kind of Unit Pengumpul Zakat (Zakat Collection Unit), and many village mosques send a percentage of their *zakat* money to the district offices. Some of the provincial BAZ have become independent organisations but still get financial support from the local government administration. Recently a number of BAZ, such as Bazis DKI Jakarta and Bazis Sumatera Utara, have proven to be professional philanthropic organisations that can compete with LAZ (Fauzia 2005).

Private philanthropic organisations are mainly established by Muslim activists as foundations and charitable NGOs. Among the leading private philanthropic organisations are Dompet Dhuafa Republika and PKPU.[10] The Department of Religious Affairs has officially recognised a number of nationwide, professional LAZ by giving them certification, leaving other medium-scale LAZ to the Zakat Collection Units, which by regulation cannot distribute the *zakat* money. In reality, however, private philanthropic organisations that are not officially recognised by the government still carry out collection, as well as distribution, activities.

Mosque-based organisations have been established by a number of big mosques, which initially included the charitable activities that they were conducting under their professional administration (later changed into foundations[11]), while other mosques include committees of Zakat Infak and Sedekah within their structures. However, a majority of mosques run charitable activities, especially at the end of Ramadan when they create a temporary committee to manage *zakat* and *fitrah* collection.

These philanthropic organisations are largely supported by community philanthropic practices. The survey found that 34% of philanthropic organisations were established after 1998, when *Reformasi* began. The majority of philanthropic organisations get their resources from the community: 78% of the organisations state they get their resources from *zakat fitrah*, 70% get their resources from *zakat mal*, 83% get *infak/sedekah* and 65% of organisations get donations from religious and public figures/leaders. Only 10% of the organisations obtain donations from Islamic organisations and 83% never get funding from charitable organisations (local or foreign). In addition, 36% of the organisations, mainly the state-based organisations, said that they get funding from government agencies.

Gender issues in Islamic philanthropic organisations

Women's participation

In general the participation of women in the structure of Islamic philanthropic organisations is low. For example, only 16.8% of the organisations have women who participate in the establishment of organisations, 24% have female executives and only 15% have female trustees.[12] This is due to the low participation of females in public activities, especially in privileged positions in a mixed gender congregation. Founders and trustees are mainly from amongst the community leaders, who are overwhelmingly male. Executives and staff may still be predominantly male but the participation of women is a little higher than among the founders and trustees.

Female participation in NGOs is higher than in state organisations. For example, the average number of female executives in state-based philanthropic organisations is between one and three women, with only 5% of state organisations having between four and seven female executives. In NGOs, however, 48% have between one and three female executives, 37% have between four and seven female executives, and 6% have more than 13 female executives. The percentage of males compared to female executives is higher in state-based organisations as compared to NGOs. State-based organisations (BAZ) have the highest percentage of male executives (94%) and hence the lowest percentage of female executives. In mosque-based organisations, 93% of executives are males, while in private organisations 85% of the executives are males.

The main reason behind this gender imbalance is the recruitment process. Within BAZ, most of the executives are selected from the staff or head of the Office of Religious Affairs at the subdistrict, district and provincial levels. As a majority of bureaucrats, especially of the Office of Religious Affairs, are men, it is not surprising that a majority of the heads and staff of BAZ are also men. LAZ, on the other hand, has a more professional and open recruitment process and as a result has a higher percentage of female executives and staff.

In Dompet Dhuafa all the founders are male; however, 36% of the executive positions (president, vice-presidents, general managers and managers) are held by women. Rachmad Riyadi, the president of Dompet Dhuafa, has stated that it was not the organisation's intention to have only men as its founders, and that the management had tried to have female members on the trustee board. The management allocates its human resources according to its needs. So, for example, almost all financial staff members are women because they are considered to be meticulous, while most of the program staff members are men because they are usually required to work in the field (interview with Riyadi, 27 June 2005).

The top management of Portal Infaq has similar characteristics. Even though all of its trustee members, consisting of Dewan Syariah and Dewan Penasehat, are men (six persons), in the Board of Founders one of the three members is a woman, while Dewan Pengurus has one woman out of its four members. One of its three managers is also a woman.

The key to having gender balance is professional management. When the organisation has professional management, female participation increases. At the same time, the attention to women recipients, women's issues and empowerment programs, such as advocacy, education and training, increases. This phenomenon is clearly evident when comparing the private philanthropic organisations with the state-based philanthropic organisations mentioned above. Therefore, when the state-based philanthropic organisations have professional management, like that of Bazis DKI Jakarta and Bazis Sumatera Utara, the level of female participation tends to increase. Another good example is Badan Amil Zakat Nasional, which was established by the government; it has solid professional management, and also a female professional, Emmy Hamidiyah, as its executive director.

Despite the general picture of low participation by women in Islamic philanthropic organisations (compared to those in other institutions like government departments and for-profit organisations such as trading corporations), women's involvement may be much higher, because philanthropic activities and organisations are regarded as belonging to the not-for-profit sector. Natalia Soebagjo, a woman philanthropist and board member of a few philanthropic organisations in Asia,[13] observes that philanthropic organisations are much more 'female' than 'male'.

> In Asia perhaps there are more women involved in the various boards of philanthropic organisations because women are stereotyped as having more time and more sensitivity towards the plight of the less fortunate. Women are perhaps also better at multi-tasking and so are able to juggle work, family and philanthropic activities better. If anything, philanthropic organisations are considered more 'female' than 'male' organisations (interview with Soebagjo, 14 June 2005).

This stereotyping may originate fiom women's roles as carers at home, extended to the public sector.

Soebagjo's opinion resembles the findings on fundraising workforce studies in the United States. These studies discovered that since the 1980s women's membership of the top-three professional fundraising organisations has increased and now the majority of their professionals are women (Conry 1991; 1998). However, the gender pay gap—where females are paid significantly less than males exists also in this non-profit sector, where the majority of its professionals are women (Mesch & Rooney 2005).

Support for orphans

The Qur'an and numerous *hadis* place special emphasis on the good treatment of orphans, and the Prophet Muhammad himself was an orphan. There is even a Qur'anic verse that condemns those believers who pray but neglect orphans, labelling them as liars towards their own religion.

> Seest thou one who denies the Judgment [to come]? Then such is the [man] who repulses the orphan [with harshness], And encourages not the feeding of the indigent. So woe to the worshippers Who are neglectful of their prayers, Those who [want but] to be seen [of men], but refuse [to supply] [even] neighbourly needs (QS 107:1–7).

The following verse further emphasises the need to behave well towards orphans.

> And serve Allah and do not associate any thing with Him and be good to the parents and to the near of kin and the *orphans* and the needy and the neighbour of [your] kin and the alien neighbour, and the companion in a journey and the

wayfarer and those whom your right hands possess; surely Allah does not love him who is proud, boastful (QS 4:36; emphasis added).

Among Indonesian Muslims, orphan support is regarded as important. Statistics show that assistance to orphans is the second most preferred form of donations after providing food assistance (see Table 3). However, it seems that the preferred form of orphan support in Indonesia is adoption. Such a practice of welcoming orphans into the family is common amongst Muslim Indonesians. Therefore, in giving to organisations, the level of donations given to orphanages is far below that which is given to religious associations, neighbourhood associations and *pengajian* (see Table 4).

Table 3: Percentage of Muslims' forms of giving

	%
Giving food	73
Giving clothes	43
Providing scholarship	17
Providing medicine/health	16
Orphan support	· 63

Table 4: Muslims' donations to organisations

Organisations	Muslim donors contributing to these organisations (%)
Women's associations	11
Sporting clubs	24
Orphanages	29
Charitable organisations	41
Youth associations	43
Schools (including *pesantren*)	46
Religious gatherings or *pengajian*	61
Village or neighbourhood associations	68
Religious associations	94

The second Qur'anic verse above has an impact on the charitable practices of Muslim Indonesians. In neighbourhood communities, orphans, along with widows, are placed in a distinct category as the beneficiaries of *zakat fitrah*. This distinction is also reflected in some philanthropic organisations. In PKPU's report, for example, donations for *yatim dan janda* (orphans and widows) are placed together with the categories of *zakat, sedekah/infak*, humanitarian funds, *wakaf* and *qurban*. The PKPU list of donors for orphans and widows reveals that female donors constitute almost the same percentage as male donors; in one case female donors are actually higher than male donors (see Table 5).

Table 5: PKPU's donors for orphans and widows

List of donors	% male	% female
Donors in January 2002	53	47
Donors in May 2005	33	67

Such statistics illustrate a well-established trend in Indonesia, where orphanages are relatively well supported by women. A good example is Tuti Alawiyah, a popular woman *da'i* (religious guru and public figure), who leads and owns the Islamic boarding school Pesantren As-Syafi'iyah in Jakarta, which specifically supports orphans. Some other *pesantren*, including the modern ones, also support orphans, mainly by waiving their education fees.

Aisyiyah, from its early formation in 1917, has also had a program for orphanages. Today Muhammadiyah and Aisyiyah organisations have 330 registered orphanages (under foundations) located all over the country (Purwana 2005:viii). In addition to these orphanages, a majority of the local Aisyiyah branches have orphan support programs. Orphan support is executed by sub-branches of Aisyiyah at the village level. For example, a sub-branch of Aisyiyah in Cirendeu village in the province of Banten has, on average, 30 children who receive scholarships on the basis that they are orphans. According to Thoyyibah,[14] these scholarships are given to orphans from elementary to senior high schools. Donations come from members of Aisyiyah and Muhammadiyah in the village (interviews with Thoyyibah, 20 August and 27 September 2005).

Giving donations to orphans is also a trend among artists and celebrities. The primary example of such benevolence on the part of a celebrity is Dorce Gamalama (Dorce Ashadi), a celebrated artist and philanthropist, who established a philanthropic foundation to support orphans. The foundation was launched on 16 January 1992 and now assists around 1,600 orphans (Gamalama 2005; Agoes 2005a; 2005b; interview with Gamalama, 13 June 2005). Gamalama supports her own foundation, Dorce Halimatussa'diyah, drawing on 40% of her income (Kurniawan 2005). The motivation behind this is religious and social, and also strongly based on her own suffering as an orphan when she was a child.[15] Thus her philanthropic activities are 'positive revenge' on her past (interview with Gamalama, 13 June 2005).

Giving and volunteering

Findings from three leading private Islamic philanthropic organisations show that there are differences between the male and female practices of giving and volunteering.

In general male donors tend to outnumber female donors because most charity is classified as 'household' charity (for example, *zakat fitrah, zakat mal* and *wakaf*) and is provided by the head of the family, who is usually the father. However, it is interesting to see that in a number of cases the percentage of female donors almost matches the percentage of male donors. The donor records of Dompet Dhuafa Republika, and PKPU, illustrate this.[16] The President of Dompet Dhuafa adds that donors who come directly to the office are mostly women. PKPU's list of donors for humanitarian funding for Aceh in January 2005 (of a total 1,042 donations) showed that the split was 65% male and 35% female (PKPU online report, January 2005). Another statistic from PKPU's donor list for *zakat mal* in the month of May 2005 showed that 57% of those who gave *zakat* were male and 43% were female (PKPU online report, May 2005).

This figure demonstrates that in urban communities such as Jakarta, where both of these organisations are based, the participation of males and females in private philanthropic institutions is well balanced. In cities a higher percentage of women earn their own incomes, and hence donations are more likely based on individual decisions as opposed to family decisions. While *zakat fitrah, zakat mal* and *wakaf* represent family contributions, *sedekah* and *infak* more likely represent individual donations. However, while *zakat mal* is representative of family contributions, *zakat* on income (one type of *zakat mal*) tends to be paid by individuals.

Male and female attitudes towards donating and volunteering differ. Female donors are more attached to the beneficiaries and are more interested in the activities of the philanthropic institutions. Therefore they tend to give donations directly to an organisation's staff and monitor closely the organisation's performance. It is therefore not surprising that it is the female donors who usually fill the offices of philanthropic organisations, as with the case of Dompet Dhuafa (interview with Riyadi, 27 June 2005).

This emotional attachment reflects the tendency for female respondents to be close to the organisations and therefore to pay more attention to the use of donations they give. Women's emotional attachment to their philanthropic contributions might be related to the claimed innate or socialised nature of women to be those who provide love and care in the home. Or it may be because women have more spare time compared to men, or because they are more careful with money. Whatever the reason, the statistics demonstrate that in general women are more likely to want to know where the money and the assistance they give will be distributed and what it will be used for (see Table 6). This attitude in turn encourages the organisations to be more efficient and transparent, thus reducing the chances of corruption or other misconduct.

Table 6: Attention to distribution of donations

Questions	Gender	Responses (%)		
		Yes	No	Don't know
Donors know where the money and the assistance will be going	Male	**55**	29	16
	Female	**68**	20	12

A comparison of the average number of male and female volunteers in philanthropic organisations reveals that they are equal. Nevertheless, in some organisations volunteering is dominated by women. Portal Infaq, a philanthropic foundation established by professionals in 2001, reported that a majority of its volunteers are women. The General Manager of Portal Infaq (Epri Abdurrahman) pointed out that the teacher volunteers sent to the devastated area of Aceh after the tsunami disaster on 26 December 2004 were mostly women (interview with Abdurrahman, 27 and 28 June 2005). Interestingly, he noted that the volunteers who work for fundraising programs are mostly career women or working women based in Jakarta. These facts contradict the assumption that women volunteer mainly because they have spare time.

In contrast to Portal Infaq, Dompet Dhuafa has many kinds of volunteer programs in which either male or female volunteers may dominate. For example, *layanan jemput zakat* (volunteers working to obtain cash donations from donors' houses or offices) are mostly men because they need to work by motorcycles to avoid traffic jams. However, volunteers working to help organise gatherings or meetings in rural communities are mostly women.

It seems that female predominance in certain kinds of volunteering is mainly a result of certain occupations being traditionally attached to women (such as teaching, caring and fundraising). For example, teaching in kindergartens and schools, as opposed to teaching in universities, is an occupation dominated by women. Besides skill and knowledge, teaching requires an element of 'caring' that is synonymous with femininity. With regards to fundraising, it is common in Indonesia for fundraising and financial positions in a majority of social and political organisations, including committees, to be given to women. The main reason for this is the perception that women are more careful and efficient in financial matters than men, and good at persuading prospective donors. Indeed, at home at least, the wives are the ones who mainly deal with financial matters.

In addition, female donations and volunteering often depend on the time available and level of income. Women who do not have enough money to donate will often give their time and skill to help. An interview with Kosirotun,[17] a female volunteer for Portal Infaq, revealed that volunteering is one of the best ways to help if one is financially limited (interview with Kosirotun, 19 July 2005). Nana Mintarni, a General Manager of Planning and Development Dompet Dhuafa, stated that the experiences of Dompet Dhuafa in rural communities revealed that female contributions usually come in the form of in-kind donations and volunteering (interview with Mintarni, 11 June 2005).

Another finding mentioned both by female philanthropists and volunteers is the *management air mata* (managing the teardrop), a term borrowed from Mintarni, that stresses the most heart-rending and saddening aspects of a particular tragedy in order to increase charitable or volunteering contributions. Indeed, alleviating poverty and misfortune is the main focus of philanthropic organisations. It is logical, then, that individuals or organisations seeking donations will play on the emotional nature of the cause they espouse. Kosirotun, who works voluntarily in fundraising, revealed that it is easy to get donations from women because they readily respond to sad stories caused by misfortunes and disaster (interview with Kosirotun, 19 July 2005). This description resembles the stereotyping of women as mentioned by Soebagjo, a female philanthropist, regarding women's participation in philanthropic organisations. Again, a 'feminisation of fundraising'—a term used by Conry (1991)—is not exclusive to Indonesia, since in the United States fundraising jobs are dominated by women, too (Conry 1998; Mesch & Rooney 2005).

Female beneficiaries

The objective of philanthropic organisations is to help the needy and work to eradicate the causes of poverty. In Indonesia there is generally no specific consideration for gender issues by the philanthropic organisations. In this regard, Rachmad Riyadi of Dompet Dhuafa explained, 'There is no attention given to gender considerations in giving assistance among philanthropic organisations. If there is a calamity, we will give attention to those who are most in need and vulnerable, the children and their mothers' (interview with Riyadi, 27 June 2005). From interviews it appears that Dompet Dhuafa and Portal Infaq have the same policy (interviews with Riyadi, 27 June 2005 and with Abdurrahman, 27 and 28 June 2005). That is, there is no specific focus on gender, but when those in most need are women, assistance will be directed towards them. Indeed, there is an assumption that the most needy are women and children.

The organisational survey revealed that the focus of philanthropic organisations towards issues specifically relating to women (women's education, family care programs, and service for mothers and babies) is low (see Table 7). Regarding these issues, private philanthropic organisations have shown more concern for long-term capacity-building programs for women and gender issues than have state-based and mosque-based organisations. The responses of different organisations concerning women's education reveal that private philanthropic organisations are more concerned with women's education (see Table 8).

Table 7: Organisations' responses as to whether they have programs related to women's issues

Questions	Responses (%)		
	Yes	No	No Answer
Education for women	18	77	5
Concern for family caring program	15	80	5
Service for mother and baby	9	86	5

Table 8. Funding of education for women according to types of organisations

	Education for women (%)
Mosque-based organisation	11
Private organisations	39
State-based organisation	24

The above findings lead to a conclusion that a professional approach to management increases the attention given to women's empowerment, at least in two fields: the selection of beneficiaries and specific programs for women.

One of the statistics derived from the Dompet Dhuafa scholarship beneficiaries' list published on its website shows that the percentage of student recipients according to gender is quite encouraging (54% male and 46% female). Mintarni explained that scholarship recipients are selected based on their academic achievements (interview with Mintarni, 11 June 2005). Although such a well-balanced sex ratio is unintentional in this case, it shows that access to information and a fair selection process may influence equality in the selection of scholarship recipients.

Women's empowerment and gender-sensitive programs

Some of the programs of private philanthropic organisations are directed at women. Dompet Dhuafa has two programs that aim to support women. The first program, called WAKALA (Wanita Kepala Keluarga), works to support widows who are the sole providers for their families, while the second program, called Sahabat Pekerja Migran (SPM), supports female workers.

WAKALA, a program set up to assist victims of the tsunami in Aceh, was launched in February 2005 in two villages of the Sigli municipality. The program provides training and capital for 75 widows who want to start their own businesses such as chicken farms, tailoring or trading enterprises (DDR 2005b). This is a long-term program, which is supervised by local personnel to increase the community's ability to support its own economic needs after the tsunami disaster.

The migrant workers' program is a new initiative that gives assistance to vulnerable female workers. Female workers, especially migrant workers, are the most likely to suffer abusive treatment, receive low payment, be deported, or be robbed while working and travelling in or out of the country. SPM has three main activities: (1) giving direct assistance to female workers in the country and abroad, such as giving assistance at airports and providing a remittance service; (2) education and economic training; and (3) advocacy and political action (part of a coalition against deportation of migrant workers). Abroad, SPM has worked actively in Hong Kong and Malaysia (DDR 2005c; interview with Mintarni, 11 June 2005).

Dompet Dhuafa has four other programs that are gender sensitive and designed on the premise that women and children are the most vulnerable in any disaster situation. The first two programs have become regular and province-wide services, while the remaining two programs are employed only in certain areas where the need exists. The four programs are, first, a free health service, intended only for the poor. The hospital through which this service is provided has sections for mothers and infants (including giving free, healthy meals) and for expecting mothers. Second, emergency assistance is provided in the form of food, clothes, shelter and other immediate needs for victims of natural disasters, such as the tsunami, earthquakes and floods, as well as other disasters such as house fires and malaria epidemics. This emergency assistance has been effective, especially in meeting gender-specific needs such as those of mothers. Third, Dompet Dhuafa provides support for improving communities' independence by lending capital to groups of households for running businesses. Mintarni states that some women's groups in West Java are the most hard-working groups and can often pay back the capital more successfully than the men's groups. Fourth, assistance is provided in conflict areas (for example in Poso), such as support and training to re-establish destroyed households and communities (interview with Mintarni, 11 June 2005).

Learning from Dompet Dhuafa's programs, it can be seen that professional management can lead to gender-sensitive activities and support for women's empowerment. Behind the activities of such philanthropic organisations is a rational approach and progressive thinking about Islamic philanthropy, which interprets beneficiaries according to the Qur'an, as outlined in the following verse:

> Alms are for the poor and the needy, and those employed to administer the [funds]; for those whose hearts have been [recently] reconciled [to Truth]; for those in bondage and in debt; in the cause of Allah; and for the wayfarer. [thus is it] ordained by Allah, and Allah is full of knowledge and wisdom (QS *9:60*).

Public and institutional surveys find that around 15% of Muslims and Islamic organisations have a positive interpretation of social justice philanthropy. Therefore, in one case, Bazis DKI Jakarta distributed donations for victims of rape and violence, as such people are seen to be 'the slave' (translated above as those in bondage) (interview with Sukanta,[18] 27 October 2003). Although there are few slaves as such in today's world, 'slave' is interpreted as persons suffering oppression. Therefore, recipients of charitable assistance, such as victims of violence and conflict and migrant workers, get strong support from professional philanthropic organisations.

Conclusion

The tradition of giving charity and volunteering differs considerably between male and female Indonesian Muslims, due to differences such as motivation, beneficiary selection and organisation selection. The difference between the sexes in this regard is certainly not 'minor and deserving of no more than passing mention', as claimed by Bowen (1999:23). Female donors have more emotional attachment to the causes to which they are making their donations. Family background, custom and wealth have become important factors behind charity and volunteering.

The expression that 'charity begins at home' is certainly the case in Indonesia, as elsewhere. Family background has influenced the practice of philanthropy amongst Indonesians. There are two distinct backgrounds that may strongly influence attitudes towards giving charity and volunteering: an extremely loving family and a family that has suffered considerably. Both of these cases may nurture feelings of empathy for others who are in unfortunate circumstances and in desperate need of assistance. The first context will no doubt teach affection towards others, and it is here that the common female function of mother or wife who teaches children at home is very important. The second background, as with Dorce's case, promotes compassion towards others as a result of reaction against one's own experience.

Custom influences philanthropic practice and vice versa. Philanthropic and charitable practices, which have been based on theological understanding and Islamic teachings, reflect a struggle for gender identity. Although there is no Islamic legal restriction regarding philanthropic giving according to gender, philanthropic practices are gendered due to the culture, which is gendered (Singer 2002:96). *Wakaf* giving and donations of large amounts of money have customarily been decided by men, who are the 'bread winners'. Now giving charity, which has usually occurred on a family basis (usually represented by the husband's name as leader of a family), is beginning to be supplemented by giving on an individual basis, where both males and females are actively involved. Orphan adoption in a family is a tradition that has a strong religious basis, where husband and wife practise charity. Charity in the form of public activities is not only done by men but also by women.

Wealth is not always the main determinant of philanthropic giving but it positively influences the giving attitude of women, since they usually do not make decisions about family expenditure by themselves, especially when the family income is limited. Working urban women usually have more freedom to spend their money, including for charity. Rural women tend to give in-kind materials and volunteer, instead of making monetary donations. In this regard, women can negotiate their lack of money in order to practise charity. The same happens in women's religious gatherings, where women practise charity collectively, as well as having access to public activities.

The social aspect of religious teachings positively encourages charity. A widely open Islamic definition that any good deed is *sedekah* provides a positive trigger for the development of philanthropic practices among both men and women. These practices have accustomed communities to understand the importance of being independent of government, and therefore of supporting civil society initiatives.

The participation of women in Islamic philanthropic institutions is interesting and encouraging. On average, women's level of participation in Islamic philanthropic institutions is low (no more than 24%), but the percentage indicates a good starting point. Participation is quite low in the state-based

Islamic philanthropic organisations, when compared to private institutions and mosque-based organisations. Private philanthropic organisations provide more space for women to be involved in their activities, and the programs of private philanthropic institutions are gender-sensitive, although old stereotyping still exists.

Women's emotional attachment to beneficiaries, as well as to philanthropic organisations, and women's tendency to want to know how their contributions are used indirectly support the transparency and accountability system of philanthropic organisations.

Even though gender and women's empowerment issues have not become the concern of most philanthropic organisations, these issues will be taken up step by step, especially by those organisations that have a more professional management approach. The more professional a philanthropic organisation is, the more aware and sensitive it is towards social and political issues.

While in many Muslim communities women have a limited role in the public sphere, philanthropic activities, such as volunteering and social work, have opened the door for Muslim women to become involved and have a role in public life, and also to gain more consideration as the beneficiaries of charitable activities. The expansion and continuing development of professionalism in philanthropic organisations in the *Reformasi* era is encouraging for the development of women's independence and gender equity.

Notes

1   The public survey used the probability sampling method employing a 3% margin of error and 95% level of trust. The respondents were chosen by a combination of multistage sampling and random sampling. Probability sampling was used, since there was no sampling framework (list of the entire Indonesian population) available in the national, provincial and district level. The only reliable sampling framework was from the neighbourhood associations (Rukun Tetangga and Rukun Warga).

2   The majority of females were 'housewives', 95% of whom were involved in family decision-making.

3   Non-probability was used, since there was no sampling framework available at all to include three different types of philanthropic organisations. The mosque-based organisations are established in almost every mosque. The total number of mosques in 2004 according to the Department of Religious Affairs was approximately 641,000.

4   Assistance was provided by Dr Graham Hepworth from the Statistical Consulting Centre of the University of Melbourne.

5   The amount of *zakat fitrah* per person was 3.5 kilograms of rice/main foodstuff or money equivalent to that. This amount was according to Islamic law, which refers to *hadis*. In Indonesia it was between Rp7,000 and Rp17,500 (equivalent to between AU$1.00 and AU$2.40). At the time of writing, AU$1.00 was equivalent to Rp7,000.

6   *Infak* is a *sedekah*, which initially was given to family members. The terms *sedekah* and *infak* are used interchangeably. *Hadiyah* (present) and *hibah* (grant) are included in *sedekah*.

7   See selected Qur'anic verses and *hadis* on philanthropy in Fauzia 2003.

8   'If ye disclose [acts of] charity, even so it is well, but if ye conceal them, and make them reach those [really] in need, that is best for you: It will remove from you some of your [stains of] evil. And Allah is well acquainted with what ye do.'

9   The *hadis*, narrated by Abu Huraira, is about the sixth kind of person (out of seven) who will get God's assistance on the day of Judgement (Bukhari, volume 1, book number 11, *hadis* number 629).

10 Dompet Dhuafa was established in 1993 by journalists working for *Republika* Newspapers (established by Indonesian Muslim Intellectual Association). PKPU (*Pos Keadilan Peduli Umat*) was established in 1999 by Muslim activists who worked for Partai Keadilan (now called Partai Keadilan Sejahtera).

11 Such as Masjid Raya Pondok Indah Jakarta and Masjid Al-Markaz Al-Islamiy Ujung Pandang, South Sulawesi.

12 Structures of organisations differ. A professional philanthropic organisation has founders, trustees, executives and staff. Some mosque-based organisations only have executive committees, without having staff.

13 Among others she is on the Board of Directors of the Foundation for Sustainable Development, Advocates of Rotary Club in Indonesia and the Governing Council of the Asia Pacific Philanthropy Consortium.

14 Hj Thoyyibah is a treasurer of Aisyiyah in the province of Banten, East section, and Chief of Aisyiyah's sub-branch in Cirendeu village.

15 Dorce was born as a male and underwent surgery to become a woman in 1983.

16 The actual figure for females is 17%, while the male figure is 18%, and anonymous is 62%. The rest represent family, organisations or no clear gender indication.

17 Kosirotun works for an oil company in Jakarta as a tax accountant.

18 Chief of Bazis DKI Jakarta.

Abdullah, M Amin 1997, 'Perkembangan Pemikiran Islam dalam Muhammadiyah: Perspektif Tarjih Pasca Muktamar Muhammadiyah ke 43' in Musawir, NM (ed), *Dinamika Pemikiran Islam dan Muhammadiyah*, Lembaga Pustaka dan Dokumentasi Pimpinan Pusat Muhammadiyah, Yogyakarta.

Abdullah, T 1971, *Schools and politics: the Kaum Muda movement in West Sumatra (1927–1933)*, Cornell University, Ithaca.

Abdullah, Taufik and Sharon Siddique (eds) 1986, *Islam and society in Southeast Asia*, Institute of Southeast Asian Studies, Singapore.

Abdurrahman, Asymuni 2003, *Manhaj Tarjih Muhammadiyah: Methodologi dan Aplikasi*, Pustaka Pelajar, Yogyakarta.

Abrar, Ana Nadhya and Wini Tamtiari 2001, *Konstruksi Seksualitas: Antara Hak dan Kekuasaan*, Kerjasama Ford Foundation dengan Pusat Penelitian Kependudukan Universitas Gadjah Mada, Yogyakarta.

Abul Husain Muslim bin al-Hajjaj al-Nisapuri 2005, *Shahih Muslim* (translation by Abdul Hamid Shiddiqui), USC, Book 5, kitab al-*Zakat*, www.usc.edu/dept/MSA/fundamentals/hadithsunnah/muslim/.

Abu-Lughod, Lila 1990, 'Can there be a feminist ethnography', *Women and Performance: A Journal of Feminist Theory* 5(1).

——1993, *Writing women's worlds: Bedouin stories*, University of California Press, Berkeley.

Adrina and Purwandari 1998, *Hak-Hak Reproduksi Perempuan yang Terpasung: Seri Kesehatan Reproduksi, Kebudayaan dan Masyarakat*, Pustaka Sinar Harapan bekerjasama dengan Program Kajian Wanita Universitas Indonesia and the Ford Foundation, Jakarta.

Afsaruddin, Asma (ed) 1999, *Hermeneutics and honor: negotiating female 'public' space in Islamic/ate societies*, Harvard University Press, Cambridge.

Agoes MD 2005a, 'Memutuskan Menjadi Wanita,' Series no III of Dorce Gamalama, www.femina-online.com/serial/dorce/srldorce3.html, accessed July 2005.

—— 2005b, 'Sejuta Warna Kehidupan Dorce Gamalama,' Series no 1 of Dorce Gamalama, www.femina-online.com/serial/dorce/srldorce1.html, accessed July 2005.

Ahmed, Leila 2000, *Wanita dan Gender dalam Islam*, Lentera, Jakarta.

Albani, Muhammad Nashiruddin al- 2002, *Cincin Pinangan: Adab Pernikahan Islami*, Najla Press, Jakarta.

Aldridge, Alan 2000, *Religion in the contemporary world: a sociological introduction*, Polity Press, Malden.

Ali, 'Abdullah Yusuf 1989, *The meaning of the Holy Qur'an*, Amana Publications, Beltsville.

Al-Qur'an [with Indonesian Language Translation], *Al-Islam*. Kingdom of Saudi Arabia. Ministry of Islamic Affairs, Endowments, Da'wah and Guidance, http://quran.al-islam.com/Targama/DispTargam.asp?nType=1&nSora=16&nAya=97&nSe g=1&l=ind&t=ind, visited in July 2005.

Al-Tabari, Muhammad Ibn Jarir 1903, *Jami al-Bayan fi Tafsir Al-Qur'an*, Al-Maymaniyah, Egypt.

Ambaretnani, Prihatini et al 1999, *Upaya Menengkatkan dan Melindungi Kesehatan Reproduksi TKIW*, Yayasan Galang bekerjasama dengan the Ford Foundation, Yogyakarta.

Amili, Ali Usaili al- 2002, *Nikmatnya Berjilbab*, Pustaka Zahra, Jakarta.

Anderson, BRO'G 1972, 'The idea of power in Javanese culture' in Holt, Claire (ed), *Culture and politics in Indonesia*, Cornell University Press, Ithaca.

Anshari, Endang Saifuddin 1986, *Piagam Jakarta 22 Juni 1945*, Rajawali, Jakarta.

Anwar, M Syafi'i 1995, *Pemikiran dan Aksi Islam: Sebuah Kajian Politik tentang Cendikiawan Muslim Orde Baru*, Paramadina, Jakarta.

Aripurnami, Sita 1996, 'A feminist comment on the sinetron presentation of Indonesian women' in Sears, Laurie (ed), *Fantasizing the feminine in Indonesia*, Duke University Press, Durham.

Aryani, Sekar Ayu et al 2004, *Pengarusutamaan Gender dalam Kurikulum di IAIN*, PSW IAIN Sunan Kalijaga bekerjasama dengan McGill-CIDA, Yogyakarta.

Aspinall, Edward 1995, *Student dissent in Indonesia in the 1980s*, Monash Asia Institute, Clayton.

Atkinson, Jane and Shelly Errington (eds) 1990, *Power and difference: gender in island Southeast Asia*, Stanford University Press, Stanford.

Aura 1999, 3(4), March.

Awwas, Irfan S 2004, 'Halusinasi Penentang Syariat Islam', http://annisa.majelis.mujahidin.or.id/artikel/hukum/halusinasipenentangsyariatislam, accessed 19 May 2005

Azra, Azyumardi 2003a, 'The Indonesian marriage law of 1974: an institutionalization of the Shari'a for social changes' in Salim, A and A Azra (eds), *Shari'a and politics in modern Indonesia*, Institute of Southeast Asian Studies, Singapore.

—— 2003b, *Surau, Pendidikan Islam Tradisional dalam Transisi dan Modernisasi*, PT Logos Wacana Ilmu, Ciputat.

—— 2004, 'Political Islam in post-Soeharto Indonesia' in Hooker, V and A Saikal (eds), *Islamic perspectives on the new millennium*, Institute of Southeast Asian Studies, Singapore.

Bachtiar, Harsja 1980 [1973], 'The religion of Java: A Commentary', *Indonesian Journal of Cultural Studies*, 5(1).

Badran, M 1994, 'Gender activism: feminists and Islamists in Egypt' in Moghadam, V (ed), *Identity politics and women: cultural reassertions and feminisms in international perspective*, Westview Press, Oxford.

Baines, Carol, Patricia Evans and Sheila Neysmith (eds) 1991, *Women's caring: feminist perspectives on social welfare*, McClelland & Stewart Inc, Toronto.

Bar, Muhammad Ali 2000, *Wanita Karir dalam Timbangan Islam: Kodrat Kewanitaan, Emansipasi dan Pelecehan Seksual*, Pustaka Azzam, Jakarta.

Barfield, Thomas 1997, *The dictionary of anthropology*, Blackwell, Cambridge.

Barlas, Asma 2002, *'Believing women' in Islam: unreading patriarchal interpretations of the Quran*, University of Texas Press, Austin.

Beatty, Andrew 1999, *Varieties of Javanese religion: an anthropological account*, Cambridge University Press, Cambridge.

Bennett, Linda Rae 2005, *Women, Islam and modernity: single women, sexuality and reproductive health in contemporary Indonesia*, RoutledgeCurzon, New York.

Berninghausen, Jutta and Birgit Kerstan 1992, *Forging new paths: feminist social methodology and rural women in Java*, Zed Books, London.

Blackburn, Susan 1999, 'Women and citizenship in Indonesia', *Australian Journal of Political Science* 34.

—— 2004, *Women and the state in modern Indonesia*, Cambridge University Press, Cambridge.

Blackburn, Susan and Sharon Bessell 1997, 'Marriageable age: political debates on early marriage in twentieth century Indonesia', *Indonesia* 63.

Blackwood, Evelyn 1995, 'Senior women, model mothers, dutiful wives: managing gender contradictions in a Minangkabau village' in Ong, A and M Peletz (eds), *Bewitching women, pious men: gender and body politics in Southeast Asia*, University of California Press, Berkeley.

—— 2000, *Webs of power: women, kin, and community in a Sumatran village*, Rowman & Littlefield, Lanham.

Boland, BJ 1971, *The struggle of Islam in modern Indonesia*, Martinus Nijhoff, The Hague.

Bowen, John R 1993, *Muslims through discourse: religion and ritual in Gayo society*, Princeton University Press, Princeton.

Bowen, Kurt 1999, *Religion, participation, and charitable giving: a report*, Volunteer Canada and the Canadian Centre for Philanthropy.

Bowie, Fiona 2000, *The anthropology of religion: an introduction*, Blackwell Publishers, Cambridge.

Brenner, Suzanne 1995, 'Why women rule the roost: rethinking Javanese gender ideologies and self-control' in Ong, A and M Peletz (eds), *Bewitching women, pious men: gender and body politics in Southeast Asia*, University of California Press, Berkeley.

—— 1996, 'Reconstructing self and society: Javanese Muslim women and "the veil"', *American Ethnologist* 23(4).

—— 1998, *The domestication of desire: women, wealth, and modernity in Java*, Princeton University Press, Princeton.

Bright, Jennifer 1999, 'Who is co-opting whom? Historical perspectives on the family planning policy in Indonesia', paper presented at American Asian Studies Conference, Boston.

Bruinessen, Martin van 1996, 'Traditions for the future: the reconstruction of traditionalist discourse within NU,' in Barton, G and G Fealy (eds), *Nahdlatul Utama, traditional Islam and modernity in Indonesia*, Monash Asia Institute, Clayton.

Bulbeck, Chilla 1988, *One world women's movement*, Pluto Press, London.

—— 1998, 'Introduction' in *Re-orienting western feminisms: women's diversity in a post-colonial world*, Cambridge University Press, Cambridge.

Burhanuddin, Jajat (ed) 2002, *Ulama Perempuan Indonesia*, Gramedia Pustaka Utama bekerjasama dengan PPIM IAIN Syarif Hidayatullah Jakarta, Jakarta.

Burhanuddin, Jajat and Oman Fathurahman (eds) 2004, *Tentang Perempuan Islam: Wacana dan Gerakan*, Gramedia Pustaka Utama bekerjasama dengan PPIM IAIN Syarif Hidayatullah Jakarta, Jakarta.

Butt, Simon 1999, 'Polygamy and mixed marriage in Indonesia: the application of the marriage law in the courts' in Lindsey, Timothy (ed), *Indonesia: law and society*, Federation Press, Annandale.

Cammack, Mark 1989, 'Islamic law in Indonesia's New Order,' *International and Comparative Law Quarterly* 38(1).

—— 1999, 'Inching towards equality: recent developments in Indonesian inheritance law,' *Indonesian Law and Administration Review* 5(1).

Canda, Edward R and Leola Dyrud Furman 1999, *Spiritual diversity in social work practice: the heart of helping*, The Free Press, New York.

Cek and Ricek 1999a, 8–14 February.

Cek and Ricek 1999b, 15–21 February.

Conry, JC 1991, 'The feminization of fund raising' in Burlingame, D and LJ Hulse (eds), *Taking fund raising seriously*, Jossey Bass, San Francisco.

—— 1998, 'Gender and pay equity in the fundraising workforce: implications for practice and policy,' *New Directions for Philanthropic Fundraising* 19.

Cooley, Laura 1992, 'Maintaining rukun for Javanese households and for the state' in van Bemmelen, S et al (eds), *Women and mediation in Indonesia*, KITLV Press, Leiden.

Coulon, C 1998, 'Women, Islam and Baraka' in Coulon, C and DC O'Brien (eds), *Charisma and brotherhood in African Islam*, Clarendon Press, Oxford.

Dahlan, Muhammad 2002, 'Sholihah A Wahid Hasyim: Teladan Kaum Perempuan Nahdliyin' in Burhanuddin, J (ed), *Ulama Perempuan Indonesia*, Gramedia Pustaka Utama, Jakarta.

Damami, Mohammad 2000, *Akar Gerakan Muhammadiyah*, Fajar Pustaka Baru, Yogyakarta.

Darwis, Khaulah binti Abdul Kadir 2002a, *Bagaimana Muslimah Bergaul*, Pustaka Al-Kautsar, Jakarta.

—— 2002b, *Istri yang Ideal*, Darul Falah, Jakarta.

Department of Information 1979, *The Indonesian Marriage Law*, Jakarta.

Dhofier, Zamakhsyari 1982, *Tradisi Pesantren: Studi Tentang Pandangan Hidup Kiai*, Lembaga Penelitian, Pendidikan dan Penerangan Ekonomi dan Sosial, Jakarta.

Djamil, Fathurahman 1994, 'Ijtihad Muhammadiyah dalam Masalah-masalah Fiqh Kontemporer', Dissertasi, IAIN Syarif Hidayatullah, Jakarta.

Djohan, Bahder 1977, *Di Tangan Wanita*, Yayasan Idayu, Jakarta.

Dobbin, C 1992, *Kebangkitan Islam dalam Ekonomi Petani yang sedang Berubah: Sumatera Tengah 1784–1847*, INIS, Jakarta.

Doi, 'Abdur Rahman I 1999, *The Qur'an, women and modern society*, Sterling Publisher Private Ltd, New Delhi.

DDR (Dompet Dhuafa Republika) 2005a, 'Donors of this week,' www.dompetdhuafa. org/english/dd.php?cat=fix&id=donatur, accessed 6 June 2005.

—— 2005b, 'Tabligh Akbar di Negeri Orang,' www.dompetdhuafa.org/english/ dd.php?cat=othernews_eng&id=11.

—— 2005c, 'WAKALA Program for tsunami victims,' www.dompetdhuafa.org/ english/dd.php?cat=othernews_eng&id=14.

Doorn-Harder, Nelly van 1999, 'Between rhetoric and reality: Aisyiyah women coping with modernization and change', paper presented at the American Asian Studies Conference, Boston.

—— 2002, 'The Indonesian debate on a woman president', *Sojourn* 17(2).

Doumato, Eleanor Abdella 2003, 'Education in Saudi Arabia: gender, jobs and the price of religion' in Doumato, EA and M Posusney (eds), *Women and globalization in the Arab Middle East: gender, economy and society*, Lynne Rienner Publishers, Boulder.

Dzuhayatin, Siti Ruhaini 1996, 'Pemberdayaan Perempuan dalam Konteks Keindonesiaan', *Media Nasyiah* 1.

—— 2000, 'Kajian Gender di Perguruan Tinggi Islam di Indonesia: Catatan dari PSW IAIN Sunan Kalijaga Yogyakarta' in Hidayat, K and H Prasetyo (eds), *Problem dan Prospek IAIN: Antologi Pendidikan Islam*, Ditbinperta Depag RI, Jakarta.

——2003, 'Agama dan Budaya Perempuan: Mempertanyakan Posisi Perempuan dalam Islam' in Abdullah, Irwan (ed), *Sangkan Paran Gender*, Pustaka Pelajar, Yogyakarta.

Dzuhayatin, Siti Ruhaini et al 2002, *Rekonstruksi Metodologis Wacana Kesetaraan Gender dalam Islam*, PSW IAIN Sunan Kalijaga bekerjasama dengan McGill-CIDA, Yogyakarta.

Effendy, B 2003, *Islam and the state in Indonesia*, Institute of Southeast Asian Studies, Singapore.

Effendy, T 2004, *Tunjuk Ajar Melayu (Butir-Butir Budaya Melayu Riau)*, Pusat Kajian Pengembangan Budaya Melayu dan PT Adicita, Yogyakarta.

Engineer, Asghar Ali 2000, *Hak-hak Perempuan dalam Islam [The rights of women in Islam]*, translated by Farid Wajidi, LSPAA, Yogyakarta.

—— 2004, *Pembebasan Perempuan*, translated by MA Nuryatno, LKiS, Yogyakarta.

Errington, Shelly 1990, 'Recasting sex, gender, and power: a theoretical and regional overview' in Errington, Shelly and Jane Atkinson (eds), *Power and difference: gender in island Southeast Asia*, Stanford University Press, Stanford.

Evans, Judith 1995, *Feminist theory today: an introduction to second wave feminism*, Sage Publications, London.

Evers-Rosander, Eva 1998, 'Women and Muridism in Senegal: the case of the Mam Diarra Bousso Daira in Mbacke' in Ask, K and M Tjomsland (eds), *Women and Islamization: contemporary dimensions of discourse on gender relations*, Berg, New York.

Faiqoh 2003, *Nyai: Agen Perubahan di Pesantren*, Kucica, Jakarta.

Fakih, Mansoer 1998, 'Diskriminasi dan beban kerja perempuan: perspektif gender,' in Bainar (ed), *Wacana Perempuan dalam Keindonesiaan dan Kemodernan*, CIDESINDO and Universitas Islam Indonesia and Yayasan IPPSDM, Jakarta.

Fananie, Zainuddin and Atiqa Sabardilla 2000, *Sumber Konflik Masyarakat Muslim Muhammadiyah-NU: Perspektif Keberterimaan Tahlil*, Muhammadiyah University Press and the Asia Foundation, Surakarta.

Fauzia, Amelia et al 2003, *Filantropi untuk Keadilan Sosial Menurut Tuntutan Al-Qur'an dan Hadis*, Pusat Bahasa dan Budaya, Jakarta.

Fauzia, A and A Hermawan 2002, 'Ketegangan antara Kekuasaan dan Aspek Normatif Filantropi dalam Sejarah Islam di Indonesia' in I Thaha (ed), *Berderma untuk Semua, Praktek dan Wacana Filantropi Islam*, Pusat Bahasa dan Budaya and Teraju, Jakarta.

Feillard, Andree 1996, 'The emergence of a Muslim feminist movement in the intellectual elite in Indonesia,' Second Eurames Conference, 4–7 July, Aix-en-Provence

—— 1999, 'The veil and polygamy: current debates on women and Islam in Indonesia,' *Moussons: recherche en sciences humaines sur l'Asie du Sud-Est* 1.

Feillard, Andree and Lies Marcoes 1998, 'Female circumcision in Indonesia: to Islamize in ceremony or secrecy', *Archipel* 56.

Firth, Rosemary 1966, *Housekeeping among Malay peasants*, Humanities Press, New York.

Foley, Rebecca 2001, 'The challenge of contemporary Muslim women activists in Malaysia', Dissertation, School of Political and Social Inquiry, Monash University.

Gamalama 2005, www.dorcegamalama.com/Dorce.html.

Gatra 2003, 'Ancaman Pidana Pasal Poligami', www.gatra.com/2003-12-07/versi-cetak.php?id=32246, accessed 23 May 2005.

Geertz, Clifford 1975, *The interpretation of cultures*, Hutchinson, London.

—— 1976 [1960], *The religion of Java*, University of Chicago Press, Chicago.

Grace, Jocelyn 2004, 'Sasak women negotiating marriage, polygyny and divorce in rural East Lombok', *Intersections: Gender, History and Culture in the Asian Context* 10, wwwsshe.murdoch.edu.au/intersections/issue10/grace.html.

Greenwood, Susan 2000, *Magic, witchcraft and the otherworld: an anthropology*, Berg, Oxford.

Hafidz, Wardah 1994, 'Feminisme sebagai counter culture', *Ulumul Qur'an* 5.

Haidlor, Ali Ahmad 2000, 'Kesetaraan Gender dan Pemberdayaan Perempuan di Pondok Pesantren', *Penamas (Jurnal Penelitian Agama dan Kemasyarakatan)* 36.

Hamidy, U 2002, *Riau Doeloe-Kini dan Bayangan Masa Depan*, Universitas Islam Riau Press, Pekanbaru.

Hari, Kurniawan 2005, 'Dorce: on duty and charity', *Jakarta Post*, www.thejakartapost.com/detailfeatures.asp?fileid=20050703.C01&irec=0.

Harsono, A 2004, *Beyond the Jilbab*, http://kyotoreview.cseas.kyoto-uac.jp/issue/issue4/article350html, accessed 2005.

Hassan, Muhammad Kamal 1982, *Muslim intellectual responses to New Order modernization in Indonesia*, Dewan Bahasa dan Pustaka Kementrian Pelajar Malaysia, Kuala Lumpur.

Hassan, Riffat 1990, 'Teologi Perempuan dalam Tradisi Islam', *Ulumul Qur'an* 1.

Hasyim, Syafiq 2001, *Hal-hal yang Tak Terpikirkan tentang Isu-isu Keperempuanan dalam Islam*, Mizan, Bandung.

Hatley, Barbara and Susan Blackburn 2000, 'Representations of women's roles in household and society in Indonesian women's writing of the 1930's' in Koning J, M Nolten, J Rodenburg and R Saptari (eds), *Women and households in Indonesia: cultural notions and social practices*, Curzon Press, Richmond.

Headley, Stephen 2004, *Durga's mosque: cosmology, conversion and community in Central Javanese Islam*, Institute of Southeast Asian Studies Publications, Singapore.

Hefner, Robert 1993, 'Islam, state, and civil society: icon and the struggle for the Indonesian middle class,' *Indonesia* 56.

—— 2000, *Civil Islam: Muslims and democratization in Indonesia*, Princeton University Press, Princeton.

Hidayat, Komaruddin and Hendro Prasetyo (eds) 2000 *Problem dan Prospek IAIN: Antologi Pendidikan Islam*, Ditbinperta Depag RI, Jakarta.

Hodgson, Marshall GS 1974, *The venture of Islam*, Chicago University Press, Chicago.

Hooker, MB 2003, *Indonesian Islam: social change through contemporary fatawa*, Asian Studies Association of Australia, Crows Nest.

Horikoshi, Horiko 1982, *Kiai dan Perubahan Sosial*, P3M, Jakarta.

Howell, JD, MA Subandi and PL Nelson 2001, 'New faces of Indonesian Sufism: a demographic profile of Tarekat Qodiriyyah-Naqsyabandiyyah, Pesantren Suryalaya, in the 1990s', *Review of Indonesian and Malaysian Affairs* 35(2).

Howell, Julia Day 1998, 'Religion' in Maidment, Richard and Colin Mackerras (eds), *Culture and society in the Asia-Pacific*, Routledge, London.

Hubeis, Aida 2000, 'Moslem women's issues in Indonesia' in Alawiyah, T (ed), *Women in Islam: past, present, future*, Badan Kontak Majelis Taklim, Jakarta.

IAIN Sunan Ampel 1970, *Lustrum I IAIN Sunan Ampel 5 Djuli 1965-1970*, IAIN Sunan Ampel, Surabaya.

IAIN Sunan Kalidjaga 1968, *Sewindu Institut Agama Islam Negeri Sunan Kalidjaga Jogjakarta 1960–1968*, IAIN Sunan Kalidjaga, Yogyakarta.

Ilchman, WF, SN Katz and EL Queen (eds) 1998, *Philanthropy in the world's traditions*, Indiana University Press, Bloomington.

Ilyas, Hamim et al 2003, *Perempuan Tertindas: Kajian Hadits 'Misoginis'*, PSW IAIN Sunan Kalijaga bekerjasama dengan the Ford Foundation, Yogyakarta.

Ilyas, Yunahar 1997, *Feminisme dalam Kajian Tafsir Al-Qur'an Klasik dan Kontemporer*, Pustaka Pelajar, Yogyakarta.

Ismail, Nurjannah 2003, *Perempuan dalam Pasungan: Bias Laki-laki dalam Penafsiran*, LKiS, Yogyakarta.

Istiadah 1995, *Muslim women in contemporary Indonesia: investigating paths to resist the patriarchal system*, Centre for Southeast Asian Studies, Monash University, Clayton.

Jabali, Fuad and Jamhari 2002, *IAIN dan Modernisasi Islam di Indonesia*, Logos, Jakarta.

Jainuri, Ahmad 1981, *Muhammadiyah Gerakan Reformasi Islam di Jawa pada Awal Abad Kedua Puluh*, Bina Ilmu, Surabaya.

—— 2002, *Ideologi Kaum Reformis: Melacak Pandangan Keagamaan Muhammadiyah Periode Awal*, Lembaga Pengkajian Agama dan Masyarakat, Surabaya.

Jamhari and Ismatu Ropi (eds) 2003, *Citra Perempuan dalam Islam: Pandangan Ormas Keagamaan*, Gramedia Pustaka Utama, Jakarta.

Jamil, N et al 2001, *Pakaian Tradisional Melayu Riau*, Bappeda Propinsi Riau dan Balai Pengkajian dan Pelatihan Dinas Kebudayaan, Kesenian dan Pariwisata Propinsi Riau, Pekanbaru.

Jaringan Islam Liberal, 'Masyarakat Terkelabui oleh Formalisasi Jilbab', http://islamlib.com/id/index.php?page=article&id=823, accessed 13 October 2005.

Jawad, Haifaa A 1998, *The rights of women in Islam: an authentic approach*, Macmillan Press, Basingstoke.

Jay, Robert 1969, *Javanese villagers: social relations in rural Modjokuto*, The MIT Press, Cambridge.

Jennaway, M 2002, *Sisters and lovers: women and desire in Bali*, Rowman and Littlefield, Lanham.

Jennaway, Megan 2000, 'Bitter honey: female agency and the polygynous household, north Bali', in Koning J, M Nolten, J Rodenburg and R Saptari (eds), *Women and households in Indonesia: cultural notions and social practices*, Curzon Press, Richmond.

Johns, Anthony Hearle 1961, 'Sufism as a category in Indonesian literature and history', *Journal of Southeast Asian History* 2(2).

—— 1995, 'Sufism in Southeast Asia: reflections and reconsiderations', *Journal of Asian Studies* 26(1).

Jones, Gavin 1994, *Marriage and divorce in Islamic South-East Asia*, Oxford University Press, Kuala Lumpur.

—— 1997, 'Modernization and divorce: contrasting trends in Islamic Southeast Asia and the West', *Population and Development Review* 23(1).

Junus, H 2002, *Engku Puteri Taja Hamidah: Pemegang Regalia Kerajaan Riau*, UNRI Press, Pekanbaru.

Ka'bah, Rifyal 1999, *Hukum Islam di Indonesia: Perspektif Muhammadiyah dan NU*, Universitas Yarsi, Jakarta.

Kadir, FA (ed.) 2001, *Fiqh perempuan. Refleksi Kyai atas Wacana Agama dan Gender*, Rahima, Ford Foundation, LKiS, Yogyakarta.

Kahn, Joel 1995, *Culture, multiculture, postculture*, Sage Publications, London.

Kalibonso, Rita Serena 1999, 'The gender perspective: a key to democracy in Indonesia', in Budiman, A, B Hatley and D Kingsbury (eds), *Reformasi: crisis and change in Indonesia*, Monash Asia Institute, Clayton.

Kandiyoti, Deniz 1988, 'Bargaining with patriarchy', *Gender and Society* 2(3).

—— (ed) 1991, *Women, Islam and the state*, Macmillan, Houndmills.

Karim, W 1992, *Women and culture: between Malay adat and Islam*, Westview Press, San Francisco.

Kartini, Raden Adjeng 1964, *Letters of a Javanese princess* (translated by Agnes Louise Symmers), Norton Library, New York.

1992, *Letters from Kartini: An Indonesian Feminist, 1900–1904* (translated by Joost Cote), Monash Asia Institute, Clayton.

Katjasungkana, Nursyahbani 1993, 'Kedudukan wanita dalam perspektif Islam', in Marcoes-Natsir, Lies and Johan Meuleman (eds), *Wanita Islam Indonesia dalam Kajian Tekstual dan Kontekstual*, INIS, Jakarta.

—— 1997, 'Pandangan Islam tentang posisi perempuan dan laki-laki dalam keluarga' in Anshori, D et al (eds), *Membincangkan Feminisme: Refleksi Muslimah atas Peran Sosial Kaum Wanita*, Pustaka Hidayah, Bandung.

Katz, June and Ronald Katz 1975, 'The new Indonesian marriage law: a mirror of Indonesia's political, cultural, and legal systems', *American Journal of Comparative Law* 23(4).

—— 1978, 'Leglislating social change in a developing country: the new Indonesian marriage law revisited', *American Journal of Comparative Law* 26.

Kazmi, F 1994, 'Muslim socials and the female protagonist: seeing a dominant discourse at work' in Hasan, Z (ed), *Forging identities: gender, communities and the state*, Kali for Women, New Delhi.

Khilmiyah, Akif 2003, *Menata Ulang Keluarga Sakinah: Keadilan Sosial dan Humanisasi Mulai dari Rumah*, Pondok Edukasi, Bantul.

Khoiriyah, Hasyim 1962, 'Pokok-Pokok Tjeramah: Pengertian Antara Mazahib dan Toleransinya,' *Gema Islam*, 13.

Kipp, Rita Smith 1993, *Dissociated Identities, Ethnicity, Religion, and Class in an Indonesian Society*, University of Michigan Press, Ann Arbor.

Kipp, Rita Smith and Rodgers, Susan 1987. 'Introduction' in Rita Smith Kipp and Susan Rodgers eds *Indonesian Religions in Transition*. The University of Arizona Press, Tucson.

Klass, Morton and Maxine Weisgrau (eds) 1999, *Across the Boundaries of Belief: Contemporary Issues in the Anthropology of Religion*, Westview Press, USA.

Koentjaraningrat 1985, *Javanese Culture*, Oxford University Press, Singapore.

Kompas 2003, 'Ideologi Pasar Dalam Tayangan Ramahan?', Ramadan, S, 27 October.

——— 2004, 'Menyosialisasikan *"Counter Legal Draft"* Kompilasi Hukum Islam', 11 October.

———2005, 'Pendapat dan Pemikiran Baru tentang Perempuan di Dalam "Muslimah Reformist"', 28 February.

Kozlowski, Gregory 1998, 'Religious authority, reform, and philanthropy in the contemporary Muslim world' in Ilchman, W, SN Katz, and EL Queen (eds), *Philanthropy in the World's Traditions*, Indiana University Press, Bloomington.

Krulfeld, R 1986, 'Sasak attitudes towards polygyny and the changing position of women in Sasak peasant villages', in Dube, L, E Leacock and S Ardener (eds), *Visibility and power: essays on women in society and development*, Oxford University Press, Delhi.

Kuypers, Sabine 1993, 'Profil Organisasi Wanita Islam Indonesia: Tinjauan dari Dalam', in Marcoes-Natsir, Lies and Johan Meuleman (eds), *Wanita Islam dalam Kajian Tekstual dan Kontekstual*, INIS, Jakarta.

Lev, Daniel 1996, 'On the other hand' in Sears, Laurie (ed), *Fantasizing the feminine in Indonesia*, Duke University Press, Durham.

Liputan 6, 2005, 'Eksekusi Cambuk Dilaksanakan', www.liputan6.com/ view/0,104109,1,0,1143087102.html, accessed 25 October 2005.

MacLeod, Arlene 1992, 'Hegemonic relations and gender resistance: the new veiling as accommodating protest in Cairo', *Signs* 17.

Magnis-Suseno, Franz 1997, *Javanese ethics and world-view: the Javanese idea of the good life*, PT Gramedia Pustaka Utama, Jakarta.

Mahmood, S 2005, *Politics of piety: the Islamic revival and the feminist subject*, Princeton University Press, Princeton.

Majalah Suara Hidayatullah 2006, http://id.wikipedia.org/wiki/Majalah_Suara_ Hidayatullah, accessed 8 March 2006.

Majlis Tarjih, PP Muhammadiyah 1972, *Adabul Mar'ah fil Islam*, PP Muhammadiyah, Yogyakarta.

——— 1980, *Bayi Tabung dan Pencangkokan Organ dalam Sorotan Hukum Islam: Keputusan Muktamar Tajih Muhammadiyah ke 21 di Klaten*, Persatuan, Yogyakarta.

Mansurnoor, Iik Arifin 1990, *Islam in an Indonesian world: ulama of Madura*, Gadjah Mada University Press, Yogyakarta.

Marcoes, Lies 2002, 'Women's grassroots movements in Indonesia: a case study of the PKK and Islamic women's organisations' in Robinson, K and S Bessell (eds), *Women in Indonesia: gender, equity and development*, Australian National University, Canberra.

Marcoes, Lies M 1992, 'The female preacher as a mediator in religion: a case study in Jakarta and West Java' in Van Bemmelen, S *et al* (eds), *Women and Mediation in Indonesia*, KITLV Press, Leiden.

Marcoes-Natsir, Lies 2000, 'Aisyiyah: between worship, charity and professionalism' in Oey-Gardiner, M and C Bianpoen (eds), *Indonesian women: the journey continues*, Research School of Pacific and Asian Studies, Australian National University, Canberra.

—— 2004, *Symbol of defiance or symbol of loyalty?*, www.qantara.de/wecom/showarticle.php/c-549/nr-5/p-1/i.html, accessed 2005.

Marcoes-Natsir, Lies and Johan Hendrik Meuleman (eds) 1993, *Wanita Islam Indonesia dalam Kajian Tekstual dan Kontekstual*, INIS, Jakarta.

Martin, Mike W 1994, *Virtuous giving. Philanthropy, voluntary services, and caring*, Indiana University Press, Bloomington.

Mas'udi, Masdar F 1993, 'Perempuan di antara Lembaran Kitab Kuning,' in L Marcoes-Natsir and JH Meuleman (eds), *Wanita Islam Indonesia dalam Kajian Tekstual dan Kontekstual*, INIS, Jakarta.

Manyhuri, Abdul Aziz [nd], *Al-Maghfurlah KHM. Bishri Syansuri: Cita-Cita dan Pengabdiannya*, Al-Ikhlas, Surabaya.

McCarthy, Kathleen D (ed) (ed) 1990, *Lady Bountiful revisited: women, philanthropy and power*, Rutgers University Press, New Brunswick.

—— 2001, *Women, philanthropy, and civil society*, Indiana University Press, Bloomington.

Megawangi, Ratna 1994, 'Feminisme Menindas Peran Ibu Rumah Tangga', *Ulumul Qur'an* 5.

Meiyenti, Sri 1999, *Kekerasan terhadap Perempuan dalam Rumah Tangga*, Kerjasama Ford Foundation dengan Pusat Penelitian Kependudukan Universitas Gadjah Mada, Yogyakarta.

Mernissi, Fatima 1997, *Beyond the veil: sex dan kekuasaan*, Al-Fikr, Surabaya.

Mernissi, Fatima and Riffat Hassan 1995, *Setara di Hadapan Allah: Relasi Perempuan dan laki-laki dalam Tradisi Islam Pasca Patriarkhi*, Yogyaka Prakarsa, Yogyakarta.

Mesch, Debra J and Patrick M Rooney 2005, 'Determinants of compensation for fundraising professionals: a study of pay, performance, and gender differences', working paper, Center of Philanthropy, Indiana University.

Miller, Donald Bruce and Jan Branson 1989, 'Pollution in Paradise: Hinduism and the subordination of women in Bali' in Alexander, Paul (ed), *Creating Indonesian cultures*, Oceania Publications, University of Sydney.

Moghadam, V 1994, 'Introduction' in Moghadam, V (ed), *Gender and national identity: women and politics in Muslim societies*, Zed Books, London.

—— 2002, 'Islamic feminism and its discontents: towards a resolution of the debate' in Saliba, T, C Allen and J Howard (eds), *Gender, politics and Islam*, University of Chicago Press, Chicago.

Moghissi, Haideh 2005, *Women and Islam: critical concepts in sociology*, Routledge, New York.

Morrison, Kenneth M 2000, 'The cosmos as intersubjective: Native American other-than-human persons' in Harvey, G (ed), *Indigenous religions*, Cassell, London.

MS, Suwardi 2003, *Alam Melayu*, Universitas Riau Press, Pekanbaru.

Mudzhar, MA 1993, *Fatwa-Fatwa Majelis Ulama Indonesia: Sebuah Studi Tentang Pemikiran Hukum Islam di Indonesia, 1975–1988*, INIS, Jakarta.

Muhammad, Husein 1999, 'Kajian Atas Kitab Uqud al-Lujain' *Tashwirul Afkar 5*.

—— 2002, 'Pesantren and the issue of gender relation', *Kultur (The Indonesian Journal for Muslim Cultures)* 2(2).

Muhammad Husein and FA Kodir 2001, *Fiqh Perempuan: Refleksi Kyai atas Wacana Agama dan Gender*, LKiS, Yogyakarta.

Mukhotib, MD (ed) 2002a, *Ketika Pesantren Membincang Gender*, YKF and the Ford Foundation, Yogyakarta.

—— (ed) 2002b, *Menghapus Poligami, Mewujudkan Keadilan*, YKF and the Ford Foundation, Yogyakarta.

—————— (ed) 2002c, *Menolak Mut'ah dan Sirri: Memberdayakan Perempuan*, YKF and the Ford Foundation, Yogyakarta.

Mukhtar, Darmiyanti 1999, *The rise of the Indonesian movement in the New Order state*, thesis, Murdoch University, Perth.

Mulder, Niels 1996, *Inside Southeast Asia: religion, everyday life, cultural change*, The Pepin Press, Singapore.

Mulia, Siti Musdah 1999, *Pandangan Islam tentang Poligami*, Lembaga Kajian Agama dan Jender, Solidaritas Perempuan and the Asia Foundation, Jakarta.

—— 2005, *Muslimah Reformis: Perempuan Pembaru Keagamaan*, Mizan, Bandung.

Mulkhan, Abdul Munir 1990, *Pemikiran Kyai Haji Ahmad Dahlan dan Muhammadiyah dalam Perspektif Perubahan Sosial*, Bumi Aksara, Jakarta.

Munir, Lily Zakiyah (ed) 1999, *Memposisikan Kodrat: Perempuan dan Perubahan dalam Perspektif Islam*, Mizan, Bandung.

Munti, Ratna Batara 1999, *Perempuan sebagai Kepala Rumah Tangga*, Lembaga Kajian Agama dan Gender, Solidaritas Perempuan and the Asia Foundation, Jakarta.

Muslikhati, Siti 2004, *Feminisme dan Pemberdayaan Perempuan dalam Timbangan Islam*, Gema Insani, Jakarta.

Muzakki, A 2003, 'Agama, Budaya Pop, dan Kapitalisme', *Kompas* 4 (18 November).

Muzium Negara Malaysia, 'Wedding culture', www.museum.gov.my/english/wedding.htm, accessed 25 October 2005.

Najib, Ala'i 2002, 'Indonesian Muslim feminist thinking: a study of schools of thought between 1900–2000', *Islamic Studies*, Leiden University, Leiden.

Nakamura, H 1983, *Divorce in Java: a study of the dissolution of marriage among Javanese Muslims*, Gadjah Mada University Press, Yogyakarta.

Nakamura, Mitsuo 1983, *The crescent arises over the banyan tree. A study of the Muhammadiyah movement in a central Javanese town*, Gadjah Mada University Press, Yogyakarta.

Nasution, Khoruddin 2002, *Status Wanita di Asia Tenggara: Studi terhadap Perundang-undangan Perkawinan Muslim Kontemporer di Indonesia dan Malaysia*, INIS, Leiden.

Needham, Rodney 1972, *Belief, language, and experience*, Blackwell Publishers, Oxford.

Newland, Lynda 2000, 'Under the banner of Islam: mobilising religious identities in West Java', *Australian Journal of Anthropology* 11(2).

—— 2001, 'Syncretism and the politics of the *Tingkeban* in West Java', *Australian Journal of Anthropology* 12(3).

The Noble Qur'an, www.usc.edu/dept/MSA/quran/, Islamic Server of MSA-USC, accessed July 2005.

Noer, Deliar 1978, *The modernist Muslim movement in Indonesia 1900–1942*, Oxford University Press, Kuala Lumpur.

Noerdin, E 2002, 'Customary institutions, *Syariah* law and the marginalisation of Indonesian women,' in Robinson, K and S Bessell (eds), *Women in Indonesia: gender, equity and development*, Institute of Southeast Asian Studies, Singapore.

Nurdin, Ali 2003, *The Muslim women's movement in Indonesia: a study of Aisyiyah's Organization, 1966–2001*, MA thesis, University of New England, Armidale.

Oey-Gardiner, M and C Bianpoen (eds) 2000, *Indonesian women: the journey continues*, Research School of Pacific and Asian Studies, Australian National University, Canberra.

Oey-Gardiner, M, M Wagemann et al (eds) 1996, *Perempuan Indonesia: Dulu dan Kini*, Gramedia, Jakarta.

Otonomi Daerah, Formalisasi Syariat Islam, dan Posisi Perempuan 2004, www.kompas.com/kompas%2Dcetak/0405/04/swara/1001500.htm, accessed 11 October 2005.

Parawansa, KI 2002, 'Institution building: an effort to improve Indonesian women's role and status' in Robinson, K and S Bessell (eds), *Women in Indonesia: gender, equity and development*, Institute of Southeast Asian Studies, Singapore.

Parianom, Bambang and Dondy Ariesdianto 1999, *Megawati dan Islam: Polemik Gender dalam Persaingan Politik*, PT Antar Surya Jaya Bersama LSK, Surabaya.

Parker, L 2005, 'Uniform jilbab', *Inside Indonesia 83*.

Payton, RL 1988, *Philanthropy: voluntary action for the public good*, American Council on Education/Macmillan, New York.

Peacock, James 1978, *Purifying the faith: the Muhammadijah movement in Indonesian Islam*, Benjamin Cummings, San Francisco.

Peletz, M 1998, *Reason and passion: representation of gender in a Malay society*, University of California Press, London.

Pemerintah Kota Pekanbaru 2001, *Lembaran Daerah Kota Pekanbaru*, Pemko Pekanbaru, Pekanbaru.

Pemerintah Provinsi Riau 2002, *Rencana Strategi (Renstra) Provinsi Riau Tahun 2001–2003*, Pemerintah Provinsi Riau, Pekanbaru.

—— 2003, *Peraturan Daerah Provinsi Riau*, Pemda Riau, Pekanbaru.

Pimpinan Pusat Aisyiyah 1994, *Tuntunan Menuju Keluarga Sakinah*, Pimpinan Pusat Aisyiyah, Yogyakarta.

—— 2000, *Suplemen Keluarga Sakinah*, Pimpinan Pusat Aisyiyah, Yogyakarta.

Pimpinan Pusat Nasyiatul Aisyiyah 1990, *Laporan Pimpinan Pusat Nasyiatul Aisyiyah pada Muktamar Nasyiatul Aisyiyah VII di Yogyakarta*, Pimpinan Pusat Nasyiatul Aisyiyah, Yogyakarta.

—— 1992a, *Keputusan Musyawarah Nasional Nasyiatul Asyiyah I Periode 1990-1995*, Pimpinan Pusat Nasyiatul Aisyiyah, Yogyakarta.

—— 1992b, *Pembinaan Akhlak Dalam Keluarga*, Pimpinan Pusat Nasyiatul Aisyiyah, Yogyakarta.

—— 1992c, *Kerangka Acuan Kajian Keagamaan dan Kewanitaan Pimpinan Pusat Nasyiatul Aisyiyah*, Pimpinan Pusat Nasyiatul Aisyiyah, Yogyakarta.

—— 1996, *Program Pelatihan Persiapan Keluarga Sakinah*, Pimpinan Pusat Nasyiatul Aisyiyah, Yogyakarta.

—— 2003, *Silabi Pelatihan Nasyiatul Aisyiyah*, Pimpinan Pusat Nasyiatul Aisyiyah, Yogyakarta.

—— 2004a, 'Konperensi Pers: Muktamar X dan Sikap Nasyiatul Aisyiyah Berkaitan dengan Situasi Politik Nasional,' 4 Novemebr 2004, Pimpinan Pusat Nasyiatul Aisyiyah, Yogyakarta.

—— 2004b, *Laporan Pimpinan Pusat Nasyiatul Aisyiyah pada Sidang Tanwir III di Surakarta, 8 Desember 2004*, Pimpinan Pusat Nasyiatul Aisyiyah, Yogyakarta.

PIRAC 2002, *Investing in ourselves giving and fundraising in Asia*, Asia Pacific Philanthropy Consortium, Quezon City.

PKPU online report, 'Daftar Donatur PKPU', www.pkpu.or.id/donasi.php?zx=8f7ed9 0c70&jenis=3&th=2005&bl=1, accessed January 2005.

Platzdasch, Berhard 2000, 'Islamic reaction to a female president' in Manning, Chris and Peter van Diermen (eds), *Indonesia in transition: social aspects of Reformasi and crisis*, Institute of Southeast Asian Studies, Singapore.

PP Aisyiyah, 'Sejarah Aisyiyah', www.pp-aisyiyah.or.id/?pilih=hal&id=13, accessed July 2005.

Prasetyo, Hendro et al 2002, *Islam and Civil Society: Pandangan Muslim Indonesia*, Gramedia Pustaka Utama bekerjasama dengan PPIM-IAIN Jakarta, Jakarta.

Program Ramadhan di TV: Pendapatan di Depan Mata 2002, www.kompas.com/ kompas-cetak/0211/10/nasional/pend28.htm, accessed 17 May 2004.

Pudjiastuti, C 2002, *Program Ramadhan di Televisi Mengulang Sukses Lama*, www. kompas.com/kompas-cetak/0211/09/daerah/prog41.htm, accessed 17 May 2004

Purwana, Muhammad et al (Tim Penyusunan dan Penerbitan Profil) 2005, *Profil Muhammadiyah 2005*, PP Muhammadiyah, Yogyakarta.

Rahardjo, Julfita and Valerie Hull 1982, *Employment patterns of educated women in Indonesian cities*, Sn, Manila.

Rahardjo, Julfita 1980, 'Women in the workforce', *Kartini centenary: Indonesian women then and now*, Centre of Southeast Asian Studies, Monash University, Clayton.

Rahman, Anita 2000, 'Moslem women's organisations: their role in attaining the benefits of development' in Oey-Gardiner, Mayling and Carla Bianpoen (eds), *Indonesian women: the journey continues*, Australia National University, Canberra.

Reenen, Joke van 1996, *Central pillars of the house, sisters, wives, and mothers in a rural community in Minangkabau, West Sumatra*, Research School CNWS, Leiden.

Republika 2005a, Dr Hj Tutty Alawiyah AS: Membalik Paradigma, www.republika. co.id/koran_detail.asp, accessed 25 October 2005.

—— 2005b, 'Hukum Islam sangat Demokratis', www.republika.co.id/suplemen/ cetak_detail.asp?mid=5&id=187997&kat_id=1, accessed 19 May 2005.

Ricklefs, MC 2001, *A history of modern Indonesia since c1200*, Palgrave, Basingstoke.

Rida, Muhammad Rashid (ed) 1973, *Tafsir Al-Manar 4*, Darul Ma'rifah, Beirut.

Riddell, Peter 2001, *Islam and the Malay–Indonesian world: transmission and responses*, Hurst & Company, London.

Robinson, Kathryn and Sharon Bessell (eds) 2002, *Women in Indonesia: gender, equity and development*, Institute of Southeast Asian Studies, Singapore.

Robinson, Kathryn 2000, 'Gender, Islam, and nationality: Indonesian domestic servants in the Middle East,' in Adams, K and S Dickey (eds), *Home and hegemony: domestic service and identity politics in South and Southeast Asia*, University of Michigan Press, Ann Arbor.

Roff, William 1985, 'Islam obscured? Some reflections on studies of Islam and society in Southeast Asia', *Archipel* 29.

Rokhmad, Abu 2005, 'KHI dan Gerakan Kesetaraan Gender', *Suara Merdeka*, 26 February, www.suaramerdeka.com/harian/0502/26/opi4.htm, accessed 19 May 2005.

Ruthven, M 2002, 'Islam in the media' in Donnan, H (ed), *Interpreting Islam*, Sage, London.

Sadli, Saparinah 2002, 'Feminism in Indonesia in an international context' in Robinson, K and S Bessell (eds), *Women in Indonesia: gender, equity and development*, Institute of Southeast Asian Studies, Singapore.

Said, Edward, 1978, *Orientalism*, Penguin, Harmondsworth.

Saliba, Therese, Carolyn Allen and Judith A Howard (eds) 2002, *Gender, politics, and Islam*, University of Chicago Press, Chicago.

Salim, Arskal and Azyumardi Azra (eds), 2003, *Shari'a and politics in modern Indonesia*, Institute of Southeast Asian Studies, Singapore.

Sanday, P 2002, *Women at the center: life in a modern matriarchy*, Cornell University Press, Ithaca.

Santosa, Edy (ed) 2002, *Islam dan Konstruksi Seksualitas*, PSWAIAIN Yogyakarta, the Ford Foundation and Pustaka Pelajar, Yogyakarta.

Sears, Laurie (ed) 1996, *Fantasizing the feminine in Indonesia*, Duke University Press, Durham.

Sen, Krishna 2002, 'The Mega factor in Indonesian politics: a new president or a new kind of presidency?' in Robinson, Kathryn and Sharon Bessell (eds), *Women in Indonesia: gender, equity and development*, Institute of Southeast Asian Studies, Singapore.

Shehabuddin, E 2002, 'Contesting the illicit: gender and the politics of fatwa in Bangladesh' in Saliba, T, C Allen and J Howard (eds), *Gender, politics and Islam*, University of Chicago Press, Chicago.

Shehadeh, Lamia Rustum 2003, *The idea of women in fundamentalist Islam*, University Press of Florida, Gainesville.

Shihab, Quraish 1999, 'Kodrat Perempuan Versus Normal Kultural' in Munir, LZ (ed), *Memposisikan Kodrat*, Mizan, Bandung.

Siapno, Jacqueline 2002, *Gender, Islam, nationalism and the state in Aceh: the paradox of power, co-optation and resistance*, RoutledgeCurzon, London.

Sinar Harapan 2005a, 'Soal "Counter Legal Draft" KHI, Masyarakat Harus Belajar Berbeda Pendapat,' 19 February.

—— 2005b, 'Pelarangan "Counter Legal Draft" atas KHI, Menteri Agama Dinilai Langgar Hak Intelektual,' 23 February.

Siregar, Ashadi et al 1999, *Media and gender: Perspektif Gender atas Industri Suratkabar Indonesia*, LP3Y and Ford Foundation, Yogyakarta.

Smith, Jane L 1998, 'The experience of Muslim women: consideration of power and authority' in Esposito, J (ed), *Islam: the straight path*, Oxford University Press, New York.

Sodik, Mochamad 2004, *Telaah Ulang Wacana Seksualitas*, PSW IAIN Sunan Kalijaga bekerjasama dengan McGill-CIDA, Yogyakarta.

Soebahar, AH and H Utsman 1999, *Hak reproduksi perempuan dalam pandangan kiai*, Kerja sama Ford Foundation dengan Pusat penelitian Kependudukan Universitas Gadjah Mada, Yogyakarta.

Soebardi, S 1976, 'The place of Islam' in McKay, E (ed), *Studies in Indonesian history*, Pitman, Carlton.

Soemandoyo, Priyo 1999, *Wacana Gender dan Layar Televisi: Studi Perempuan dalam Pemberitaan Televisi Swastai*, LP3Y dan Ford Foundation, Yogyakarta.

Soewondo-Soerasno, Nani 1955, *Kedudukan Wanita Indonesia dalam Hukum dan Masyarakat*, Timun Mas, Jakarta.

Stacey, Judith 1988, 'Can there be a feminist ethnography?', *Women's Studies International Forum* 11(1).

Stange, Paul 1990, 'Javanism as text or praxis', *Anthropological Forum* 6(2).

Steenbrink, Karel A 1974, *Pesantren, Madrasah. Sekolah: Pendidikan Islam dalam Kurun Moderen*, LP3ES, Jakarta.

Steinberg, Richard and Mark Wilhelm 2003, 'Giving: the next generation—parental effects on donations', working paper, Centre on Philanthropy, Indiana University.

Stivens, M 1996, *Matriliny and modernity: sexual politics in social change in rural Malaysia*, Allen & Unwin, Crows Nest.

Stoler, Ann 1977, 'Class structure and female autonomy in rural Java', *Signs: Journal of Women in Culture and Society* 3(1).

Stowasser, B 1998, 'Gender issues and contemporary Qur'an interpretation' in Haddad, Y and J Esposito (eds), *Islam, gender, and social change*, Oxford University Press, New York.

Subhan, Zaitunah 1999, *Tafsir Kebencian: Studi Bias Jender dalam Tafsir Al-Qur'an*, LkiS, Yogyakarta.

Subono, Nur Iman and Gadis Arivia 2003, *Perempuan dan Partisipasi Politik: Panduan untuk Jurnalis*, Diterbitkan atas kerjasama Yayasan Jurnal Perempuan dan the Japan Foundation, Jakarta.

Sullivan, Norma 1987, 'Women, work and ritual in a Javanese urban community' in Pearson G and L Manderson (eds), *Class, ideology and woman in Asian societies,* Asian Research Service, Hong Kong.

—— 1994, *Masters and managers: a study of gender relations in urban Java,* Allen & Unwin, St Leonards.

Sumarni, D and L Setyowati 2000, *Pelecehan Tenaga Kerja Perempuan,* Kerja sama Ford Foundation dengan Pusat Penelitian Kependudukan Universitas Gadjah Mada, Yogyakarta.

Supanto 1999, *Kebijakan Hukum Pidana Mengenai Pelecehan Seksual,* Kerja sama Ford Foundation dengan Pusat Penelitian Kependudukan Universitas Gadjah Mada, Yogyakarta.

Surur, Miftahus 2005, 'Belajar dari Pembatalan "CLD" KHI', www.kompas.com/kompas-cetak/0310/06/swara/605838.htm, accessed 12 December 2005.

Suryakusuma, Julia 1996, 'The state and sexuality in New Order Indonesia' in Sears, L (ed), *Fantasizing the feminine in Indonesia,* Duke University Press, Durham.

—— 2004, *Sex, power and nation: an anthology of writings 1979–2003,* Metafor Publishing, Jakarta.

Swara 2004, 'Mempertanyakan RUU yang Bias Jender', 11 October, www.kompas.com/kompas-cetak/0310/06/swara/605838.htm, accessed 23 May 2005.

Syafruddin, Didin 1994, 'Argument Supremasi atas Perempuan: Penafsiran Klasik QS al-Nisa: 34', *Ulumul Qur'an* 5.

Tahido, Huzaemah 1993, 'Konsep Wanita Menurut Al-Qur'an, Sunah dan Fikh' in Marcoes-Natsir, L, et al (eds), *Wanita Islam dalam Kajian Tekstual dan Kontekstual,* INIS, Jakarta.

Tambiah, Stanley Jeyaraja 1990, *Magic, science, religion, and the scope of rationality,* Cambridge University Press, Cambridge.

Thalib, Muhammad 2005, Draft KHI Versi Gender Lecehkan Syari'at Islam, www.hidayatullah.com/index.php?option=com_content&task=view&id=1451, accessed 19 May 2005.

Tibi, Bassam 2002, *The challenge of fundamentalism: political Islam and the new world disorder,* University of California Press, Berkeley.

Tim PSW IAIN Sunan Kalijaga 2002a, *Membentuk Keluarga Bahagia,* PSW IAIN Sunan Kalijaga bekerjasama dengan McGill-CIDA, Yogyakarta.

—— 2002b, *Menuju Keluarga Bahagia,* PSW IAIN Sunan Kalijaga bekerjasama dengan McGill-CIDA, Yogyakarta.

—— 2002c, *Menuju Pernikahan Maslahah dan Sakinah,* PSW IAIN Sunan Kalijaga bekerjasama dengan McGill-CIDA, Yogyakarta.

—— 2002d, *Relasi Ideal Suami-Istri,* PSW IAIN Sunan Kalijaga bekerjasama dengan McGill-CIDA, Yogyakarta.

—— 2003a, *Anotasi Dinamika Studi Gender di IAIN Sunan Kalijaga 1995-2003*, PSW IAIN Sunan Kalijaga bekerjasama dengan McGill-CIDA, Yogyakarta.

—— 2003b, *Dekonstruksi Gender: Kritik Wacana Perempuan dalam Islam*, PSW IAIN Sunan Kalijaga bekerjasama dengan McGill-CIDA, Yogyakarta.

Umar, Nasaruddin 1999a, *Argumen Kesetaraan Gender: Perspektif Al-Qur'an*, Paramadina, Jakarta.

—— 1999b, *Kodrat Perempuan dalam Islam*, The Asia Foundation, Jakarta.

Vreede-De Stuers, Cora, 1960, *The Indonesian woman: struggles and achievements*, Mouton, The Hague.

Wadud, Amina 1994, *Wanita di dalam Al-Qur'an*, Pustaka, Bandung.

—— 1999, *Qur'an and woman: rereading the sacred text from a woman's perspective*, Oxford University Press, New York.

Wardhana, V 2002, *Televisi dan Prasangka Budaya Massa*, ISAI, Jakarta.

Washburn, K 2001, 'Jilbab, Kesadaran Identitas post-Kolonial dan Aksi Tiga Perempuan (Jawa)' in Monika F (ed) *Perempuan Postkolonial dan Identitas Komoditi Global*, Penerbit Kanisius, Yogyakarta.

Weedon, C 2004, *Identity and culture: narratives of difference and belonging*, Open University Press, New York.

Whalley, L 1993, *Virtuous women, productive citizens: negotiating traditions, Islam, and modernity in Minangkabau Indonesia*, dissertation, University of Illinois, Illinois.

White, Sally Jane 2004, *Reformist Islam, gender and marriage in late colonial Dutch East Indies, 1900–1942*, dissertation), Australian National University, Canberra.

Wieringa, Saskia 2002, *Sexual politics in Indonesia*, Palgrave Macmillan, Basingstoke.

Wilhelm, Mark et al 2004, 'The intergenerational transmission of generosity', working paper, Center on Philanthropy, Indiana University.

Williams, L 1998, *Wives, mistresses, and matriarchs: Asian women today*, Allen and Unwin, St Leonards.

Woodcroft-Lee, C 1984, 'Some perceptions of Indonesian women under Islam' in Dixon, Suzanne and Theresa Munford (eds), *Pre-industrial women: interdisciplinary perspectives*, Australian National University, Canberra.

Woodward, Mark (ed) 1988, 'The Slametan: textual knowledge and ritual performance in Central Javanese Islam', *History of Religions* 28(1).

—— 1996, *Toward a new paradigm: recent developments in Indonesian Islamic thought*, Arizona State University.

—— 1991–92, 'Javanism, Islam and the plurality of ethnography', *Anthropological Forum* 6(3).